Institutional Attitudes
Instituting Art in a Flat World

Pascal Gielen (ed.)

Antennae
Valiz, Amsterdam

With contributions by

Kenny Cupers
Bart De Baere
Ann Demeester
Jimmie Durham
Alex Farquharson
Mark Fisher
Pascal Gielen
Marc Jacobs
Sonja Lavaert
Thijs Lijster
Isabell Lorey
Markus Miessen
Chantal Mouffe
Gerald Raunig
Patricia Reed
Nicolaus Schafhausen
Blake Stimson

[redacted]

Institutional Attitudes: Instituting Art in a Flat World

Pascal Gielen (ed.)

[redacted]

[redacted]

Introduction When Flatness Rules

Pascal Gielen

Today's networked society offers us many wondrous possibilities of information, communication, mobility, and flexibility. It also has a special latent side effect: it makes the world flat. Time-honoured hierarchies, traditions, elites, canons, and forms of 'grandeur' are subject to eroding movements that have a tendency to always gravitate towards mediocrity. A rhizome is not a root, so it can hardly take root. In short, today's networked society has a problem with verticality. It hurts to look up, and those who turn their gaze towards the sky are finding it difficult to estimate differences in height. The democratization of art, for instance, suggests that anyone can have an opinion about the quality of a work of art; and the popularization of democracy assures that the same value is attached to all statements about society. Neoliberalism, flowing freely through the veins of the global network, uses evidence-based policy, audits, modulation, and neo-management to guarantee the dominance of only one hierarchy: that of numbers, capital, or quantities, which effectively makes every quality relative. All qualities are expressed in terms of quantity, making any quality interchangeable with, or at least comparable to, any other quality. This belief in a measurable society is constantly transmuting qualities into quantities. The well-substantiated argument for democracy, for instance, is converted into a liberal representative democracy that takes its lead from the numbers of anonymous voters only. The value of media and organizations is determined by the size of their audience or turnover, respectively, and educational quality is translated into numbers of competencies and contact hours.

In such a flattened world, art institutions are finding it hard to survive. After all, institutions traditionally represent verticality, historic profundity, canons, tradition, values and dignity, 'grandeur', stability, and certainty. Within the fluent network society, these qualities too are subjected to being expressed in terms of measurable quantities by measuring output and public outreach and by counting the number of organized events. Institutes, which represent institutions, are thus reduced to being tactical operative organizations in a competitive world, just competitors among many others. Within that context, they are finding it increasingly difficult to hold up the pole of the big top, which leads to less space and less height.

In this book, various authors explore the future identity of art institutes and therefore that of THE Institution as well. Will they be able to create verticality again? Is this desirable? And if so, what would this new verticality look like? Or is it better to develop horizontal strategies in order to react more advantageously to the new flat world? Can institutes make room for a type of quality that follows a different logic from that of numbers? Which strategies can they develop to achieve this within today's networked society? These are the questions this book addresses, by looking at some of the values that are attributed to art institutes but are in danger of being lost in the current context, including: criticism, participation, responsibility and historical awareness.

Most contributions in this book focus on classic art institutions such as museums, criticism and art schools. They obliquely discuss previous developments in the art world around institutional critique and the New Institutionalism and then look at the present and towards the future. The issue of verticality and the institute is also regarded within a wider social framework. After all, although the focus of *Institutional Attitudes* is on the classic art institutions, other traditional institutions such as the State, criticism (and public opinion), education, etc. are under pressure as well.

In the first part of the book, 'Transforming Attitudes', a sociologist, a philosopher and an artist address the changing attitudes of art institutions. Over the last three decades, not only museums but art academies and art criticism as well have undergone a profound transmutation. Museums and schools have been redefined within a context of competitive market relationships, and criticism as a 'verticalization activity' seems to have lost its function. Various authors have declared the 'death' or the 'end' of criticism in the last decade. In his contribution, philosopher Thijs Lijster takes notice of that analysis but also makes some important comments. Inspired by Michel Foucault, and especially by Luc Boltanski, he arrives at the proposition that criticism could draw on the imaginative realm of the art work to pretend that a meta-position outside of society is possible; and from that position, criticize society as a whole. So critics have the possibility of taking up a vertical position again by making the art work their ally.

Cultural sociologist Pascal Gielen starts off this first section by placing that idea in a broader social context. For him too, the imagination that finds its place in art, among other things, is an important tool for distinguishing between the real world and an imagined, or fictional 'reality'. Precisely because of our ability to 'see the world through a double lens', we can take up a vertical perspective 'outside' of society while still remaining within it. Not

[redacted]

just museums and art academies, but just about any institution that was shaped in the modern age, such as the family, public opinion, the legal system and politics is now under pressure to give up this vertical perspective. Over the past thirty years, it has been made increasingly difficult for them to pursue their own ideals and develop their own imaginative horizon.

Institutions shouldn't allow that horizon to be shrunk by the free market economy, as Jimmie Durham argues in his contribution. He sketches an impression of his own experiences within the art world of the last few decades. Art fairs have proven to be more successful than biennials. Should we resign ourselves to this commercialism? Art institutions will only be able to survive in this horizontal world as guardians of autonomy and self-referential value regimes if they, like the market, break through their own boundaries and intervene in other social domains.

Although this first part of the book outlines a few escape routes from the dire situation in which art institutions find themselves nowadays, the main focus is on a critical analysis of the current horizontal condition of the art institutions.

The contributions in the second part then turn our attention to possible strategies to escape this deadlock. Political philosopher Chantal Mouffe advocates the development of strategies for art institutions to become allies. Institutions should not be discarded but on the contrary be used as sites for agonistic politics in which social conflicts are made productive. We should become engaged with art institutions to undermine the imaginary environment of the consumer society.

In their search for possible strategies, political scientist Isabell Lorey and author Mark Fisher take a closer look at the methods of the Occupy Movements. For Lorey the Occupy Movements stand for an exodus from vertical, unifying institutionalization, which is an important break with the exisiting order of the dominant (Western) representative democracy. But this movement needs a constituted power. In the eyes of Lorey new vertical condensations and new institutions are necessary. The constituent process has to create openings for horizontal social and political practices again and again because 'horzontality itself does not exist without aspects of verticality', according to Lorey.

Fisher comes to the conclusion that horizontal strategies are not really effective in bringing about a fundamental social change. Horizontal strategies don't work, or only partly. What we need is a new verticality — an authority even — to achieve structural change, without confusing authoritarianism with authority. The functioning of the Occupy Movement does however offer some valuable lessons for today's art world and art organizations.

With the same intention, philosopher Sonja Lavaert takes a fresh look at the role of institutions in the works of the philosophers Paolo Virno and Giorgio Agamben. She also comes to the conclusion that institutions are necessary and so rejects the idea that they have become irrelevant. However, Lavaert makes an important differentiation with regard to this book's general proposition. She admits that 'there is something wrong with current institutions, but this is not because we live in a flat world. The problem is rather the reverse: institutions can only be established and questioned in an open, enlightened, horizontal and democratic space.'

Blake Stimson also underlines the importance of the Enlightenment for the institution. In his focus on archives, this art scholar and theorist states that archives do not simply exercise power by determining and fixating meanings. They also preserve and guard the possibility and promise to 'un-fixate' meanings. This is what he calls 'the tender spot for the archive'. It means that especially in this institution's deep dungeons, knowledge and power can be separated. In that respect, institutions play a crucial role in realizing freedom. 'If we wish to be free, then there is nothing better we can do than insist upon systems, rules, enclosures, and institutions that redirect the unbridled sovereignty of politicians, bankers, and ourselves. Freedom from domination — particularly, at this moment in much of the world, freedom from the ruthless domination of the market — depends on such institutionality', says Stimson.

Part Two is called 'Horizontal Strategies?', with a question mark that is there for a reason, as this part seriously discusses horizontal strategies as a possible escape route for art institutes while upholding the value of the institution as such.

The thing is, though, that institutes are obliged to operate differently nowadays and that is why the third and final part of this book, 'Instituting in a Flat World', presents a number of concrete examples from practice. Whereas the Belgian historian Marc Jacobs looks at the past, studying the workings of the Republic of Letters to find possibilities for the art institutions of today, British museum director Alex Farquharson presents a real action plan. He defines a handful of attitudes and techniques that art institutions today should observe if they want to intervene in the current political and economic context. In a collage of text and dialogue, architect Markus Miessen a.o. outlines his methods with the Winter School Middle East as a mobile institution. The agonistic 'approach' described by Mouffe is a great inspiration in his practice of confronting the 'flattening' pressure on institutions to participate in all sorts of cultural activities and policies.

The concrete examples and recommendations in this third part are preceded by a theoretical introduction to the central theme of the book. The philosopher Gerald Raunig provides a wider referential frame for all these endeavours: within the new social context, it is imperative to articulate a political project that creates and feeds the 'common'. The 'art institutions of the common', as Raunig calls them, will no longer reproduce the traditional canon but neither will they lapse into a competitive struggle of introducing ever-new canons or trends. On the contrary, art institutions will have to offer a platform for political-aesthetic experiments that convincingly demonstrate that there are viable alternatives to the current short-term thinking of the market hegemony.

And so *Institutional Attitudes* starts with a critical analysis of the social context in which art institutions operate today in Part 1, explores possible new strategies and the potential of institutions in Part 2 and presents a concrete definition of tasks ahead in Part 3. It is up to today's art institutions themselves to either accept the challenge or not.

Institutional Attitudes is the result of a symposium of the same title that was organized in 2010 in the Beursschouwburg of Brussels by the Roosendaal Committee. The afterword by Bart De Baere, Ann Demeester, and Nicolaus Schafhausen provides further information about the history and aims of this association. De Appel, MuHKA and Witte de With, the members of the committee at that time, took the initiative to continue the debate in the form of a publication. I am very grateful to all of them for their trust in me and for giving me every freedom to develop this idea. Not only was this a chance to continue and extend the symposium in Brussels, it also provided an opportunity to frame the subject in a wider historical, economic and political context. In broadening the discursive material, this publication hopes to make a substantial contribution to the current debate on the role of art institutions in a globalized, flat society. In the first place, the book hopes to offer support to art organizations that wish to better define their own position in society in order to be able to develop the most effective strategies.

When flatness rules, we all feel the need to stand up to get some air. It is exactly this breathing space that *Institutional Attitudes* hopes to create.

[redacted]

Part I
Transforming Attitudes

Institutional Imagination

Instituting Contemporary Art Minus the 'Contemporary'

Pascal Gielen

It is only because of our ability to 'see the world through a double lens' that we can conceive of both the natural world and culture as being different than what they are in reality. Because we can distinguish between the real world and an imagined, or fictional 'reality', change and innovation are within the realm of human possibility. Regardless of whether such change means progression or regression, our ability to oscillate between non-fiction and fiction is crucial in imagining other worlds, in being creative, in presenting different models of society or in addressing ecological issues. The empirical 'reality' of an imaginary world allows for both daydreaming and the forging of the most utopian plans. The sobering return from this fictional world to reality then generates the chance to try out these things. Imagination may well be one of the few remaining possibilities for us to escape from a quagmire by pulling ourselves up, like Baron von Münchhausen, by our own hair. As social scientists know only too well, individuals, groups and organizations are always *within* society. They cannot escape from it, especially since our society has become a 'global village'. Only the power of imagination can bring about such an exodus. Or perhaps we should use the neologism 'inodus' here, coined by the Italian artist Michelangelo Pistoletto (2009), because the power of imagination enables us to simultaneously be in the world physically while escaping from it mentally. This is why it is like an escape *into* the world. Daydreaming during meetings, making holiday plans while teaching a class, but also collectively brainstorming about the reorganization of a company posits a different, imaginable world within this one. The imaginary is therefore certainly not only an individual affair. Like Karl Marx's 'general intellect', there is such a thing as collective imagination.

This universal — or at least human — possibility of taking ourselves to an imaginary place is not without risk, however. There is, for instance, the danger of not planning a return trip to reality, which may lead to isolation, unworldliness and sometimes even complete madness on an individual level. On a collective level, an escape from the real world may result in the most esoteric of cults or radical revolutionary movements. No wonder then that the powers that be — in the past, mainly the church, and nowadays, to a considerable degree the State — have always concerned themselves with this imaginary space. However, regimes of power are always relatively powerless when face-to-face with the imaginary. No law, no dark dungeon, is so efficient that it can completely root out the dissident, dangerous or undermining power of the imagination. Individuals may be chained and tortured, entire segments of the population may be excommunicated or banned to ghettos, and still their thoughts will be free. Those who want to control imagination or more or less streamline it without liquidating humanity itself must therefore come up with an ingenious plan indeed. It is very difficult to eradicate 'wrong' thoughts. At best they can be contained, and the most efficient way of doing this from a position of power is by embarking upon the imaginary path as well. In short, fiction is best combated with fiction.

It shouldn't come as a surprise, then, that both the church and the State have in the past invested enormous amounts of time, money and effort in producing images and telling stories, in consecrating and nationalizing art and history, and even in 'sacralizing' and 'patriotizing' natural resources and geographic areas. Religion and nationalism both use the imaginary extensively to create a certain reality. In doing so, they have tried to quarantine that which can also always be otherwise, at least when they deem it threatening to their own existence.

It is well known that institutions have always played a crucial role in mediating between the real world and the imagined world. Whereas the Church moderated the contact between heaven and earth by means of rituals, images of saints and liturgy, with the advent of the modern age museums and educational institutions took it upon themselves to propagate national treasures and heritage, among other things. However, the secularization that went on during the modern age led to yet another important role for these institutions. According to most social scientists, during the nineteenth century the world — the Western world in the first place — became subdivided into social subsystems or value regimes. Not only did the separation of Church and State originate in the modern age; so did the increasing differentiation of politics, justice, science, economics, art and family life. Institutions also served to guard the boundaries between these value regimes relatively strictly. The university, for instance, as the institutionalization of science, had to take care that the objectifying methods within its walls could not be undermined by religion, money or power. Likewise, the court had to safeguard that its verdicts were reasonable and just and that judges were not blinded by wealth or by any form of superstition. In nascent democracies, the

[redacted]

parliamentary system and its concomitant suffrage were meant to safeguard that politicians put the public interest first and were not manipulated or pressurized by their own position, family or business relations. Art institutions such as academies, museums, galleries and journals, finally, had to protect the imaginary space of the artist against political and religious propaganda or commercialism.

So, in the modern world, institutions would guarantee the 'purity' and proper functioning of their own social domain to a large degree. They also provided the much-needed backbone and ethics for the negotiations between value regimes, for instance between art and the market, art and politics or art and family life. Finally — and perhaps most importantly — institutions mediated, each for their own world, between reality and fiction. In this way, each institution upheld the values, and especially the ideals, of its own world, from absolute justice in law to fair competition in the economy to *l'art pour l'art* in the arts — all of them ideals and value narratives that were constructed at this time. Institutions became the pillars of the modern world, as it were. They established value regimes that represented and maintained a higher goal worth striving for. The fact that these goals were rather lofty and belonged more to the realms of utopia and fiction was no problem. On the contrary, it enabled people who wished to be in these institutions to live meaningful lives. The preordained goal gave their lives a clear direction, and so we might call institutions 'verticalization machines'. They not only generated an imaginary height, but also a historical depth, a foundation to stand on. This is because institutions are always also 'con-stitutions'. They spring from the Latin 'con-' or 'com', from acting communally. The path to the imaginary world is organized collectively, and its associated values are guaranteed and sanctioned by a collective. In this respect, institutions generate — or used to generate — a sense of certainty, even of safety and security. However, for the same reason they could also seem very rigid, hierarchical and overwhelmingly authoritarian. In combating anomy, institutions tend towards social claustrophobia.

Institutional Critique

The two waves of institutional critique that we have seen in the art world so far can be partly understood as a dissatisfaction with claustrophobia. In a broader sense, the scepticism in regard to classic institutions is based on their oppressive navigation between the world of non-fiction and that of fiction. During the first wave of institutional critique in the 1970s, artists such as Michael Asher, Robert Smithson, Daniel Buren, Hans Haacke and Marcel Broodthaers seemed to be gasping for breath. They literally wanted to break open the museum in the name of imagination and democracy. Individual freedom and creativity were pitted against a bourgeois morality and the canon of art history. The second generation, from the 1990s, which included protagonists such as Fred Wilson and Andrea Fraser, became mired in a wider institutional art field, as described by the cultural sociologist Pierre Bourdieu, among others. Within this field, artists cannot escape the power game and find themselves caught in a Weberian iron cage. In the words of the American cultural theorist Brian Holmes:

> This situation of a critical process staking itself for its object recently led Andrea Fraser to consider the artistic institution as an unsurpassable, all-defining frame, sustained through its own inwardly directed critique (Fraser, 2005). Bourdieu's deterministic analysis of the closure of the socio-professional fields, mingled with a deep confusion between Weber's iron cage and Foucault's desire 'to get free of oneself', is internalized here in a governmentality of failure, where the subject can do no more than contemplate his or her own psychic prison, with a few aesthetic luxuries in compensation. (Holmes, 2009: 58)

This failure of institutional critique is also caused by the very ambivalent attitude of artists towards their own institutions. As noted earlier, institutions are vertical, tightly organized hierarchical value regimes that guard their boundaries with other value regimes such as that of religion, the market or politics precisely because they are so inflexible. Critique of the institution is only possible thanks to the shelter of that same institution and the values it represents. At the same time, such critique always also threatens to erode institutional boundaries, making it increasingly difficult for the institution to provide this collective shelter. With its call for more democracy and less hierarchy, institutional critique has in the meantime opened the door to a flat world in the art world as well. The breaches it has made in the institutional walls of the modern era have let in other value regimes that have eroded not only its own hierarchy but also its own dignity. This was possible because the critique was mainly of a negative nature, an attack that offered few alternatives or new strategies. If there were to be a third wave of institutional critique nowadays, it could only succeed by making the time-honoured modern values of the art institution its ally. The art institution that was the target of modern and postmodern critique no longer exists. It has been transmuted and eroded to such an extent that it has become unrecognizable when compared to thirty years ago. If critique is to be effective at all, it has to have a clear focus. It therefore makes sense to first take a closer look at the transmutation of at least two art institutions: the art academy and the museum.

Crumbling Pillars

The classic nineteenth-century museums provided depth by presenting history, offered a stepladder by way of an exemplary canon and provided 'grandeur' to anyone exhibiting there, and even to those wandering around in them. The consecration of the actual work of art could only take place in relation to the deep wells of history. In art education, there was a similar hierarchical relationship between those who knew and those who did not (yet) know. The classic relationship between master and pupil was a vertical one in which the place of law and authority was clear. The pupil had to climb the proverbial ladder and try to become the equal of his or her master. Only then did the ritual patricide become possible. But what is important here is that learning was *climbing*. Climbing the ladder of a rather self-assured wisdom. And aspiring students were only willing to do so if teachers had some 'grandeur' that earned them respect (even if this 'grandeur' was sometimes artificially upheld by the institutions that embedded them). At the same time, museums and art academies offered a yardstick for measuring creativity. Teachers who felt that they discerned talent in a pupil not only relied on vast experience but also on a healthy dose of intuition and subjectivity — especially when dealing with a modern artist. In other words, in the relationship between master and pupil there was also always an element of 'not-knowing' (Laermans, 2012).

The important point is that institutions such as museums and academies, in spite of their subjectivity and 'not-knowing', did erect a relatively objectifiable hierarchy of values. This hierarchy had little to do with the quantitative hierarchy of visitor numbers, number of competencies, output data and other evidence-based measurement material of the flat world. Creation and the potential for creativity simply do not lend themselves to being calculated or recorded in such a logic of numbers. On the contrary, having a lot of money or public acclaim has in the past not always proven to be the best guarantee of good art, creation and innovation. To create something means to place oneself outside of the measurable measure. Artists must withdraw themselves from the flat plane and, by much trial and error, make themselves stand upright. Classic institutions came in handy here because they, with their experience of depth, could somehow point the way up. All this navigating of course carried no absolute guarantees for a successful result, but it did offer an adequate view of the horizon. And perhaps it was precisely this concurrence of rigidity, history, ignorance and faith within the institution that offered creativity its chances in the past.

Without trying to romanticize their function — the history that institutions carry with them can also be crushing and the bureaucracy they embrace can be too rigid to allow for any rebellion or literal 'uprising' — one can safely say that classic institutions at least stood for a hierarchy of values that assessed and measured creativity differently from the way it is done in the present dominant system of measuring investment and output. The latter reduces quality to quantity and erases the former in the process. Any numerical calculation makes differences in quality relative, after all. It generates quantitative comparability and the interchangeability of qualities by making an abstract distinction in grades. Once the abstraction is made, literally anything can be related to anything else, and relationships therefore become relative and interchangeable too. By contrast, rising up, or creating something, requires absolute faith and blind intuition, but also needs a solid cultural ground to stand on. And that is exactly what the classic institutions provided.

After the 1999 Bologna Agreement, not only did the educational arena in Europe become highly uniform and rational, it was also redefined as a market space where educational institutes fiercely compete for students, outbidding each other in offering easily interchangeable competencies. Within this system, students are treated like little entrepreneurs, while the relationship between

[redacted]

teacher and pupil takes the form of a contract. Much has already been said elsewhere about the transmutation of education (see, for instance, Masschelein and Simons, 2006, and Gielen and De Bruyne, 2012). What matters here is that under the neoliberal hegemony, the classic institution is being eroded. One of the causes is that it is losing its own cultural hierarchy in the shadow of market logic. What was once regarded as highly functional for educating articulate citizens, creating 'cultivated' people, now fades into dysfunctionality under the dogma of profitability. And, as the German philosopher Peter Sloterdijk argues:

> ...because schools over the last few decades could no longer muster the courage to be dysfunctional – a courage they had continually demonstrated ever since the seventeenth century – they became empty selfish systems, focused exclusively on the norms of their own operational management. They now produce teachers that are only reminiscent of teachers, subjects that are only reminiscent of subjects, students that are only reminiscent of students. At the same time, schools become 'anti-authoritarian' in an inferior way, without ceasing to exercise formal authority. (Sloterdijk, 2011: 447)

The implementation of an anti-authoritarian educational model does indeed run remarkably parallel to the introduction of a formal authoritarian neo-management model, which, as in other institutions, deconstructs the traditional cultural hierarchy of verticality by submitting it to the law of numerical measurability. According to Sloterdijk, the overturning of verticality into horizontality, and of book culture into net culture, also generates a kind of controlled 'jungle pedagogics' within education, whereby 'interdisciplinarity' is the buzzword that eradicates all disciplines (and thus depth — 'time to dig deep', as Richard Sennett [2008] would say).

We should not be fooled by these loud calls for professionalization. After all, in art schools these calls are often answered by inserting some marketing and management subjects, which inevitably leaves less time for teaching the proper creative subjects.

As a result, students rapidly switch from one specific skill to a completely different area of knowledge. Such jungle pedagogics thus often have the opposite result of what was intended and result in the de-professionalization of the creative profession. The aim of all this is to deliver 'broadly employable' or 'polyvalent' students, multi-purpose individuals who follow just one important imperative: that of adaptation or anticipation. 'Adaptivity' and 'flexibility' are after all the highest goods in a flat network world. The main thing is that such an educational model loses all performativity. Educational institutes become organizations that no longer deliver a surplus of autonomous personalities and idiosyncratic skills, for which society (and the economy) needs to generate new space. On the contrary, schools obligingly follow the demands of the market 'to be more closely linked to the professional practice'. However, as schools are always lagging behind in following these economic trends, and as it is also impossible to guess what the demands of a fluctuating labour market may be in five years' time, education covers itself against such fluctuations by delivering multi-purpose or 'polyvalent' subjects. Whether they are as characterless as traditional multi-purpose venues is best left an open question. The point is that by 'tuning into' the market, schools lose all performativity (and authority) to make their own mark and therefore no longer provide a spine to those who wish to stand up straight and undertake some daring creative act.

And what about museums, then? That is a more familiar story. Beginning in the 1970s, the function of the museum has slowly but surely been eroded by the rapid succession of temporary exhibitions and biennials, introducing a structural amnesia in the field of art, causing it to suffer from a loss of depth (Gielen, 2009). Over the past few decades, the museum 'unlearned its ability to hook up with the artistically most ambitious level of the previous generations', again according to Sloterdijk (2011: 449). Paradoxically, the ideology of creativity has consistently fought the institution of the museum. If artists and other protagonists of the institutional critique as mentioned before, had been aware thirty years ago that they were undermining their own institutional foundation, then perhaps they would have changed their tune completely. Or at least they would have chosen a better strategy. Still, such an analysis is not altogether fair and correct. On the road of their slow criticism (slow, as they were always starting from a very ambivalent attitude towards the museum) they were after all overtaken at high

[redacted]

velocity by a speeding neoliberalization. It quickly found ways to profit from the work done by the institutional critique by taking over its jargon of 'creativity' (which would squash the museum), 'innovation' (which would slow the museum down) and 'flexibility' (which would make the museum rigid). This takeover by neoliberalism took place in a rather 'unseemly' manner, and the 'anti-institutionalists' from before hardly even recognized it anymore. Only the converts to neoliberalism — and there was no shortage of them in the 1990s — still saw some similarity between the critique from before and the opportunism that now ruled.

Mostly, however, the neoliberal engine has set a new operational framework in motion in the art world. Or rather, it deftly hitches a ride, even enhancing operations that were initiated in the art world with the best intentions and much idealism. This of course refers to the hegemonial shift from the museum to the biennial and the symbolic displacement of the artist by the so-called 'independent' curator. Artists who still aim for immortality and who take up a position as bohemians outside of society, hoping for recognition in the hereafter, are today ridiculed for their conviction. It is only the here and now that counts. Or rather, not the here and now, but the very near future on this flat foundation. The artist can no longer stand outside of or above the world. Because many contemporary artists still regard creation as 'standing upright', rising above everyday things, they are summarily dismissed in the contemporary flat world. The creative worker of today is not so much a trapeze artist but more of a (social) networker. In the world of visual art, the latter coincides wonderfully well with the 'independent' curator mentioned earlier. He mingles with the audience, wanting both to show and be seen. Sloterdijk calls it the shift from 'art as production power (including the ballast of the 'great masters') to art as exhibition power' (2011: 449). It's all less and less about creating and more about exhibiting.

In this exhibitionistic turn, it should hardly come as a surprise that the workshop or the atelier is losing importance or that studios cease to exist (Davidts et al, 2009). In the flat world, this space of digging deep, of reflexivity and 'slowness' or verticality, but also of isolation and dealing with materiality, is predictably exchanged for an immaterial discourse that is all about mobility, and the institution dissolves in a network structure. 'Mobilism', 'nomadism', 'travel', 'planetary drift', 'exodus', 'transport', 'links', 'chains', 'loops', 'neurons', 'in touch', 'relational', 'connection', 'communication', 'distribution', 'redistribution' are but a handful of notions used by curators and a growing horde of creative workers to describe and sell their activities. While curators — both in their exhibitions and in general — pour out criticism of the perverse excrescences of late capitalism by the bucket load, the majority of people in the art world dance perfectly in time to the tune of the neoliberal climate. This lack of self-reflexivity — at least publicly — is quite remarkable. The same goes for the notion of the rhizome or that of the network. It is usually embraced, and endowed with a romantic touch. The hero of network thinking is of course the nomad, which again emphasizes the rosy side of mobile man. This nomad, however, is not a strider but a swimmer — and one with gills, if we are to believe the Italian author Alessandro Barrico (2011).

Flat Wet World

Mobility and networking are today part of the art world's doctrine, and in fact that of the entire world of professionals. Artists who stay at home in their studios are morally reprehended and accused of localism. They nourish false illusions on an island where they still have solid ground beneath their feet. But nowadays artists are either international or they are nobodies. Curators are connected or they are nobodies. These may sound like the ground rules of the contemporary art world, but they are also the adages of global late capitalism, which has, over the past few decades, effortlessly invaded the artistic realm through cultural and creative industrialization. This late capitalism, by the way, has a lot to gain from us seeing ourselves as mobile actors in a fluid networked world. Individuals as well as organizations feel that their true selves are 'corporate identities on the open sea', as Sloterdijk says in his writings about globalization (2006: 90). Time, labour, and even love become liquid if we are to believe Zygmunt Bauman (2009).

So, those who imagined that they still had solid ground beneath their feet when the flat world was created were very much mistaken. The flat world is a wet one. It is one big pool of $H2O$ in which we paddle around as if on water bikes. Or, to put it more pathetically, we are floating in a swimming pool, treading water in an airless, liquid, late-modern age, hoping to find some sort of direction (or meaning). Whereas collective institutions — the welfare state prominent among them — used to guarantee the stability of the cruise ship on the open ocean, today our living and

[redacted]

working environment is made up mainly of rubber rings floating about with the occasional small lifeboat and a limited number of luxury yachts thrown in.

This is especially true of creative working environments. Creative workers have been thrown into deep existential waters with treacherous currents. Therapists, personal coaches and other social-psychological workers are supposed to help us get used to our new living environment. This mental support force is entrusted with the noble task of relieving entrepreneurial creative people from their fear of drowning. Those who still think that they can rely on the traditional ground that institutions used to offer are merely delusional. With no clear idea of the future, creative individuals are bouncing from one wave to the other and have no choice but to practice freestyle swimming. Occasionally they may find a precarious rubber ring to keep their head just above water, but the creative entrepreneurs have to inflate it themselves and the slightest puncture will burst it wide open. Hopefully, the double wall of the insurance policy will then keep them afloat for a little while longer. In a flat world with neither God nor secular collective solidarity structures, these entrepreneurs are indeed very much left to their own devices.

This 'immanism' of liberal representative democracy, as the French philosopher Jean-Luc Nancy calls it (1991), regards society as the sum of independent individuals, who are finding it increasingly difficult to forge relational ties. A flat, wet world that looks upon itself as a network presupposes quite specific characteristics and makes certain demands of the people who are floating about in it. In a neutral definition, a network consists of interconnected points. It can only exist because there are connections, as we know from the actor-network theory. When those connections are broken, the rhizome evaporates with them. The word 'evaporate' clearly indicates the weakness of a network configuration within a wet playing field and evokes the volatile or at least temporary nature of such social connections. What's more, within a liberal network economy these temporary collaborations are controlled by competition. This is why project-like thinking is so dominant in the current order. People only temporarily drift together, to then float collectively while realizing a project, after which their swimming lanes often diverge again. Relationships arise because there is a collective goal for a short while. This is why sociologists call this *goal-instrumental action*. This thinking in terms of networks and projects is not limited to the field of creative labour but has become part of society in general. Nowadays, for instance, project developers determine to a large extent the look of our cities and living environments, and even the nuclear family is seen as a temporary educational project for children, at the conclusion of which parents can go swim their separate ways again.

The best functioning units within wet networks are not collectives or large, unwieldy cruise ships. It is not unions, social classes, groups, political parties, institutions or families that set the course, but entrepreneurial individuals — even in their rubber rings. The maximum collective unit that matters is the team, precisely because in a team all members can be called to account for their *individual* responsibility and effort. Individuals are more flexible, more mobile, slicker, wetter and more 'adaptive' than rigid collective structures on dry land, and that makes them very suitable for the water society. It is also why 'independent' curators have a better market position in today's art world than do collective museum structures with their local artistic, political, social and economic embedding and historical and art-historical obligations. One of the reasons is that the 'independent' curator can provide the manoeuvrability of a speedboat, whereas institutions are as unwieldy as mammoth tankers. Just like an entrepreneur, this player stays dynamic by constantly keeping a watchful eye on the potential competition from other curators and fluently anticipating it. The curating boom with its worldwide culture of selection and contests fuels this competitive mood even more. Just like independent entrepreneurs, curators who wish to keep their heads above water take their destiny into their own hands, never give up and respond with a problem-solving attitude to every new challenge that the surrounding oceans throw at them. Indeed, in the flat wet world, creativity is often equated with 'problem-solving', which is something else entirely than causing problems or, rather, *problematizing* issues, a task that was until recently reserved for the artist or dabbler.

Over the past two decades, the art world has increasingly come to define itself as part of the network society outlined above. It should be no wonder, therefore, that a lot of the jargon mentioned here can be found in today's exhibition catalogues. The word 'network' is ubiquitous and the careers of curators and artists are treated like a succession of temporary projects. Art schools, museums and biennials, as well as the cultural cities in which they

[redacted]

operate and produce, also define themselves as enterprises competing with each other for artistic, political and economic prestige. Their symbolic weight is reflected in visitor numbers, audits and other measurements, and their potential for creativity is expressed in this quantifying logic as well.

The Ideology of Realism

It would be too simplistic to condemn the network idea as a purely ideological concept. Within the present-day economy, however, it is increasingly being appropriated and deployed to serve the neoliberal hegemony. This is certainly true for labour relations, but also for the reorganization of education, the media, politics and relationships in the art world. Also, the whole network discourse is instrumental in completely redrawing the lines between the public domain, the labour sphere and the domestic sphere. To use the network concept as a purely neutral or descriptive term, as Bruno Latour does in his ethnographic work, or to flirt with it — often accompanied by some choice phrases by Gilles Deleuze — as happens in the art world, is to ignore or suppress the ideological appropriation of the notion of networking. It can only lead to sticking one's head in the sand.

As mentioned earlier, the current context of production by creative entrepreneurs is characterized by a high degree of individualization or de-collectivization of project work in a fluent network structure. The ambiance of this production context and the always youthful enthusiasm with which it is embraced, and even 'scientifically legitimized' under the guise of individual independence, makes the art world especially sensitive to neoliberal value regime. Those ideas cater to the desire of cultural producers to act autonomously, in full freedom. Creative capitalism of course tells its protagonists that they are, or at least should be, in control of their own lives and working conditions. It is their moral obligation. In exchange for this opportunity for self-regulation, the artist as well as the curator is prepared to offer her or his virtuosity cheaply, and sometimes even for free. The desire for autonomy, fuelled by the neoliberal appeal for realism and 'personal responsibility', eventually leads to 'self-precarization'. Artistic entrepreneurs take risks and neglect institutional securities (disability insurance, pension funds, etcetera), believing they can take care of these things themselves. Within these parameters, work offers the experience of a unique chance for self-realization, and that is exactly why labour is easily offered at low rates. In their urge to realization, entrepreneurs take up a sensible or realistic position in order to obtain their goals efficiently. In this secularized religion of 'self-realism', it is no coincidence that the root word 'real' fits in well with neoliberalism's call for more realism and the neo-manager's watchfulness over the realizability or feasibility of a proposed project. Utopia and excessive imagination is out of the question in this ideology of realism. Worse still, whatever cannot be measured is soon set aside as impracticable and too utopian. The urgent call for an awareness of reality obliterates the breathing space for an awareness of what is possible. Entrepreneurs, who are themselves the employers of their own labour, regard the realization of their objectives as real, and in the process *real*ize themselves. However, the belief in 'self-realism' often gets these employers/ employees into trouble. Political scientist Isabell Lorey has outlined the ambivalent situation into which these cultural and creative entrepreneurs manoeuvre themselves:

> This financing of one's own creative output, enforced and yet opted for at the same time, constantly supports and reproduces the very conditions in which one suffers and which one at the same time wants to take part of. It is perhaps because of this that creative workers, these voluntary precarized virtuosos, are subjects so easily exploited; they seem able to tolerate their living and working conditions with infinite patience because of the belief in their own freedoms and autonomies, and because of the fantasies of self-realization. In a neoliberal context, they are so exploitable that, now, it is no longer just the State that presents them as role models for new modes of living and working. (Lorey, 2011: 87)

Because classic bourgeois institutions offered many collective guarantees for the self-realization of the individual, that individual could also take more risks. Institutions guaranteed a collective safety net, as it were, for possible 'excesses'. But more importantly, institutions had a certain autonomy in defining their own reality

[redacted]

and so kept other yardsticks for measuring reality at bay. The classic art academy, for instance, shielded not only its students but its very subject, i.e. art, from the economy as well as from politics. As a result, students and teachers alike saw themselves as belonging to a different — sometimes perhaps naïve — world, but at the same time, this enabled them to measure themselves against an alternate reality. In other words, the isolation of the ideal art academy, with its risk of unworldliness, served the purpose of being able to see the world as also always possibly otherwise.

The artist-entrepreneur as outlined above can hardly appeal to this collective embedding in the institution anymore. Because the artistic risks that they take are hardly safeguarded by institutions as yet, they will simply be more careful before sticking out their necks. What's more, because art institutions are less and less able to build and protect their own value regime in an auto-referential way, artists are increasingly positioning themselves according to a measurable economic reality within the current neoliberal hegemony. This not only causes them to take less risks, but also means that the grace period for 'unprofitable' artistic experimentation is shortened. In other words, artists are forced to score in the short run and to avoid risks whenever possible. In the free market — which is an institution as well — the exchange between non-fiction and fiction is organized quite differently from the way this is done within the classic art institution. Whereas the latter related fiction to eternal life or at least to a lasting cultural contribution, the former stresses the importance of surviving in the here and now. And even more than that: within the hegemony of the market, making a cultural contribution is seen within the fiction of endless accumulation. The Sign of cultural eminence in a faraway future may be told directly from the present financial surplus value of the cultural product.

So, the free market cherishes its own fictions and its own utopia, as was wonderfully demonstrated by the Dutch philosopher Hans Achterhuis (2010). The only difference is that it regulates the exchange between non-fiction and fiction differently than the art institution and thereby generates a different reality. However, by persuading us that there is only one liveable reality possible, neoliberalism slips into the ideology of realism, as Mark Fisher has explained quite subtly (2009). Only that which can be calculated is manageable, and only that which is manageable is realistic and real. It should come as no surprise that such dogmatic realism produces evermore calculable art for the market.

Auditing Imagination

The possible exchange between non-fiction and fiction is not only shrinking because of the erosion of art institutions. As is well known, other social institutions such as education, the media, health care and the justice system are also being measured within the parameters of evidence-based policy. Today, they are all submitted to an audit industry that tries to reduce risk through standardized technologies for monitoring and measuring output. Through the audit, specific value regimes that used to be managed and controlled auto-referentially by institutions are now related to other value regimes, to values that often have little to do anymore with their original ideas about quality. Audits are therefore not passive instruments of inspection, but, as the economist Michael Power states, active players with specific ideas about quality and accountability. Institutions are thus made auditable and are being structured according to the needs of monitoring systems (1994: 7). Each audit ritual starts with a self-evaluation report, the sort of institutional confession in which an organization scans itself critically. The institution 'sincerely' shows all of its own positive and negative sides, but in doing this it also learns how to *imagine* itself in an alternate way. Values like justice, beauty, artistic innovation, imagination, health or intelligence, to name a few, are very hard to demonstrate to outsiders if they are not expressed in measurable units. For instance, it is much harder to prove to auditors that the art on display has a lot of quality or is even socially relevant than it is to present attendance figures or point to the *number* of reviews published about an exhibition. Says Power:

> The consequence is a displacement in the terms of government discourse, from service-specific values of teaching, care and so on to more abstract, financial and quantitative categories.... Audits do as much to construct definitions of quality and performance as to monitor them. (1994: 13 and 25)

And so the audit introduces into the institution its own values, such as efficiency, rationality and transparency, and especially the idea that

[redacted]

what is produced within the institution and what the institution stands for can indeed be measured and inspected. What's more, the auditors do this while pretending to be apolitical, according to Power. Formalizing and codifying audit processes does indeed generate a cosmetics for and of institutions that is highly interchangeable. The most diverse institutions are beginning to 'imagine' themselves in a similar manner for the outside world, the more so because they assume that this is a manner that is at least understood. The audit promises transparency, after all. In doing so, however, institutions are denying their own specificity and are taking less and less effort to explain it.

This uniformization of the public image of sometimes quite different institutions has the effect that laymen think they can really instantly understand their specific values and institutional value hierarchies. Through the re-codification of art, health care, etc. in quantitative terms, their qualities appear to be related and therefore interchangeable. This illusion of 'instant understanding' of a world or value regime (an illusion which is maintained by the mass media, by the way) makes people feel that they don't need to move anymore, that hardly any effort is required to get from one world to another. It makes it all the more difficult to still see *the* world from a fundamentally different perspective or value regime. Those who do not understand that institutional worlds can be radically different, that there are irreconcilable value hierarchies, limit for themselves the possible routes between the real and the imagined world. They do not realize, for instance, that the same artefact becomes a radically different reality when it is addressed and treated from a religious, economic, artistic, educational, political or legal value regime. All these worlds are reducible to the rule of efficiency and the unity of the number. And the institutions themselves have taught this to the outside world by imagining themselves in a way that is 'understandable' to auditors and the mass media. In doing so, they have also reduced the gross global possibilities of imagination.

Intervention beyond the Contemporary

Looking at the attitude of art institutions historically, it is obvious that in general they take a relatively passive stance. In the nineteenth century, when geopolitics ruled, they became instruments of the prevailing nationalism and when neoliberalism arrived on the back of globalization, museums and other art organizations became 'contemporary' and easily switched to legitimizing themselves with business figures, numbers of visitors and output measurements. Although these public legitimizations and imaginations sometimes deeply affected the auto-referential values of the institutions themselves, it looks as if a core of authenticity has remained intact somewhere deep down. As institutions increasingly start to behave as corporate organizations, the modern imagining of artistic values remains present for the time being. However slick, cunning, competitive and profitable art institutions may themselves behave these days, for the time being the memory of something like artistic autonomy or even transgression, but especially imagination, is still kept alive. Art still cherishes the idea of *that which can always also be otherwise imagined*, an idea it has upheld since the advent of the modern age. Meanwhile, this idea has been adapted by advertising, abused by post-Fordism and digested by cognitive capitalism, which is centred on the accumulation of immaterial assets. Art *knows*, however, that this is not about true imagination or an absolute possibility, as it is still breathing this artistic utopia through the cracks and fissures of its institutions. For now, the art world remembers only too well that it was the inventor of the route between fiction and non-fiction from the beginning of the modern era. It even, thanks to the existence of the art institution — even in its current, sometimes completely degenerated form — relatively safeguards the knowledge of the distinction between fiction and non-fiction. And also thanks to the art institution, we are aware that this distinction between reality and imagination is an aspect of all worlds — so also of the worlds of politics, science and economics.

If a third wave of institutional critique is to succeed, it will have to make that modern truth of art, which lies buried within the art institution like a public secret, the motor of its critique. Paradoxically, this means that institutional critique must accept the institution as its ally. Not the institution in its present organizational, operational and sometimes opportunistic form, but the institution as a value regime and keeper of an imagined ideal. However, if institutional critique is to prevent this ideal from being completely lost, it will have to 'de-pacify' the institution. Just as the market today is overflowing its banks, the art institution will have to go beyond its own borders to intervene in the world. It would be an illusion to think that we can keep neoliberalism from penetrating the walls of the institutions. What's more, it would be

[redacted]

reactionary to defensively withdraw again to one's own temple in the spirit of the modernist ideal. Rather, art will have to burst at the seams and break into 'alien' social domains such as the domestic domain of the private home, into the familiar spheres of its peers in art academies and studios, into civil space and the political arena and, yes, into the free market and ruling neoliberalism.

To do this, institutional critique should first and foremost imagine its own values according to its own logic — so, no longer via the imagination demanded by auditors and other accreditors or the mass media. Art will then tactically respond to the colonization of both the public and domestic sphere by the neoliberal market logic by developing counter models for those same domains. For instance, where market logic now occupies the domestic space with home entertainment and precludes individual creativity there, museums and biennials will break this creativity open again via the Internet, workshops for children, volunteer work and all sorts of means by offering unformatted and non-pre-programmed possibilities. Among peers and within the walls of the schools, the art institution will juxtapose the call for entrepreneurship, marketing and management with a political discourse. It will teach students to self-reflexively understand that this currently prevailing call is ideologically biased and that it offers but one imagined reality within a whole kaleidoscope of possibilities.

It will also teach them that being an artist is not an individual fate, such as proclaimed by entrepreneurship, but that they can fall back on collective structures of solidarity. Nowadays, for instance, some artist-in-residence and biennial circuits already make up an alternate economy of bartering, exchange and services. Within the value regime of the market, the art world is building on these far-from-neoliberal transactions. It is beginning to oppose the property laws of the creative industry with the free rights of the creative commons, for example.

The art institution will also no longer try to lure an audience through all kinds of marketing strategies by asking it what it wants. On the contrary, the institution will start to tell its audience, in the public domain, what it *should* want, if that audience wants to preserve its imaginative powers. The journey from one world to another sometimes needs to be jumpstarted. In the recent past, institutions seemed almost embarrassed to take on a truly guiding role, to suggest designs for communality based on their own value frameworks. The fear of coming across as patronizing or pedantic has paralyzed their social performativity.

From the very moment that art started calling itself 'contemporary' (everything that is made now is contemporary and therefore has no historical depth, but neither does it have a future), it not only lost its verticality. By applying such sterile self-labelling (which by the way is remarkably in tune with the movement in the 1970s through the mid 1980s towards post-Fordism and neoliberalism), art lost its own voice. Everything that is made today can be labelled 'contemporary' and this automatically disqualifies anything that was made yesterday. Contemporary art refuses to make a clean break with the past, precisely through an uncomplicated forgetting. But in its embrace of the hyper-current, art above all lost the vigour to really concern itself with history. The intoxication of the contemporary leaves no time for solidification and so everything remains fluid. In its desire to be 'with it', to 'keep up with the times' and not, like the historical avant-garde, be *ahead* of its time, contemporary art gave up on any utopian plan to really intervene in the world. In short, the route from fiction to non-fiction was closed. Contemporary art has exiled itself to a safe island within the white walls of the purely imaginary, where anything is possible as long as it makes no claims to reality.

If the art institutions are to survive, they will have to pitch their tents outside of these walls. The tent poles will no longer reach the unassailable heights of the pillars, but they will be unquestionably vertical. Adapting and anticipating in the flat wet contemporary can only be forsaken by intervening again from verticality, not with the ambition of 'keeping up with' but of 'staying ahead of'. Not for the sake of being fashionable, but simply because society needs imagination. This, by the way, is the difference between fashion or trends and art. Fashion, if it wants to sell, cannot afford to be too far ahead of its time, while art has not yet completely given up its right to a visionary sluggishness, at the risk of being perpetually unmarketable and ethereally un-contemporary. A third wave of institutional critique can only succeed if it uses its imagination to be critical from a really distant future perspective. This means taking an upright stance to shake off and destroy the indifferent and blind contemporaneity of current art institutions. It must, in other words, not follow the world but intervene in the world. Only then will it be able to write history again. It is only through such 'creative destruction' (Schumpeter, 2010) that art institutions can secure their social mission for the

[redacted]

future. Only then will the prediction that the Danish-French artist Thierry Geoffroy wrote on his tent at *Documenta 13* come true: 'The Emergency will replace the Contemporary'.

Bibliography

Achterhuis, Hans. De utopie van de vrije markt. (Rotterdam: Lemniscaat, 2010.)
Barrico, Alessandro. De Barbaren. (Amsterdam: De Bezige Bij, 2011.)
Bauman, Zygmunt. Liquid Love: On the Frailty of Human Bonds. (Stafford: Polity Press, 2009.)
Benjamin, Walter. 'The Author as Producer'. In Thinking Photography, ed. by Victor Burgin, p. 15-31. (London: McMillan, 1980.)
Bourriaud, Nicolas. 'Altermodern'. In Altermodern: Exhibition Guide, ed. by Fiona Gaskin and Kirsteen McSwein. (London: Tate Publishing, 2009.)
Corsten, Marie-José, Pascal Gielen, and Luigi Coppola. '"The Cleverness of Spirituality". An Interview with Michelangelo Pistoletto'. In Being an Artist in Post-Fordist Times, ed. by Pascal Gielen and Paul De Bruyne, pp. 55-67. (Rotterdam: NAi Publishers, 2009.)
Davidts, Wouter, and Kim Paice. The Fall of the Studio: Artists at Work. (Amsterdam: Valiz, 2009.)
Fisher, Mark. Capitalist Realism: Is There No Alternative? (Winchester: Zero, 2009.)
Gielen, Pascal. The Murmuring of the Artistic Multitude: Global Art, Memory and Post-Fordism. (Amsterdam: Valiz, 2009.)
Gielen, Pascal, and Paul De Bruyne, eds. Being an Artist in Post-Fordist Times. (Rotterdam: NAi Publishers, 2009.)
Gielen, Pascal, and Paul De Bruyne, eds. Teaching Art in the Neoliberal Realm: Realism versus Cynicism. (Amsterdam: Valiz, 2012.)
Holmes, Brian. 'Extradisciplinary Investigations: Towards a New Critique of Institutions'. In Art and Contemporary Critical Practice: Reinventing Institutional Critique, ed. by Gerald Raunig and Gene Ray, pp. 53-61. (London: MayFly Books, 2009.)
Laermans, Rudi. 'Disciplining Thought vs. Nimble Thinking: Possible Stakes of Teaching Theory'. In Teaching Art in the Neoliberal Realm: Realism versus Cynicism, ed. by Pascal Gielen and Paul De Bruyne, pp. 145-64. (Amsterdam: Valiz, 2012.)
Lorey, Isabell. 'Virtuosos of Freedom: On the Implosion of Political Virtuosity and Productive Labour'. In Critique of Creativity: Precarity, Subjectivity and Resistance in the 'Creative Industries', edited by Gerald Raunig, Gene Ray, and Ulf Wuggenig, pp. 79-90. (London: MayFly Books, 2011.)
Masschelein, Jan, and Maarten Simons. Globale immuniteit: Een kleine cartografie van de Europese ruimte voor onderwijs. (Leuven: ACCO, 2006.)
Nancy, Jean-Luc. The Inoperative Community. (Minneapolis, MN: University of Minnesota Press, 1991.)
Power, Michael. The Audit Explosion. (London: Demos, 1994.)
Schumpeter, Joseph A. Capitalism, Socialism and Democracy. (London and New York: Routledge, 2010.)
Sennett, Richard. The Corrosion of Character: The Personal Consequences of Work in the New Capitalism. (New York and London: Norton & Company, 1998.)
Sennett, Richard. The Craftsman. (New Haven, CT: Yale University Press, 2008.)
Sloterdijk, Peter. Het kristalpaleis: Een filosofie van de globalisering. (Amsterdam: SUN, 2006.)
Sloterdijk, Peter. Je moet je leven veranderen. (Amsterdam: Boom, 2011,) translated from the German: Du mußt dein Leben ändern [You Must Change Your Life], (New York: Polity Press, 2013.)

[redacted]

Where is the Critic?

Thijs Lijster

In 1910, the Salon des Indépendants in Paris exhibited a painting by a mysterious young Italian painter named Joachim-Raphaël Boronali. Nobody had ever seen or heard of him before. The painting, titled *Et le soleil s'endormit sur l'Adriatique*, was a brightly coloured abstract work. In the accompanying manifesto, Boronali named his new style 'Excessivism'. Critics debated the quality of this new work, and discussed whether it could indeed be the next step in painting. In the meantime, newspaper reporters went looking for the 'man behind the work'. When they eventually found him, however, it turned out to be a donkey answering to the name of Lolo. Its owner, the novelist Roland Dorgelès, had attached a brush to the donkey's tail in order for it to create its masterpiece. In this way, Dorgelès wanted to unmask the empty rhetoric of art criticism.

Art critics traditionally have a bad reputation. Like other major art institutions, such as museums and academies, art criticism represents verticality, differentiating between good and bad and judging in the name of history. But much more than is the case with the other institutions, verticality in art criticism is fixed in a single figure: the art critic. This is why critics are considered elitist, mandarins and know-it-alls. They are the sourpuss spoiling the festive premiere or exhibition. Especially among artists, critics are held in low esteem. Their opinion of critics, expressed in Dorgelès' practical joke, is perhaps most waspishly formulated by the Irish playwright Brendan Behan: 'Critics are like eunuchs in a harem; they know how it is done, they've seen it done every day, but they're unable to do it themselves.'[1] Consequently, artists usually ignore critics, or, at times, fear them.

Who will mourn the extinction of these armchair experts? For this is what we increasingly hear: the critic is moribund. Critics from all corners — the visual arts, performing arts, literature, and academic as well as magazine critics — give witness to a crisis. In recent years, numerous publications have proclaimed or heralded the 'end of' or 'farewell to' criticism, or the 'death' of the critic.[2]

Who killed the critic? Like detectives, sociologists and historians have searched for clues to find out who or what could be held responsible for the demise of the critic. Meanwhile, another question forces itself upon us: is the death of the critic a blessing or a curse? For while criticism, like museums and art academies, is experiencing the dire consequences of our increasingly 'flattening' world, its decline is seldom mourned. More often than not, the critic is considered a relic of a less democratic age, which we are happy to have gotten rid of. Why do we need critics once we can decide on our own what we like and do not like?

In this essay, I will first analyze the disappearance of the critic. Next, I will argue that the decline of criticism cannot so easily be considered a symptom of democratization. I think the figure of the critic can still play an essential role in a democratic public sphere. In the final part, I will discuss how we might rethink the figure of the critic.

Rise and Fall of the Critic

At first sight, it seems absurd to state that art criticism is facing extinction. Aren't newspapers filled daily with reviews of exhibitions, performances and movies? Isn't art criticism practiced in catalogues, glossy magazines, and, last but not least, innumerable weblogs on the Internet? James Elkins, in his pamphlet *What Happened to Art Criticism?* (2003), agrees that much is written about art, but in his view, this massively produced art criticism is also massively ignored: 'Art criticism is flourishing, but invisibly, out of sight of contemporary intellectual debates. So it's dying, but it's everywhere. It's ignored, and yet is has the market behind it.'[3] Catalogues are skimmed through during a visit to a museum; reviews are read half-asleep during breakfast. In Elkins' view, little of what is written really impresses its audience, while the chances of art criticism penetrating into academic discussions on art history or aesthetics are rare. The reason for this, he argues, is the lack of a common ground for art criticism: critics throw around adjectives such as 'deep', 'disturbing', or 'Lacanian', but behind this jargon there seldom is a real theoretical paradigm or foundation. Present-day art critics, Elkins argues, are reluctant or unwilling to take a step back from the here-and-now, as famous critics from the past still dared to do.

Elkins points to an interesting problem in his pamphlet, but he does not really answer the question posed in the title. Although

1 Quoted in: Rónán McDonald, *The Death of the Critic* (London: Continuum, 2007), p. 9.
2 Cf. Maurice Berger, ed., *The Crisis of Criticism* (New York: The New Press, 1998); James Elkins, *What Happened to Art Criticism?* (Chicago: Prickly Paradigm Press, 2003); Raphael Rubinstein, ed., *Critical Mess: Art Critics on the State of Their Practice* (Lenox, MA: Hard Press Editions, 2006); McDonald, op. cit.; James Elkins and Michael Newman, eds., *The State of Art Criticism* (New York: Routledge, 2008).
3 Elkins, op. cit., p. 2.

[redacted]

he sketches a convincing image of the situation of present-day (visual) art criticism, he does not tell us how art criticism has ended up in this awkward situation. Many theorists have thought about this problem. One might divide their arguments into three possible answers. First, there are those who explain the death of the critic within the much broader context of the decline of the public sphere, which is the cradle and natural habitat of the critic. Then there is a second category of authors who relate the disappearance of the critic to the depoliticization and self-devaluation of art, which, they argue, was obligingly followed by criticism. Finally, there are those who argue that the critic is dying because of a rupture in criticism itself, between academic and journalistic criticism.

Authors such as Jürgen Habermas and Richard Sennett belong to the first category.[4] They have famously described how the eighteenth century witnessed the emergence of a public sphere, as a realm between state authority and private interest. In this sphere, the modern figure of the critic was born. Interestingly, however, the primal history of the critic shows him or her to be a 'horizontal' rather than a 'vertical' being. Part and parcel of the late eighteenth-century tendency to abjure a rule-based aesthetics (consider, for example, Kant's *Critique of Judgment*), critics are primarily defined not by their knowledge of the rules, but by their taste, an *a priori* faculty accessible to every (rational) human being. This idea of taste, Habermas argues, determines the 'dialectical task' of modern critics. On the one side, they are the educators of the public, but on the other side, they speak on the public's behalf, since their judgment of taste has claims to universality.

This a priori egalitarian and democratic notion of criticism contained an emancipatory political impetus from the very beginning. In principle, everyone can have, and should be allowed to develop, an adequate judgment of taste. This means that the classical *rules* of beauty, personified by the taste of nobility, lose their force of law. Art criticism is, in other words, from the outset a political phenomenon. It both presupposes and stimulates a public sphere where individuals can meet as equals. It is suspicious of authority; that is, of any kind of authority whose source is not available to all people.

As Habermas and Sennett argue, the public sphere disintegrated over the course of the nineteenth and twentieth centuries. The same free market that once conditioned the public sphere now turned against it, as private interests and consumption got the upper hand over public discussion and emancipatory ideals. Habermas argues that the pseudo-public sphere of cultural consumption has replaced the 'artistic public sphere'. Art has become, on the one hand, a leisure activity dominated by the cultural industry, while on the other hand the artistic avant-gardes have turned it into a domain exclusively accessible only to a select group of connoisseurs. The public, he argues, is thus split 'into minorities of non-publically reasoning specialists and the big mass of publically receiving consumers'.[5] According to this line of argument, in short, the death of the critic is an epiphenomenon of this decline of the public sphere. Critics lose their publics, which increasingly prefer consumption above critical judgment. Moreover, with the rise of the mass media, critics lose their traditional mediating function: in a mass-mediated society, no one can claim to be 'better informed' than anybody else.

Not everyone agrees that we can blame the market and mass media for the death of the critic. In *l'Adieu à la litterature* (2005), the French theorist William Marx blames the artists and critics themselves.[6] In this controversial work, he poses the question of how is it possible that literature, which was once held in such high regard, could have become so marginalized. While Voltaire was still considered a hero in the eyes of a wide audience, literature and art today play no important role within public debates and are even cut out of school programmes. To describe how it could have come this far, he divides the history of literature after 1700 into three phases: 'expansion', 'autonomization' and 'devaluation'.

The first phase, expansion, is propelled by the nineteenth-century Romantic notion of the 'sublime', which has its origins in eighteenth-century art philosophy (e.g., Burke and Kant). According to this theory, poets are not merely craftspeople, but some sort of high priests who have access to a higher truth through the magical powers of language. And while poets are considered priests, critics become their temple guards. Famous critics began to judge works of art not merely by the extent to which they followed the rules of the classics, but also by the extent to which they expressed a moral and social meaning.

4 **Jürgen Habermas,** Strukturwandel der Öffentlichkeit. Untersuchungen zu einer Kategorie der bürgerlichen Gesellschaft **(Berlin: Neuwied, 1962); Richard Sennett,** The Fall of Public Man: On the Social Psychology of Capitalism **(New York: Knopf, 1977).**
5 **Habermas, op. cit., p. 210.**
6 **William Marx,** l'Adieu à la litterature **(Paris: Minuit, 2005).**

[redacted]

The second phase begins with a farewell to precisely this idea of the moral and social relevance of literature, most notably in the doctrine of *l'art pour l'art.* According to Marx, 1857, the year of the trials against Flaubert and Baudelaire, marks a turning point. While nowadays these trials are often considered to have emerged from a primitive form of state censorship and petite-bourgeois moralization against art, Marx argues that in fact the prosecutors attached more importance to literature than did the accused. While the prosecutors still considered art to be a gateway to a higher truth or a better world, the authors and their defenders had erected a wall between beauty on the one side and truth and morality on the other.

This wall only got higher and higher towards the end of the nineteenth century, when the decadent movement even considered art as being hostile to life. This is where, Marx argues, the third phase sets in: devaluation. Poets like Paul Valéry and Hugo von Hofmannsthal lament the utter senselessness and powerlessness of poetic language, and its inadequacy to express human experience and feelings. Their conclusion is that one should learn how to be silent. In Marx's view, this essentially comes down to poetic suicide.

Where were the critics when this happened? Marx describes how criticism, which in his view should have distanced itself from literature when it committed suicide, instead imprisoned itself, together with literature, in the poetic form. By consequence, it too lost its relationship with the outside world. Roland Barthes, the famous French critic, once wrote that criticism is essentially equal to art, but while this statement was applauded as criticism's emancipation from its parasitical status, Marx argues that it in fact meant that criticism had chained itself to a sinking ship.

William Marx provides an interesting perspective on the development of the history of literature and criticism, and the way their social function and position changed throughout the past centuries. One of the strengths of his arguments is that he does not point to the 'usual suspects' of youth culture, television or the Internet to explain the devaluation of criticism, but blames the artists and critics themselves for this marginalization. If they cannot or will no longer explain what their function and importance is, why should the public bother?

However, the strength of this original and controversial position is at the same time a weakness. One could argue that

Marx himself makes the mistake he accuses literature of: he has too little attention for the outer-literary reality. Neither the elevation of the poet as priest, nor the doctrine of *l'art pour l'art* can be solely explained from the writings of Kant. These are not purely inner-literary developments. To understand them, one has to consider the social, political, economic, and technological contexts — the fall of the *Ancien Régime*, the rise of the middle class, the invention and development of the printing press. Likewise, to understand what Marx calls the 'devaluation' of literature one cannot ignore the introduction and increasing democratization of new media.[7]

This brings us to the third explanation of the disappearance of critics, namely a schism in criticism itself. Rónán McDonald, in his *The Death of the Critic* (2007), observes that the public critic as described by Habermas has been ripped apart. The two halves consist of a specialized, but also obscure, impenetrable and non-evaluative, academic criticism on the one side, and an accessible but superficial journalistic criticism on the other. McDonald accuses both the ivory tower of academia and the 'slums' of journalism and the 'blogosphere' of the death of the critic.

Academic criticism, as some theorists argue, is the result of the critic's shift in allegiance, occurring in the nineteenth century. While the critic of Habermas' public sphere represents (or at least pretends to represent) first and foremost the *sensus communis* of the public, or even of the entire community of humanity, the later critic's loyalty lies first with the work of art. This estrangement from the public already begins with Romanticism. The German Romantics argued, for instance, that criticism has no goal or purpose outside the realm of art itself, while British Romanticism gave birth to the figure of the 'sage', a prophet-like man of letters speaking from transcendent heights.[8] And although the avant-gardes of the twentieth century turned their attention to the public, their works are actually directed towards a public as they believe it should be. As Boris Groys writes:

7 Apart from this, Marx is very selective in his use of examples. Twentieth-century authors that clearly do not fit into the third phase of 'devaluation', such as Breton, Brecht or Solzhenitsyn, are neglected or only mentioned in passing.

8 Terry Eagleton, *The Function of Criticism: From The Spectator to Post-Structuralism* (London: Verso, 1984), p. 39.

[redacted]

> Now it is not the observer who judges the art work, but the art work that judges – and often condemns – its public.... Every individual is free to place himself, against the rest of the public, on the side of the art work – to number himself among those constituting the new humanity. Several art critics of the historical avant-garde did just that. In place of the critic in the name of society arose social critique in the name of art: The art work doesn't form the object of judgment but is instead taken as the point of departure for a critique aimed at society and the world.[9]

The critic, in other words, now sides with a *future* humanity. He or she is no more the spokesperson for the public, but rather considers the public as the enemy. This is no less the case for the avant-garde critic than it is for the conservative critic, who regards the general public as barbarians standing at the gates of culture, threatening the precious goods of art. While cultural mass-consumption is on the rise, the critic increasingly focuses on a small circle of kindred spirits.

During the nineteenth century, the university formed an important condition for this shift in loyalty. National awareness stimulated the founding of departments of national cultural and literary history, forming a harbour of refuge for critics. There they could safely neglect the public, leaving it to the graces of newspapers and magazines. But this independence and emancipation came with a price of isolation and alienation. In leaving the public sphere behind, critics also lost the political function they still had in the eighteenth century. Terry Eagleton writes:

> The academicization of criticism provided it with an institutional basis and professional structure; but by the same token it signalled its final sequestration from the public realm. Criticism achieved security by committing political suicide; its moment of academic institutionalization is also the moment of its effective demise as a socially active force.[10]

Ever since, academic criticism has had to defend itself against charges of 'uselessness', both from within and outside academia's walls.[11] In the meantime, the position of the remnants of criticism in journalism did not go unquestioned either. The newspaper, traditionally the home of the critic, was challenged by other mass media. Art criticism was hardly considered a form of entertainment by the general public, and publishers increasingly favoured artist interviews over critical essays. This tendency is related to a breakdown of the traditional division of labour between artist and critic. The historical avant-gardes heralded the 'age of manifestoes', during which artists themselves provided the theoretical framework for their artistic practice. Finally, and most importantly, democratization and egalitarianism (which in the eighteenth century, as we saw, made modern criticism possible in the first place) gradually led to a fundamental distrust of anybody who attempted to impose standards with which to evaluate art and culture for the public. Nobody has to be told what they should like or dislike; everybody considers themselves entitled to their own opinion. Of course, such an environment is fatal for the traditional role of the critic, who, after all, pretends to be better informed than the average person, and hence better equipped to make judgments of taste. But if the crisis of criticism is indeed part of an increasingly 'horizontal' culture, why should we lament it? Why do we need it?

Why Criticism?

I have already pointed to the paradoxical situation that arises from the fact that although many agree that criticism is in crisis, it also seems to be thriving. Art is discussed not only in the traditional media (journals, magazines and newspapers), but also widely on the Internet. There are numerous weblogs where people interested in art and culture share their tastes and opinions. Shouldn't we conclude that the death of the critic is a mere symptom of the increased democratization of taste? Shouldn't we say, paraphrasing Joseph Beuys, that today everyone is a critic? The public's taste is now more than ever a force to be reckoned with. Some even argue that it is impossible to distinguish between tastes and values. The

9 Boris Groys, *Art Power* (Cambridge, MA: MIT Press, 2008), p. 112.
10 Eagleton, op. cit., p. 65.
11 See for instance Martha Nussbaum, *Not for Profit: Why Democracy Needs the Humanities* (Princeton, NJ: Princeton University Press, 2010).

[redacted]

British literary critic John Carey, for instance, claims that nobody can tell another person what to like or dislike, or what should be considered art. In his view, something is (good) art as soon as someone considers it as such.[12]

One should always be suspicious of gratuitous hymns to 'the people's power'. McDonald rightfully argues that an increase of public participation in discussions on art and culture is not necessarily as democratic as it might seem. To be sure, criticizing a seemingly democratic development is a hazardous enterprise. Many an intellectual cannot resist the temptation to lapse into hysterical lamentations over ubiquitous dumbing-down and to wailingly digress upon the 'eternal standards' of beauty. Such warnings of the vulgarization and corrosion of aesthetic standards will not do critics any good, for they themselves were born, as we have seen, out of resistance to an elite culture, opposing traditional standards of perennial and classic beauty. Contempt about the vulgarity of the 'blogosphere', moreover, ignores the fact that today there is actually a lot of qualitatively high standard art criticism on the Internet. I would argue that the divide between traditional criticism and journalistic and weblog criticism is not the same as that animating the old discussion of high versus low culture. Furthermore, there is no reason why a serious criticism of that which passes for 'low' culture — pop music, movies, comics, television series, etc. — should not be possible.

So the question is not one of determining between high and low culture, but whether the judgment of the critic, as a skilled, trained and experienced observer, is more legitimate or valuable than the opinion of any other average person. Or is beauty and aesthetic quality in the eye of the beholder? These are ancient philosophical questions, lacking a definitive answer, but they gain renewed urgency, since everyone in the debate answers them explicitly or implicitly. McDonald argues that the democratic aura that glows around the dictum that 'everyone is entitled to their own opinion' is false. The Internet, he argues, has to cope with the practical problem that it is incredibly vast. Therefore, artistic and literary weblogs have to specialize and subdivide in innumerable little niches, each covering a part of the artistic field. But because of that, people roaming the Internet are often searching for, and confronted with, a reflection and affirmation of their own taste and opinions. This, he argues, is the exact opposite of the traditional role of criticism, which disputes prejudice and threadbare standards of taste, shedding light on the new, the strange and the unfamiliar.

McDonald's point seems to be confirmed by the fact that the traditional authority of professional critics has largely been taken over by celebrities. A now famous example is that of Oprah Winfrey, who managed to take Tolstoy's *Anna Karenina* to the top of the *New York Times Bestseller List* in 2004, after having praised and recommended it in her talk show and 'book club'.[13] To be sure, it is quite an accomplishment to get millions of people to read (or at least buy) a classic nineteenth-century novel of nearly a thousand pages. Still, the aesthetic quality of the novel is clearly not what is at stake here (since with the same ease, Oprah turns the next New Age self-help book also into a bestseller). The point is that the public would rather take the advice of a 'personality' or 'celebrity' it feels comfortable with, than that of a professional critic. Seen in this way, the idea that everyone can be a critic does not have the emancipatory or democratizing effect ascribed to it. If we are only searching for the affirmation of our own likes and dislikes, if we only listen to those people with whom we agree beforehand, this rather leads to conservatism and dogmatism than to emancipation and democratization.

Many theorists lamenting the decline of criticism argue that critics should once more be thoroughly *critical*, in other words, that they should once more dare to make value judgments. McDonald, for instance, argues that we should be reminded of the Greek root *kritos*, which means judge or judgment. He concludes: 'If criticism is to be valued, if it is to reach a wide public, it needs to be evaluative.'[14] Likewise, critic Raphael Rubinstein in an essay mentions the result of a questionnaire among critics, of whom seventy-five percent considered value judgments the least important of their tasks as a critic. Rubinstein expresses his amazement at this outcome and argues that 'it's not enough to simply present the things you like in isolation, that even in a radically multipolar artistic environment, value judgments must somehow be made and articulated'.[15] He does not tells us, however, *how* these value judgments should be made, (his 'somehow' has an almost desperate

12 **John Carey,** What Good are the Arts? **(London: Faber and Faber, 2006).**
13 **Jim Collins,** Bring on the Books for Everybody: How Literary Culture Became Popular Culture **(Durham: Duke University Press, 2010).**
14 **McDonald, op. cit., p. 149.**
15 **Rubinstein, op. cit., p. 33.**

[redacted]

undertone), nor does he show how this would help lift critics out of their marginal position.

In my view, however, the solution of making value judgments cannot match the compelling way in which theorists like Habermas, Eagleton and McDonald have illustrated the crisis of criticism. The way they define the problem of the decline of criticism rules out such an easy solution in advance. Obviously, the marginal position of the critic is not merely due to his or her lack of evaluative judgment, but is entangled in the very structure of society. The critic can judge all he wants, but if no one listens to him, it will certainly not help him. If the critic's judgments are to be of any consequence, he shall have to deal with that problem first.

In order to do so, we have to realize once more that art critics should be considered first and foremost in their public role, more specifically, in their role as intellectuals. Neither the work of art nor the aesthetic experience are private affairs for them. This means that the judgment of critics is not a mere 'culinary' matter, but forms the nexus between private experience and the public sphere. Neither should critics be thought of, as is sometimes suggested, as the guardians of the artistic canon. An artistic canon conceived of as a pantheon of 'masterpieces' resembles a butterfly collection: it might be beautiful, but it is still dead. Rather, critics are able to renew the life of reified art works, by reconnecting them to living experience. As the German philosopher and critic Walter Benjamin once rhetorically asked: 'For what is the value of all culture if it is divorced from experience?'[16] In Benjamin's view, the function of the critic is not conservation but actualization. Criticism is what he calls an intervention in the 'afterlife' of a work, which means not only an intervention in the historical reception of a work, but also an intervention through social, cultural or political debates by critics themselves.

Up until now, however, we have only moved our question around without actually answering it. If we are to conceive of critics as 'intellectuals', then what is an intellectual? Antonio Gramsci already argued that being an intellectual has nothing to do with one's intellectual capacities. In the same way that not everyone who fries an egg now and then is for that reason a cook, everyone may have certain intellectual capacities, but 'not all men have in society the function of intellectuals'.[17] The intellectual, in other words, is a social role certain individuals take upon themselves, and which in turn is attributed to them by the public. This implies that an intellectual is only an intellectual if he or she is recognized as such.

This, of course, is precisely the problem of the contemporary critic. In the eighteenth-century coffee houses and salons, as we are told by Habermas, a critic still had authority, representing the *sensus communis*, speaking on behalf of all and to all. Are there still critics today who are able to claim such an authority, and are recognized as such? In my view, one should be wary of the scent of nostalgia that tends to cling to eulogies of the eighteenth-century public sphere. Obviously, the critic who spoke on behalf of all and to all never existed in the first place. He spoke primarily on behalf of the other visitors of the salon, not for dockworkers and dairymaids. If there is one thing to learn from critical theory, it is that there is no such thing as a free-floating intellectual.

There are many ways a critic might relate to his public. In my view, a return to the times in which the taste of the many was dictated by the few is neither possible nor desirable. But neither am I convinced that everybody should be their own critic, an idea which, as I have argued, is only seemingly democratic. In the final part of this essay, I will try to present new ways in which intellectuals can relate to their audience, drawing on the ideas of Michel Foucault and Luc Boltanski.

The Critic as Intellectual

What is the role of the intellectual? In an interview in 1977, Michel Foucault introduces a distinction between the 'universal' and the 'specific' intellectual.[18] The universal intellectual is the type of intellectual that has been dominant throughout Western history. This is the intellectual inhabiting Habermas' coffeehouses: the prophet or *homo universalis* who speaks on behalf of everyone and in everybody's interest. According to Foucault, this intellectual had its source in law: 'The "universal" intellectual derives from the jurist or notable, and finds his fullest manifestation in the writer, the bearer of values and significations in which all can recognize themselves.'[19] Even the Marxist intellectual, though he or she

16 **Walter Benjamin,** Selected Writings: Vol. 2, 1927-1934 **(Cambridge, MA: Belknap Press, 1999), p. 732.**
17 **Antonio Gramsci,** Selections from the Prison Notebooks **(New York: International Publishers, 1971), p. 9.**
18 **Michel Foucault,** Power/Knowledge: Selected Interviews & Other Writings, 1972-1977 **(New York: Pantheon Books, 1980), p. 126ff.**
19 **Ibid., p. 128.**

[redacted]

acts as the representative of a certain class (an 'organic' intellectual, in Gramsci's terms) claims such a privileged access to universal values. The proletariat, after all, was in Marx's view the bearer of the universal interest of mankind, and the (party) intellectual spoke on its behalf.

Foucault argues that the late twentieth century witnessed the disappearance of the figure of the universal intellectual — even though in some circles there still existed a certain desire for prophets — and the dawn of a different kind of relationship between theory and praxis. This relationship is embodied by the figure of the 'specific' intellectual. Unlike universal intellectuals, specific intellectuals do not pretend to be neutral bystanders, but are conscious of their involvement in a system of power — the laboratory, the university, the hospital, the asylum, etc. They are specialists, but specialists who are aware of the social, moral or political impact of their field of research. As Foucault tells us, the atomic scientists after the Second World War (e.g. Oppenheimer and Einstein) can be considered the first examples of this new intellectual. They intervened in a public debate about nuclear weapons, and could only do this because of their highly specialized scientific knowledge and their unquestioned authority in their field. But one might also think of Foucault himself as a specific intellectual, who intervenes in a specific regime of truth production, namely psychiatry. The specific intellectual, in short, is not the one who judges on behalf of humanity as a whole, but the one who translates his or her specialized knowledge to debates in the public sphere.

Many contemporary public discussions on urgent questions such as climate change, humanitarian crises, financial crises, and genetic research, indeed ask for intellectuals who have specialized knowledge of these fields. Foucault is right to note that the position of universal intellectuals, the category to which the art critic traditionally belonged, is increasingly contested. Does this mean that we should think of the critic as a specific intellectual instead? At first sight this seems implausible, since, as Foucault argues, biology and physics are the privileged fields of the specific intellectual. Still, the art critic is a specialist too, namely in the field of art. This may seem a field where matters less urgent than nuclear power, climate change, and genetics are at stake. However, the domain of art should be considered an arena where artists experiment with, and raise questions about, matters concerning values, traditions, identity, and culture. Art works address and raise questions that concern us all, even though for most of us this is not immediately transparent. Art critics, as specific intellectuals, mobilize their expertise on the context, concepts, and/or history of art to facilitate the place of art in the public sphere.

Foucault, however, points to a danger faced by the specific intellectual, namely 'the danger of remaining at the level of conjectural struggles, pressing demands restricted to particular sectors'.[20] Indeed, if specific intellectuals are only concerned with (political) issues concerning their own field of research, more general and structural problems might be neglected. This is precisely the reason, I would argue, that there are still many intellectuals who pretend to speak on behalf of some universal value, which makes Foucault's claim that the universal intellectual has disappeared at least empirically contestable.[21] Rather, intellectuals intervening in public debates have to act *both* as specific and as universal intellectuals. They mobilize the specific knowledge of their fields, but also claim to represent universal human values, acting both as translator and as judge. We might think of the figure of the art critic as such a combination of a specific and universal intellectual: he has a specialized knowledge of a certain field of research, namely the field of art, but this field of research is particularly concerned with human values, self-reflection, and culture.

The privileged viewpoint, the alleged 'bird's-eye view' of the intellectual remains a problem, however. How can the critic steer between the Scylla of claiming a universal judgment and the Charybdis of being merely one among a cacophony of opinions? Perhaps here the art critic could learn something from critical social theory, where debates on the status, authority, and task of critique have gained a new urgency in recent years. One of the most promising contributions to this debate is Luc Boltanski's *On Critique* (2011).[22] Boltanski makes a distinction between a 'critical sociology of domination' and a 'pragmatic sociology of critique'. The programme of a critical sociology of domination presumes that sociologists can give an adequate description of power relations within society.[23] Critical sociology, furthermore, believes that

20 Ibid., p. 130.
21 See also René Gabriëls, *Intellectuelen in Nederland: Publieke controversen over kernenergie, armoede en Rushdie* (Amsterdam: Boom, 2001).
22 Luc Boltanski, *On Critique: A Sociology of Emancipation*, trans. Gregory Elliott (Cambridge, MA: Polity Press, 2011).
23 Boltanski identifies this programme with the work of Pierre Bourdieu, of whom he was a student.

[redacted]

social theory poses a challenge to forms of domination. It attributes to itself, in other words, an emancipatory potential and task.

Boltanski argues that a critical sociology of domination faces several problems. First, the actors figuring in critical sociology might themselves be utterly oblivious to the forms of domination described by sociologists. To account for this possibility, critical social theorists assume that these actors are being deceived (i.e. that they have 'false consciousness'). This means, however, that sociologists necessarily underestimate, or even ignore, the critical capacities of the actors they are analysing. There is, in other words, an 'asymmetry between the sociologist enlightened by the light of his science and ordinary people sunk in illusion'.[24] This asymmetry lies at the basis of a second problem. In Boltanski's view, critical sociology not only overestimates its own range of vision, pretending to know people better than they know themselves, but it also overestimates its own emancipatory potential, which contradicts its utter contempt for people's critical capabilities.

The programme of a pragmatic sociology of critique responds to the asymmetry present in the programme of critical sociology.[25] Pragmatic sociology of critique is not primarily interested in its own critical perspective, but rather in 'observing, describing, and interpreting situations where people engage in critique'.[26] This means observing the way in which actors find themselves confronted with indignation, stress, and social tests, of how they deal with these, and how they justify their actions. Critique, in this view, is not a meta-perspective, but is what is happening in people's everyday lives. This approach has several drawbacks too, however. Placing the actors' own critique at the centre, the pragmatic sociology of critique is dependent on what Boltanski calls the actors' 'sense of reality'. Actors have a sense of what they consider 'normal', and this sense will determine the extent to which they experience feelings of indignation and anxiety, and hence the extent to which they are tempted to criticize what they consider the sources of these feelings. Indeed, pragmatic sociology of critique might be right in arguing that critique is happening all the time, but the scope of it is often quite local. Boltanksi argues that, with the exception of revolutionary situations, 'ordinary people rarely call into question… the general framework in which the situations that provoke their indignation and protests are inscribed'.[27]

What is lacking in a pragmatic sociology of critique, then, is what Boltanski calls a 'sense of totality', or in other words, a perspective from which the general framework can be questioned and criticized.[28] This is where a pragmatic sociology of critique could learn from the tradition of critical sociology. Hence, Boltanski argues that a new framework of critical social theory should take into account both the 'overarching' perspective and the 'pragmatic' perspective:

> From the overarching programme this framework would take the possibility, obtained by the stance of exteriority, of challenging reality, of providing the dominated with tools for resisting fragmentation.... But from the pragmatic programme such a framework should pay attention to the activities and critical competences of actors and acknowledgement of the pluralistic expectations which, in contemporary democratic-capitalist societies, seem to occupy a central position in the critical sense of actors, including the most dominated among them.[29]

This is not the place to elaborate on Boltanski's proposal concerning critical social theory. I merely want to note that his line of reasoning might also be fruitful for our discussion on the public role of the critic of art and culture too. Drawing a parallel with Boltanski's distinction between critical sociology and pragmatic sociology of critique, we can distinguish between two ways in which critics can relate to their public. On one side, we have the authoritative critics of yore, who autonomously pass their judgment on the work of art, and posit their taste and opinion on the public as the only viable and reasonable one. On the other side are

24 Boltanski, op. cit., p. 23.
25 This programme was introduced by Boltanski and Laurent Thévenot in *On Justification: Economies of Worth*, trans. Catherine Porter (Princeton, NJ: Princeton University Press, 1991).
26 Boltanski, op. cit., p. 24.
27 Ibid., p. 32.
28 Ibid., p. 33.
29 Ibid., p. 48.

[redacted]

the cultural theorists who are merely interested in how people engage with art and culture, refusing to discuss the value of these kinds of practices. From the perspective of the latter framework, the judgment of the critic would be as viable as anybody else's.

Following Boltanski, we might imagine a form of criticism that draws from both frameworks. Such a form of criticism would know that there is no Archimedean point outside of culture or society from which to criticize it. It would be aware of the fact that it is itself thoroughly embedded in that culture, and therefore takes into account the place of cultural phenomena in social institutions as well as in people's everyday lives. But such a criticism might also draw on the imaginative realm of the art work so as to pretend *as if* a meta-position was possible. From that position, it can develop a 'sense of totality', in Boltanski's terms. By means of the art work, the art critic is able to question that totality, to 'challenge reality' and to open up a perspective from which the social whole might be criticized.

Conclusion

It is sometimes argued that since there are no longer any fixed artistic rules or values, judgments or opinions concerning art are therefore completely subjective and hence art criticism is no longer possible. This is a *non sequitur.* On the contrary, an actual *debate* on art is possible only once we have dispensed with an aesthetics of rules, as Kant already saw. And even if we agree that artistic values are historical, transient and contingent, it does not follow that we live in an aesthetic 'vacuum'. Such a line of reasoning degrades our 'personal' opinions about art to a mere private matter. It fails to appreciate the public character of our views on art and culture — not only the extent to which these views are constituted by public discussions, but also the extent to which we generally desire to *make* these views public.

Art criticism is the name for the public exchange of aesthetic experiences and aesthetic judgments. Stressing the importance of criticism might be thought to imply that art is something for the happy few. The opposite is the case, however. As I have discussed, art criticism has its cradle in the modern public sphere. It does not presume fixed hierarchies or relations of authority, but rather starts from the premise that anyone can marvel over, reflect upon and argue about art. It is an emphatically democratic institution. But from this it does not follow that the critic's views are 'just' another opinion: as specialists of art, critics function as mediators between the individual aesthetic experience and the public sphere. They lay bare the historical and social experience that lies hidden in historical as well as contemporary works, connecting it to the experiences of their public. Drawing on specific works of art, they reflect and comment upon questions of culture, identity and tradition — questions that have, to a certain extent, always existed, but which gain urgency in the light of present-day debates. A critic, then, is a *medium* in the strict sense: he or she stands on the threshold of past and present, of private and public, of the artistic domain and the public sphere.

Finally, some might fear that an emphasis on the public role of art critics might jeopardize the autonomy of art. My point is not, however, that artists should be engaged in social and political debates. Commitment is here expected not primarily from the artists, but from the spectators, in so far as they should recognize the work of art as *always already* involved in these debates. Works of art are mediums of experience, which have something valuable to say about their world. Today, the distance of art from the public sphere has reached a point where Plato's dream of banishing art from the *polis* has all but come true. The function of the art critic today consists of making the aesthetic experience a matter of public concern once again.

[redacted]

The Place of Art in Art Places

Jimmie Durham

[redacted]

I've been trying to watch what happens in art systems; trying to be an anthropologist (trying to pretend to be disinterested).

In the beginning of the 1990s there was a surge of new curators, and so they often seemed to feel 'powerful'. Most artists perceived them as arrogant with little substance to back up the arrogance. It was simply as though a 'surplus' of artists had developed, and therefore the curators could pick and choose. They had to be competitive against each other, of course, but were more or less imaginative enough to create temporary spaces, events and shows; even finding enough money to stage them. They had ways of talking which sounded like they had control of the discourses on art, but again with little substance. I remember a young woman in New York admonishing me for continuing to make 'identity art' when it was so obviously passé (they were keen on knowing when things had become passé). I had not heard the term 'identity art' before, and did not imagine I was guilty of it. So many of their exhibitions had the most insipid selections — 'fluffy art', some of us called it — stuff that bothers no one but had the requisite symbols and signs of sophistication.

The mists did not clear, even though the spaces and curators evaporated. By the turn of the century, the art markets had inflated themselves. I suspect this had more to do with the rapid growth in the number of rich people in the US and Europe, through speculation with money, the Internet and real estate, than with actual reasons of art. Anyway, artists and their galleries began to sell more work at higher prices.

In a poorer art system, curators had focused on power. In this new system, galleries began to make strange deals with museums and other institutions. These transactions continue to develop in complexity, it seems, but I have no idea with what results. There is more bad art around (yet there would be, because more artists will always also mean more bad artists). As soon as this is committed to the page, however, an obvious result glares out: more bad art is made. We need only look at the publishing world. More bad books are published than good books because the money follows the lowest-common-denominator phenomenon of what people buy. We can see this even more easily in the magazine racks — more copies of the stupider magazines are sold than any others, even to the point that in many airport shops which stock thousands of magazines, nothing even vaguely reasonable is available. There is a larger market for stupidity. The principle also holds true for the art markets. When I ask why so many stupid books are written in the first place, I must also ask why so much stupid art is made. It is more sellable.

In the 1980s in New York, it was extremely rare for artists to live by the sale of their art. Claes Oldenburg worked at the Cooper Union library into the late 1970s. Artists worked as teachers, construction workers, film projectionists, with no stigma attached to the need for money. Did that mean that more of them could be more careful with their work? I think so. New York in the 1980s was kind of a silly place. It was not a golden age. But there was public support for art — never enough, seldom going to the right places, but much happened nevertheless. So many public art spaces! They were not meant to be cost-effective. When we applied for funding from the city, state or federal government agencies, we did not need to show how large an audience we planned to attract to a given event, and we did not need to show that we could sell tickets or otherwise make money independently.

I left New York in 1987, though, and already government agencies were shutting down and private corporations were using their funding of arts organizations for advertising and for tax rebates. Phillip Morris, Hugo Boss, Seagram and others started giving awards to artists as advertising.

From Mexico, and later from Europe, I began to lose touch and interest in these affairs. Then last year I received a request to participate in a group show at a new museum in New York. It seemed to be completely corporate — a commercial enterprise from the beginning. It was a little depressing; I was still thinking about museums from the position of how they might be improved. Suddenly caught off guard, but why? The USA has privatized most of its prisons, many public schools and much of its military. I guess I just wasn't quite ready for a commercial future.

In the harbours of Hamburg and Nantes, a growing number of giant mahogany and other tropical hardwood tree trunks arrives every month. They are used for making designer yachts. Friends who vacation in Greece and Italy report more and bigger yachts every year. This is because more young men have more extra money. The number of new millionaires and billionaires in the USA is worse than impressive. But there is no money in governments and we are in an ecomomic depression. All over Europe, hospitals are in bad condition, understaffed and underfunded. Shouldn't we assume that the health of the people is a primary

[redacted]

concern of governments? They say they must cut back on health-care and on social services, on nonessentials. I cannot figure out what is the actual case.

There is high unemployment in most of Europe, and not much production in general. More people who do have a job work in 'service industries' like restaurants. Fewer people do artisanal, construction or factory work. It looks as though people no longer see work as a central part of their lives. It looks like life has become only social, without the sociality. We go to the shopping mall, maybe join Facebook. If you become a plumber, you might join a union, go to the annual plumbers' picnic in the summer, the New Year's party. Friends might come over to play dominos. One's job might have some substance. Even now in Italy, there are men who are waiters. They've been doing the job without drudgery for years and are expert at it. Proud and cheerful. The new waiters, who have the job only temporarily while searching for something better, are not necessarily more socially or economically mobile.

It is as though the purpose of education is now to keep us from being plumbers, carpenters, mechanics or waiters. And we see, even though I do not understand it, so many young people becoming suddenly rich. We should all become rich, and not work. Well even if we could, it would not be a success. The rich artist is not necessarily the successful artist; was it her objective to become rich? Too paltry a goal to imagine for art, or for writing. When we think of books, of writing, we must really be thinking of our own individual reading. It is not necessary to be judgemental, to say what is good and what is bad. I might admire the work of Phillip Roth while Carolyn dislikes it, but neither of us will agree to be ripped off by books written and produced only for the market. I mean to say in part that art has at many levels, beginning with artists ourselves, become more and more tainted. Infected by commercial stuff.

Easy to say that we have allowed this situation to develop by our complacency. But no one has been complacent. Art systems, and again artists in particular, are famous for being non-joiners, for not being activists. But there is also the situation of not knowing what to do. It is at least fifteen years ago that I began to hear complaints from curators, from people in academies and institutions about the then-developing trend of governments putting the arts in the same basket as sports and leisure. There were, I'm sure, protests from many people. To no avail. As Foucault wrote, 'Stupidity gathers stupidity from every source as it rolls and sweeps along.' In the academies, so many people became worried over their jobs and/or their funding and accreditation if they did not closely obey rules that were distant from reality and commercial at heart. In the UK, this started under the Thatcher government, which was impervious to public opinion.

In 2012, I was invited to Brussels along with other artists to have a discussion with the European minister for arts, sport and leisure. That premise itself could not have been discussed. The framework, so detrimental, could not be on the agenda. Some years ago, I got angry audience responses for my objections to a 'blockbuster' show of Jackson Pollock's work. It was the disrespect for the work that I was objecting to, though; the spectacle wherein media hype causes thousands of people to stand in line for a three-second, crowded glimpse of Pollock's work.

Do I care if a book is a bestseller or not? The bestsellers are almost always nonsense. That might be depressing, but it is not a mystery. Practically every museum now has staff that will cheerfully brag about the success of a show by citing the number of visitors. We might complain about commercialism, yet we rent it, try to buy it. Under these rules, with these aims, a private corporate museum established for the purpose of making money will certainly be more successful than a clumsy, underfunded state-sponsored one. We need look only at how art fairs now generate more enthusiasm than the biennales — and, they are commercially successful.

The time when we might have tried to reason with governments and money systems has past. The new corporate museums will arrive in your area soon. Right away, there will be forward-looking professionals who say: 'It's really not so bad. Doing a surprisingly good job.'

[redacted]

Part II
Horizontal Strategies?

Institutions as Sites of Agonistic Intervention

Chantal Mouffe

I.

How to envisage forms of aesthetic resistance in societies where the production of symbols has become a central goal of capitalism? Should we agree with those who claim that, through the development of the creative industries, individuals have become totally subjugated to the control of capital? In their view, not only consumers but also producers of culture have been transformed into passive functions of the capitalist system. They are prisoners of the culture industry, dominated by the media and entertainment corporations. If this were the case, we would have to accept the post-political motto that 'there is no alternative' and abandon the hope that it is possible to bring about an alternative to neoliberal hegemony.

Fortunately, this pessimistic diagnostic is far from being shared by those engaged in artistic and cultural practices. In fact, it is increasingly being challenged by a variety of views which, while acknowledging the profound transformation brought about by the current Post-Fordist stage of capitalism, argue that these new forms of production allow novel types of resistance, to which artistic practices could make a decisive contribution. However, when it comes to envisaging the form that this resistance should take, we find important divergences. One of the main disagreements concerns the spaces in which resistance should be deployed and the type of relation to be established with the institutions. Should critical artistic practices engage with the current institutions with the aim of transforming them, or should they desert them altogether? An influential approach advocates what can be called a strategy of 'withdrawal'. It claims that the institutions of the art world have become complicit with capitalism and that they can no longer provide a site for critical artistic practices. Under Post-Fordist conditions, artists working inside the system are totally instrumentalized and, transformed into businesspersons, bound to contribute to the reproduction of the system. Resistance is still possible but can only take place outside the institutions.

It is interesting to note that this position, which is characteristic of a variety of authors influenced by the Autonomist tradition, acknowledges the growth of the culture industry already pointed out by Adorno and Horkheimer, but interprets it in a very different way. As is well known, Adorno and Horkheimer saw the development of the culture industry as the moment when the Fordist mode of production finally managed to enter the field of culture. For them, this evolution represented a further stage in the commodification and subjugation of society to the requisites of capitalist production. Adorno saw art as the only place where autonomy was still possible. It is this possibility that has now been eliminated by the advances of the commodification process, according to the pessimistic view mentioned at the beginning of this paper.

Post-Operaist theorists, influenced by the Italian Autonomia movement that stresses the proactive role of workers' struggles in the development of capitalism, see the transition from Fordism to post-Fordism in a very different way. Paolo Virno, for instance, asserts that the culture industries have played an important role in the process of transition between Fordism and post-Fordism.[1] It is where new practices of production emerged which led to the overcoming of Fordism. They represent, he says, the matrix of post-Fordism. Indeed, with the development of immaterial labour in advanced capitalism, the labour process has become performative, mobilizing the most universal requisites of the species: perception, language, memory and feelings. Contemporary production is now 'virtuosic' and productive labour in its totality appropriates the special characteristics of the performing artist. In his view, this transformation opens the way for new forms of social relations in which art and work exist in new configurations. Under Post-Fordist conditions, the objective of critical artistic practices should be to contribute to the development of the new social relations which are made possible by the transformation of the work process. Their main task is the production of new subjectivities and the elaboration of new worlds that would create the conditions for the self-organization of the multitude.

Such a view of the role of artistic practices goes together with a conception of radical politics formulated in terms of 'exodus'. This strategy of exodus comes in different versions, according to the way the future of the multitude is envisaged, but they all share the conviction that the traditional structures of power organized around the Nation State and representative democracy have today become irrelevant, and that they could eventually disappear. Hence the belief that the multitude can ignore the existing power structures and concentrate its efforts in constructing alternative

1 **Paolo Virno,** *A Grammar of the Multitude: For an Analysis of Contemporary Forms of Life* **(Los Angeles, CA: Semiotext(e), 2004).**

[redacted]

social forms outside the State power network. Any collaboration with the traditional channels of politics like parties and trade unions are to be avoided. The majoritarian model of society, organized around a State, needs to be abandoned in favour of another model of organization presented as more universal. It has the form of a unity provided by common places of the mind, cognitive-linguistic habits and the general intellect. This is why the various theorists of the 'exodus' approach are adamant that political action should aim at withdrawing from existing institutions and freeing ourselves from all forms of belonging. Institutional attachments as deemed to constitute obstacles to the new non-representative forms of 'absolute democracy' suitable for the self-organization of the multitude.

What such an approach forecloses is an immanent critique of institutions, whose objective would be to transform them into a terrain of contestation of the hegemonic order. The very possibility of a counter-hegemonic struggle to disarticulate the constitutive elements of neoliberal hegemony, with the aim of establishing a new power configuration, is precisely what is rejected by this approach. All institutions are perceived as monolithic representatives of the forces to be destroyed and every attempt to transform them is dismissed as reformist illusion. The strategy advocated is one of 'desertion' and of the creation of new social relations outside the existing institutional framework.

In the artistic and cultural domain, such an approach implies that critical artistic practices can only have efficacy if they take place outside cultural institutions. To imagine that museums, for instance, could provide a site for critical political intervention is, according to such a view, to be blind to the manifold of forces — economic and political — which make their very existence possible. The strategy, here again, is to ignore them and to occupy other spaces, outside the institutional field.

Such a perspective is, in my view, profoundly mistaken and clearly disempowering because it impedes us from recognizing the multiplicity of avenues that are opened for political engagement. To believe that existing institutions cannot become the terrain of contestation is to ignore the tensions that always exist within a given configuration of forces and the possibility of acting for subverting their form of articulation.

Contrary to this strategy of 'withdrawal from institutions', the strategy that I want to advocate is a strategy of 'engagement with institutions'. This strategy is informed by a theoretical approach that brings to the fore the discursive character of the social, and reveals how it is through a multiplicity of discursive practices that 'our world' is constructed, a construction that is always the result of a particular hegemony.[2] This theoretical approach reveals that society is always politically instituted and that what is called 'the social' is the realm of sedimented political practices, practices that conceal the originary acts of their contingent political institution. As the temporary and precarious articulation of contingent practices, every order is the expression of a particular structure of power relations. What is at a given moment accepted as the 'natural order' is always the result of sedimented hegemonic practices. Things could always have been otherwise and every order is predicated on the exclusion of other possibilities. This is why it is always susceptible of being challenged by counter-hegemonic practices that will attempt to disarticulate it so as to establish a different hegemony.

I submit that this approach is particularly fruitful for apprehending the relations between art and politics because it highlights the fact that the hegemonic confrontation is not limited to traditional political institutions but that it also takes place in the multiplicity of places where hegemony is constructed, i.e. the domain of what is usually called 'civil society'. This is where, as Antonio Gramsci has argued, a particular conception of the world is established and a specific understanding of reality is defined, what he refers to as the 'common sense', providing the terrain in which specific forms of subjectivity are constructed. Gramsci also emphasized the centrality of cultural and artistic practices in the formation and diffusion of this 'common sense', highlighting the decisive role played by those practices in the reproduction or disarticulation of a given hegemony.

From the standpoint of the hegemonic approach, artistic practices have a necessary relation to politics because they either contribute to the reproduction of the common sense that secures a given hegemony or to its challenging. Critical artistic practices are those which, in a variety of ways, play a part in the process of disarticulation/rearticulation which characterizes a counter-hegemonic politics. This counter-hegemonic politics aims at targeting the institutions which secure the dominant hegemony in

2 For a presentation of this approach, see Ernesto Laclau and Chantal Mouffe, *Hegemony and Socialist Strategy: Towards a Radical Democratic Politics* (London: Verso, 2001).

[redacted]

order to bring about profound transformations in the way they function. This strategy of a 'war of position' (Gramsci) is composed of a diversity of practices and interventions operating in a multiplicity of spaces: economic, legal, political and cultural. The domain of culture plays a crucial role in this war of position because, as we have seen, this is one of the terrains where the 'common sense' is built and subjectivities are constructed. In the present conjuncture, with the decisive role played by the culture industries in the capitalist process of valorization, the cultural and artistic terrain has become of strategic importance. Indeed, artistic and cultural production is vital for capital reproduction. This is due to the increasing reliance of Post-Fordist capitalism on semiotic techniques in order to create the modes of subjectivation which are necessary for its reproduction. The forms of exploitation characteristic of the times when manual labour was dominant have been replaced by new ones which constantly call for the creation of new needs and incessant desires for the acquisition of goods. They rely on the joint forces of advertising and the 'creative industries' for producing fantasy worlds through which the identity of the consumer is constructed. To buy something today is to enter into a specific world, to identify with a certain culture and become part of an imagined community. To maintain its hegemony, the capitalist system needs to permanently mobilize people's desires and shape their identities; and the cultural terrain, with its various institutions, occupies a key position in the process of commodification. To challenge this system, a counter-hegemonic politics must imperatively engage with this terrain and target the forms of identification that provide the conditions for the reproduction of Post-Fordist capitalism.

This requires a very different strategy to the one of 'withdrawal from institutions' advocated by the first conception that we examined. Critical artistic practices do not contribute to the counter-hegemonic struggle by deserting the institutional terrain but by engaging with it, with the aim of fostering dissent and creating a multiplicity of agonistic spaces where the dominant consensus is challenged and where new modes of identification are made available. I am convinced that a conception of radical critique fostering a strategy of 'engagement with institutions', instead of 'withdrawal from institutions', is absolutely crucial for challenging neoliberalism and envisaging the conditions of a radical democratic.

I would like to make clear that I am not arguing in favour

of a purely institutional conception of politics or for a relegation of critical artistic practices to the traditional domain of the art world, but for an articulation of different modes of political intervention in a multiplicity of places. There exists a great variety of ways of bringing about agonistic spaces, and they can emerge both inside and outside institutions. The hegemonic approach envisages radical politics as an articulation of parliamentary with extra-parliamentary struggles and aims at establishing a synergy between parties and social movements. In the specific domain of artistic practices, such an approach challenges the view that institutions cannot be transformed and that resistances can only develop and be successful outside them, and it encourages a diversity of interventions, inside and outside the traditional world of art. In our post-political times, where the dominant discourse tries to occlude the very possibility of an alternative to the current order, all the practices that can contribute to the subversion and destabilization of the hegemonic neoliberal consensus are welcome. As I will argue in a moment, museums, for instance, can under certain conditions provide spaces for an agonistic confrontation and it is a mistake to believe that artists who choose to work with them cannot play a critical role and that they are automatically recuperated by the system.

While asserting the continuing relevance of more traditional modes of artistic intervention, the approach that I advocate also acknowledges the significance of the various forms of artistic activism which have recently flourished. By putting aesthetic means at the service of political activism, this 'artivism' can be seen as a counter-hegemonic move against the capitalist appropriation of aesthetics in order to secure its valorization process. In its manifold manifestations, artivism can certainly help in subverting the post-political common sense and in the creation of new subjectivities. For instance, various modes of artivist intervention influenced by the Situationist strategy of 'détournement' like the Yes Men are very effective in disrupting the smooth image that corporate capitalism is trying to impose, bringing to the fore its repressive character. One could also mention a variety of urban struggles like 'Reclaim the Streets' in Britain, the 'Tute Bianche' in Italy, the 'Stop Advertizing' campaigns in France or the 'Nike Ground-Rethinking Space' in Vienna. There exist a great variety of types of artistico-activist practices and of modes of 'communication-guerilla', and those are only a few examples.

[redacted]

II.

How to visualize the future of the museum within such a framework? Could it contribute to the undermining of the imaginary environment of the consumer society? My view is that, far from being condemned to play the role of conservative organizations dedicated to the maintenance and reproduction of the existing hegemony, museums and art institutions could be transformed into agonistic public spaces where this hegemony is openly contested. To be sure, the history of the museum has been linked since its beginning to the construction of bourgeois hegemony, but this function can be altered. As Wittgenstein has taught us, signification is always dependent on context, and it is use which determines meaning. This is also true for institutions, and we should discard the essentialist idea that some institutions are by essence destined to fulfil one immutable function. In fact, we have already witnessed how, following the neoliberal trend, many museums have abandoned their original function of educating citizens about the dominant culture and have been reduced to sites of entertainment for a public of consumers. The main objective of those 'post-modern' museums is to make money through blockbuster exhibitions and the sale of a manifold of products for tourists. The type of 'participation' that they promote is based on consumerism, and they are actively contributing to the commercialization and depoliticization of the cultural field.

However, this neoliberal turn is not the only possible form of evolution; and another one can be envisaged, leading in a progressive direction. There might have been a time when it made sense to abandon the museums to open new avenues for artistic practices. But under the present conditions, with the art world almost totally colonized by the markets, museums could become privileged places for escaping the dominance of the market. As several theorists have pointed out, the museum, which has been stripped of its normative role, could be seen as a privileged place for art works to be presented in a context that allows them to be distinguished from commercial products. Visualized in such a way, the museum would offer spaces for resisting the effects of the growing commercialization of art.[3]

To rethink the function of the museum on those lines would represent a first step towards envisaging it as a possible site for countering the dictatorship of the global media market. It is interesting to note that such a move dovetails with other attempts to reclaim public institutions which have been targeted by neoliberalism. Think for instance of the change of attitude of a part of the European left with respect to the institutions of the welfare state, whose bureaucratic nature they used to criticize. This was no doubt a justified critique, but after they have been dismantled by neoliberal governments, many people have begun to realize that those institutions also constituted important forms of protection against the forces of the market and that their privatization had not represented a democratic advance. Similar considerations could be made towards the role of the State which, after years of demonization, has been re-evaluated during the 2008 financial crisis. Unfortunately, instead of intervening by imposing more regulations on the banks and promoting more redistributive policies, the State has simply come to the rescue of the financial sector. However, if the power relations had been different, things could have taken another direction. What this episode reveals is the necessity of the hegemonic struggle within existing institutions. I believe that the conclusion that we need to draw from these events with respect to the nature of public institutions is that, instead of celebrating the destruction of all institutions as a move towards liberation, the task for radical politics is to engage with them, developing their progressive potential and converting them into sites of opposition to the neoliberal market hegemony.

As far as museum and art institutions are concerned, there are already several offering different examples of the strategy of 'engagement with' that I am proposing. One of the best known is the Museu d'Art Contemporani de Barcelona (MACBA), which under the direction of Manuel Borja-Villel (who now heads the Reina Sofía in Madrid) succeeded in creating a new model of the museum.[4] Between 2000 and 2008, various projects informed by critical pedagogy were launched to recover the educational role of the museum, and its role as a constituent part of the public sphere. With the aim of proposing an alternative reading of modern art, the MACBA started to develop a collection and organize temporary exhibitions that privileged artists and art scenes that had been neglected by the dominant discourse on artistic modernity.

3 See for instance, Boris Groys, 'The Logic of Equal Aesthetic Rights', in *Art Power* (Cambridge, MA: MIT Press, 2008) pp. 13-22.
4 An excellent overview of the activities of the MACBA during those years is found in 'Experiments in a New Institutionality' by Jorge Ribalta in *Relational Objects: MACBA Collections 2002-2007* (Barcelona: Actar, 2010).

[redacted]

Among the many notable shows the museum mounted during this period were *Philippe Thomas: Readymades Belong to Everyone* (2000); *Art and Utopia: Restricted Action* (2004); *A Theatre without Theatre* (2007); and *Be-Bomb: The Transatlantic War of Images and All That Jazz. 1946-1956* (2007-2008). Another objective of the MACBA was to establish a vibrant relation between the museum and the city, and to provide a space for debate and the expression of conflicts. Looking for ways in which art could make a significant contribution to a multiplication of public spheres, it encouraged contacts between different social movements. For example, *The Direct Action as One of the Fine Arts* workshops organized in 2002 (and coordinated by Jordi Claramonte) brought together artist collectives and social movements to examine possible forms of connecting local political struggles with artistic practices. Several workshops were organized around topics such as precarious labour, borders and migrations, gentrification, new media and emancipatory policies. A further example of collaboration with the new social movements was the *How do we want to be governed?* project, conceived as a counter-model to the 2004 Universal Forum of Cultures launched by the City Council of Barcelona. While taking culture as an alibi, the true objective of this forum was a real estate operation to promote the urban renewal of the city's seafront. Curated by Roger M. Buergel, the *How do you want to be governed?* exhibition took place in several areas of the site to be remodelled. It was an exhibition in process, combining artistic work and social dynamics and involving debates with the neighbourhood movements.

The experience of MACBA represents a radical alternative to the modern and the post-modern museum, but many other types of initiatives would be worth mentioning. A particularly interesting one is the recently established 'L'Internationale', which consists of long-term collaborative projects between several progressive art institutes in order to collectively use their collections and archives to take issue with the dominant narratives in the art world and to build new plural narratives. The aim of this network, organized by five institutions — the Moderna galerija in Ljubljana, Slovenia; the Julius Koller Society (SJK) in Bratislava, Slovakia; the MACBA in Barcelona; the Van Abbemuseum in Eindhoven, The Netherlands; and the Museum van Hedendaagse Kunst Antwerpen (MuHKA) in Belgium — is defined in the following way: 'In place of the global hegemonic ambitions of the largest contemporary art institutions, L'Internationale proposes collaboration between museums, each with its specific collection focus and history, as a way to instigate transnational, plural cultural narratives.' This kind of network is in its first stages and would need to be enriched by partners outside Europe, but it suggests a promising way for art institutions to join together in the struggle against the hegemonic discourse.

What is really at stake in this debate about how to deal with institutions such as the museum is the nature of the political and its relation with artistic practices. According to the modernist view, a structural affinity exists between the political and the artistic avant-garde, but such a view needs to be relinquished. Its claim that the radical move consists of the destruction and radical negation of tradition and requires exit from all institutions, political as well as artistic, is not suitable for the task facing radical politics today. The challenge to neoliberalism needs to be envisaged as a 'war of position' (Gramsci) consisting of a variety of counter-hegemonic interventions whose objective is to disarticulate the nodal points through which the dominant hegemony is secured, so as to construct a more democratic one. The sites where this counter-hegemonic struggle should take place are multiple; however, in the current conditions of Post-Fordist capitalism, the field of artistic and cultural practices clearly constitutes a key area.

As Luc Boltanski and Eve Chiapello have shown in *The New Spirit of Capitalism*, capitalists have managed to capture the demands for autonomy made by the new movements that developed in the 1960s, harnessing them to secure the conditions required by the new mode of capitalist regulation.[5] They were able to neutralize the subversive potential found in the aesthetic strategies of the counterculture: the search for authenticity, the ideal of self-management and the anti-hierarchical exigency, transforming them into new forms of control which have replaced the disciplinary framework of the Fordist period. To this hegemonic move by capital, it is urgent to oppose a counter-hegemonic one, which opposes capitalism's programme of total social mobilization. Instead of deserting public institutions, the challenge is to find ways to use them to foster political forms of identification and make existing conflicts productive. By staging a confrontation between

5 **Luc Boltanski and Eve Chiapello,** The New Spirit of Capitalism **(London and New York: Verso, 2005).**

[redacted]

conflicting positions, museums and art institutions could make a decisive contribution to the proliferation of new public spaces fomenting agonistic forms of participation where radical democratic alternatives to neoliberalism could be imagined and cultivated.

[redacted]

On Democracy and Occupation

Horizontality and the Need for New Forms of Verticality

Isabell Lorey

Only a few months before the major protests broke out in Portugal, Spain and Greece in the Spring of 2011, no one in the 'West' spoke so euphorically of democracy. Democracy is the form of government that is perceived as 'normal' and taken for granted, and in the past decade it has become, most of all, a top 'Western' international export that has contributed, not leastly, to the legitimization of several wars. It is said that the best of all possible forms of government is to be found in the West: democracy, as a high degree of freedom and the rule of law in which 'the people' purportedly rule themselves.

Political struggles in the past decades were not primarily arranged around the central signifiers of democracy. Social and political movements mostly focused on exploitative and discriminatory conditions, fighting for more recognition and visibility on the legal and symbolic levels, specifically against the backdrop of democratic societies. Democracy supplied the self-evident framework within which the struggles took place. It was not so much a matter of newly inventing democracy, but rather of criticizing or reforming existing democratic conditions.

That changed in 2011. The mass protests in Tunisia and Egypt, the so-called 'Arab Spring' at the beginning of that year, came as a complete surprise to the West and were followed with great sympathy in many places. From a Western perspective, this revolution appeared wholly unforeseeable, and yet comprehensible as belonging to the pattern of 'Western' political development: in the Arab Spring, people were fighting for the introduction of democracy in order to finally rid themselves of long-lasting conditions of oppression. The struggles were directed against their respective rulers, until they had been overthrown and chased out. And yet from a traditional Western view, neither these successes nor the first relatively free elections were able to establish the kind of democratic conditions for which millions had taken to the streets.

Beyond this schematization of democracy — which is not unusual historically — strange things were happening in the Casbah Square in Tunis and the Tahrir Square in Cairo. The many who assembled there elected no leaders; they set up sit-ins and camps, and with support from friends and neighbours, in no time organized an infrastructure in the central public square. They assembled regularly, exchanged ideas, supported one another despite their different social positions and hierarchies of gender, religion and education, and protected one another so that it was even possible to live in the square, not only during the day, but also at night and for several days and weeks — although not without being directly or indirectly exposed to State force and resisting it.

These inventive political and social practices, which not only happened during the occupation of Tahrir Square, gave rise to a historically specific spark, which was able to spread in Europe and the USA as well. The occupiers in Cairo did not simply demand the end of dictatorship and the replacing of it with democracy. With the occupation of the squares, with assemblies, with the public exchange of ideas, they invented a battle strategy in which certain non-representationist and alternative forms of democracy were practised to introduce democracy. The activists in Tahrir Square did not want to import a complete package of representative democracy, but instead began fighting by changing public space. They did so specifically by developing not only new political practices, but also new socialities, new ways of living at the same time. Practices already started becoming evident here which were also to be observed in the 15M movement in the squares of Spain, and were then called 'horizontalism' in the Occupy Movement. Not only were the local squares occupied, but new democratic social and political practices were also invented in the occupations, the assemblies and in the organising. These practices were not oriented to those of representative democracy.

'They do not represent us' and 'They call it democracy, but it is none' were slogans that could be heard not only in the Puerta del Sol in Madrid and read on banners in May and June of the year 2011. Sol is no longer a geographical place, but rather an 'unexpected event', writes Marta Malo in *texts from the #Spanishrevolution*. 'It is not a matter of taking the street anymore, it's a matter of making the square.'[1] And Amador Fernández-Savater recorded the statement from the 15M movement: 'The democracy we want is already the organization of the square itself.'[2] Within only a few days, the main squares of more than sixty Spanish cities were occupied.

1 Marta Malo, 'Sol, or when the impossible becomes unstoppable', in texts from the #spanishrevolution, www.edu-factory.org/wp/spanishrevolution/#unstoppable; for all the texts published in English on the website of the Edu-Factory network, see: www.edu-factory.org/wp/spanishrevolution/.

2 Amador Fernández-Savater, 'Notes from #acampadasol (1)', in Texts From the #Spanishrevolution, www.edu-factory.org/wp/spanishrevolution/#acampadasol.

[redacted]

The movements of the precarious, called the 'indignants' from Spain to Portugal and Greece after the bestseller by Stéphane Hessel, related to the revolutions in Tunisia and Egypt and concatenated again and again with the slogan 'Real Democracy Now'. Non-representationist practices were not a wholly new invention; they have historical genealogies, not only in anarchism, but also in the Zapatist movement of the 1990s, and the anti-globalization and EuroMayDay movement of the 2000s. Yet the protests of the precarious in 2011 went far beyond the leftist social-critical spectrum. And there was more to it: this was a matter of collective political practices, which in 2011 were testing forms of non-representational democracy in countries of representative democracy to an unusually great extent.

Respectively and together, these breaks in different places signify an exodus from the given forms of democracy and can be understood on a theoretical level as the emergence of a constituent power.

> It is time to ask ourselves whether there does not exist, from a theoretical and practical point of view, a position which avoids absorption with the opaque and terrible essence of the State. In other words, whether there does not exist a viewpoint which, renouncing the perspective of those who would construct the constitution of the State mechanistically, is able to maintain the thread of genealogy, the force of constituent praxis, in its extensivity and intensity. This point of view exists. It is the viewpoint of daily insurrection, of continual resistance, of constituent power. It is a breaking-with, it is refusal, it is imagination, all as the basis of political knowledge.[3]

Constituent Power Beyond Representation

Discourses of legal and state theory on the 'sovereignty of the people' resemble one another in the thrust of their arguments: constituent power is only imaginable as uniforming and unifying the many into *one* 'people', a people that presumably cannot be assembled in its multitude and heterogeneity and must therefore be represented. The 'will' and the representatively conveyed agency that are associated with the constructions of the one 'people' conform to the logic of juridical sovereignty. In the occidental tradition of democracy, there obviously has to be a nexus, no matter how it is weighted, between the people, law, sovereignty and representation, which has to construct the multitude as a threat in crucial places and ward it off. A constituent power of the many, not tamed into 'a people', beyond sovereignty, law, and representation, is thus excluded from the realm of the imaginable, because it is associated with non-governability, disorder and chaos.

In contrast to these positions, we must relinquish the understanding that 'the people' must be embodied in a certain place or in a certain way in a democracy. Neither the constitution nor the individual law, neither representation nor an institutional place is capable of covering the democratic process that is at stake. All these forms of embodying 'the people' reduce and striate the practising of democracy. The 'democratic will' cannot be represented, it cannot be embodied in a juridical institutionalized power — neither as a law-giving constituent force nor as the constituted force of the law or of representation. Practising democracy always overshoots juridical logic and eludes it, but in this logic it is not possible to leave the *demos* indeterminate, contingent and arbitrary.

We are accustomed to situating political agency in an area which only becomes political when it is structured by representation, in other words by constituted power. The many are integrated into political order through conditions of participation and obedience. As a crowd, they cannot be left behind, disinterested or resigned to the representative-democratic form of domination, because this would not only undermine its legitimation, but also lead to the danger of rebellion. The constituent power that could emerge then is not infrequently imagined as an absolute threat to existing order, as a destructive and simultaneously creative force, which is capable of initiating a major revolutionary event and implementing an act of (suspending) constitution. This force is at the beginning of every political order, but it must then be tamed or neutralized in order to maintain this order. For this reason, the permanent potentiality of the constituent power of the different

3 Antonio Negri, 'Constituent Republic' (1993), trans. Ed Emery, in *Revolutionary Writing: Common Sense Essays in Post-Political Politics*, ed. Werner Bonefeld (New York: Autonomedia, 2003), pp. 245-53, here p. 251.

[redacted]

many is kept out of the theoretical framework that explains the political order, and located in an area beyond this order. Within existing orders, political agency is usually only considered constituted power when it is linked to representation and unifying organization. A constituent power that conversely rejects mediation through representation and does not transcend existing order — in other words, one to which power and domination relations are immanent — is usually regarded as unpolitical and negated as process. A decisive reason for this is that political agency is still always conceived as being separate from other societal dimensions: as public agency, it is separated from the private sphere, but especially also from the social sphere. In contrast to this, the focus on a constituent power of the many, which is understood as being processual and immanent, means looking at the resistive and society-changing power of everyday actions, social relationships, ways of living together, ways of life and, most of all, modes of subjectivation. All of these are relations that are generally not taken into consideration in political theory and not regarded as political agency.

Following from Marx, Deleuze and Foucault, Antonio Negri proposes an interpretation of constituent power that is not a unique act, neither an act of establishing a constitution nor one of revolution as a major, eruptive event linked to taking over domination. In contrast, the constituent power of the many is a process, according to Negri, that cannot be closed and cannot be limited.[4] In a process of creation and invention like this, it is not possible to fence in the radical heterogeneity of the multitude in the identity of 'a people'. In other words, every democratic constituent power is clearly based on the strength of the many. If the potentiality and power of the multitude is only conceived of as a unit, what is lost is that 'the strength is not based only on the large number, but is instead one of the "many", of singularities and differences'.[5]

Horizontality as Common Self-Governing

As Marina Sitrin and others have shown, the instrument of horizontality has been practised by various movements since the Argentinian revolution of 2001 and has been updated by the Occupy Movement.[6] The Spanish M15 movement also attempted to implement practices of horizontality in its assemblies.

Horizontality is not an ideal concept, but is instead linked with practices of real and presentist democracy.[7] Some would say it is a form of direct democracy, but that would be too reductionist, because it involves more than voting and participating in issues in an otherwise indirect representative form of rule. It is a matter of alternative democratic practices, which do not supplement representative forms of democracy in the sense of 'good governance', but rather change the structures and ways of thinking associated with representative democracy, and seek to break with it in order to develop a different society.

Horizontality cannot be implemented according to a certain plan; it often results from the necessity of having to decide on common concerns, the necessity of governing oneself, because representationist structures fail and are to be distrusted. Horizontality primarily seeks to break down and break through existing hierarchies. It is a central instrument of unmediated, non-representationist self-government and collective decision-making about common concerns, without turning to existing institutions and posing demands, without electing representatives to make decisions on the behalf of others. In making these kinds of common decisions, however, there is no attempt to establish a new form of sovereignty in the modern sense of self-lawgiving, similar to a second order of law of 'the people'. Nevertheless, it does involve social regulation, new forms of organising, new modes of subjectivation, a mutual 'becoming-related'. Common modes of self-government are involved, which break through hegemonic forms of governmentality (in other words, of being governed and making oneself governable).

It is not unusual for horizontal practices to be (mis-)understood as being fundamentally anti-institutional and posited

4 Cf. Antonio Negri, *Insurgencies: Consistuent Power and the Modern State*, trans. Mauriza Boscagli (Minneapolis, MN: University of Minesota Press, 1999), pp. 29-32.

5 Ibid., p. 308.

6 Cf. Marina Sitrin, ed., *Horizontalism: Voices of Popular Power in Argentina* (2005) (Oakland, CA and Edinburgh: AK Press 2006); Marina Sitrin, 'The Chills of Popular Power: The First Month of Occupy Wall Street', in *This Changes Everything: Occupy Wall Street and the 99% Movement*, ed. Sarah van Gelder and the staff of YES! magazine (San Francisco: Berrett-Koehler Publishers, 2011), pp. 27-32; Marina Sitrin, 'Some Issues with Horizontalism', *Occupy! An OWS-Inspired Gazette* 3 (2012), pp. 30-32; Marina Sitrin, 'Pulling the Emergency Brake', *Tidal: Occupy Theory, Occupy Strategy* 2 (March 2012), pp. 6-7; on horizontality, see also Marianne Maeckelbergh, *The Will of the Many: How the Alterglobalisation Movement is Changing the Face of Democracy* (London: Pluto Press, 2009).

7 See Isabell Lorey, 'Non-Representationist, Presentist Democracy', trans. Aileen Derieg, transversal: '#occupy and assemble∞', September 2011, http://eipcp.net/transversal/1011/lorey/en.

[redacted]

in opposition to vertical structures, which mark hierarchies and characterize institutions. With this anti-State understanding, however, discussions about the perception of ordering differences, privileges, and relations of inequality (that is to say, the knowledge of and reflection on hierarchizations) can also be de-legitimized within the practices of self-government, because they can disrupt a desired harmony of horizontality.

Horizontal practices are often preceded by a common exodus out of hegemonic domination conditions, enabling a new way of dealing with one another: a break, a refusal, effecting a breach for something new, an exodus out of the predominant dispositions of time and distributions of space, which can materialize in occupations and assemblies. In this context, the occupation signifies a blockade of familiar, hegemonic streams of traffic, one that is not interested in pacification or a confrontation with State power, but rather in opening up and enabling the development of a constituent power in self-organising.

Horizontality does not simply assert the equality of all participants because everyone has a voice, a vote. The equality of votes every time votes are cast does not correspond to equality in the way an individual raises their voice. Not everyone can speak in the same way or is accustomed to clarifying their own position to others in public; some need more time than others until they begin to speak. Not everyone is listened to in the same way just because of the claim of horizontality. In order be able to make common discussions possible, speaking for oneself often has to be learned. Horizontality is not an instrument for making everyone present the same, but rather an instrument for creating a social space in which everyone feels empowered to speak and take part in common challenges as a different and similar singularity, a space in which privileges and inequalities can be consciously dealt with, and heterogeneous ways of speaking and opinions have to be endured. In this sense, horizontality is not a programme that immediately cancels out and ends hierarchies and verticalities. Instead, it opens up a process in which verticalities are specifically not negated, but must first be recognized in order to change them. Verticalities, hierarchizations, unequal social positions, hegemonic structures and State modes of governing constitute the bodies and the minds that come together in a horizontal togetherness, and they are not simply shaken off through the act of exodus and refusal. The art of common self-government in horizontality proceeds from the governmental ways of the self-government of the individuals, in whom social conditions are (re-)produced in the ambivalence between subjugation and empowerment.

The challenge consists in making differences even possible in political practice, in their non-graduated, non-identitarian multiplicity, which means communicating, arguing and living with people without defining them. Allowing multiplicity, which transgresses in many ways the hierarchizing differentiations of structures of inequality through categorizations based on gender, class, sexuality, origins, race, is not a question of the 'right' consciousness. Instead it is an everyday, ongoing practice that first must be learned. This is loaded with conflicts, tedious and does not immediately or always succeed, and what it means to tolerate and accept multiplicity, on the basis that all are equal, also has to be concretely negotiated. Horizontality is a processual practice that takes time and patience. It is a practice that breaks open the hegemonic logics of social and political order and modes of subjectivation, and it is specifically not a practice that can be met with a pattern of a moralistic order of 'proper' behaviour. Differences that are not hierarchized are based on and arise in the relationships between the participants. This does not at all mean that unbounded inclusion is a goal with horizontality, that everyone can participate, regardless of the opinions they hold and how they behave toward others. Instead, it is a matter of relative inclusion: for instance, anyone who expresses non-negotiable racist or sexist positions, anyone who cannot accept the basic preconditions of mutual respect and equality, can be excluded from the assemblies, the compositions of the manifold many. One art consists specifically in not allowing dogmas about behaviour or speaking to arise, but rather in the practice of continually negotiating what horizontality means in each concrete composition, in which new democratic practices are to be developed. A further art, starting from governmental techniques of (self-)governing, consists in not slipping into the neoliberal logic of the economic efficiency of diversity, in which people are deployed according to their abilities to where they seem to be the most effective. Horizontality is based not on representation, but rather on affirmation — not in the sense of uncritically confirming, but rather as empowering. The various participating singularities are affirmed with their (potential) abilities. Striving for horizontal relationships in assemblies and other gatherings is a challenge that does not take place

[redacted]

without conflicts. Conversely, confrontations and struggles are immanent to this means of developing new democratic practices. Halting them would mean halting the motor of the process of horizontality. Horizontality is never the end or the goal itself, but rather always only a means, an instrument in a process of common self-government, in a process of enabling something more. Horizontality is the tool to impel answering the question of how a way of organising is possible, which does not revert to the logics of representation and State institutions. Horizontality is a means of self-organising, but not a form of organization itself. It is not a model that can simply be implemented, but rather orients itself in practice to the understanding that there are no models for what must first be invented in a process in which horizontal relationships are an important means.[8]

Horizontality cannot be contrasted per se with institutionalization and verticalization, because in the practice of common self-government it has to be possible to invent new political and social institutions, new institutions of the common, which do not separate the political from the social and the economic, do not leave politics and State solely to a realm of the political that is considered autonomous, as it traditionally happens in the bourgeois-capitalist form of domination. Exactly this tradition is reproduced, if horizontal social gatherings are considered a civil society that opposes the State.

If it is a matter of new forms of society in the assemblies and gatherings, new ways of living together and new ways of organising that, then questions of social labour and production conditions must also be raised, questions of current precarization and the distribution of labour. Many presentist democratic practices are to be found in the democracy movements of 2011, which propel this process and invent the future. These practices are also presentist because they implement no programme and no idea. Instead, they have to be negotiated with others in concrete situations of confrontation and newly invented again and again. The point is not to take over power, but rather to continually open up a presentist space of possibility for the unpredictable, anarchic invention of the future, the re-organization of a commonality — a process that is in no way linear. To further design and organize this, new forms of verticality are needed, which build on non-representationist practices of horizontality and do not halt the process of a constituent power.

Occupy Arts

Many people participating in the Occupy Movement came from the art field and offered their tools, their skills, their time and their resources. This certainly did not mean just designing posters and flyers or producing photos and videos. Many of them were organizers in the movement, and as facilitators they arranged the public space, for example, in such a way that horizontal practices could become possible. It is not sufficient to call them 'art-activists', as though art and activism could be separated and only conjoined temporarily when public political agency is called for. In a Gramscian wording, one could speak of organic cultural producers. 'Art is simply a number of abilities that are needed to resist power, domination.'[9] This does not mean that every artistic practice is to be understood as resistive, but rather that cultural production represents a sociality that can become a practice, which rejects existing modes of (self-)government and invents new forms of sociality. Media, for example, become direct action in Occupy Wall Street. In the second edition of the magazine *Tidal*, in keeping with horizontal practices it says:

> Radical strategic media is more than viral YouTube videos; it ... pushes the limits of traditional formulas, story structures, and methods of communication. It's about creating content that asks questions rather than provides answers.... We must create alternative media outlets that incorporate decision-making processes that reflect the balanced, fair and non-exploitative world we wish to create.[10]

It is also about the use of creativity beyond a logic of valorization, in which subjectivation has become economicizable. In the context of Occupy, many activists moving in the art field and working in cultural production in different groups, such as

8 Cf. Colectivo Situaciones, 'a group of political and militant reflection' (in Sitrin, ed., *Horizontalism*, pp. 53-55).

9 Nato Thomson in an interview on *Living as Form*, 'a book about socially engaged art' that he edited, www.labkultur.tv/blog/interview-mit-nato-thompson-zu-living-form-ein-buch-ueber-sozial-engagierte-kunst.

10 Katie Davison, 'Media as Direct Action', *Tidal: Occupy Theory, Occupy Strategy* 2 (March 2012), pp. 26-27, here p. 27.

[redacted]

Arts & Labor or *Occupy Museums*, have massively questioned the production conditions, funding or collections in art institutions. In direct actions, they have often loudly criticized the intransparency of budgets, the distribution of work, and especially the low wages, thus putting the precarization of cultural producers back on the agenda in a way that has not happened for many years in the USA. The aim of the direct actions is also to problematize, again and again, the vertical logics of art institutions. They collect either in the logic of authorship (objects tied to names) or of cultural heritage (as colonial appropriation) and they are based on economic structures, of which hierarchizations form the supporting pillars of the institution. Institutional critique in the sense of horizontality can project and suggest conflicts and confrontations in the institutions, to change not only the conditions of working (together), but also the exhibiting and consuming of art.[11]

Following the heyday of the camps in Autumn 2011, the curators of the 7th Berlin Biennale, which took place in early Summer 2012, travelled not only to New York and invited *Occupy Museums*, among others, to take part in an 'autonomous section' of this art festival.[12] The curators, Artur Żmijewsky, Joanna Warsza, and the group Voina, had stepped forward 'to make art political' and to suspend the separation between art and activism.[13] Art should take part in social changes, advance them, and not be so often concerned with 'presenting ideas that no one has any intention of putting into practice', as Żmijewsky writes in the foreword to the festival publication *Forget Fear.* The Biennale was intended to be the project to show ways out of the 'vicious circle of creative impotence'[14], and to present art that is 'clever and creative enough to get involved in social transformation processes'[15] — a principally laudable project that is a rare exception in the art field with its aspirations.

'Members' not only of Occupy, but also from the Spanish M15 movement and other activist contexts were invited, 'who have contributed to the recent ideological upheaval'. According to Joanna Warsza in a section titled 'Performative Democracy', 'the exhibition hall of the KW Institute for Contemporary Art was to be *turned over to them as representatives*'.[16] The terms 'membership', as though a closed association were involved, and 'representatives', as though representational critique were not a topic of discussion, already indicate the difficulties of an institution-critical art project in the functional adaptation of these new democracy movements. 'Turning over' art spaces cannot elude a steered space policy either, when elsewhere it is a matter of occupying public space in common and of its horizontal transformation.

In the 'non-curated' 'autonomous section', the invited activists had financial and logistical support for exchange and actions — which was not only the curators' concept, but also the practice of the activists. 'The curators have nothing to say here. If we want to, we can join them and collaborate — but only in a situation where our voices carry the same weight, and in which no power hierarchy forces others to act in a certain way.'[17] However, this possibility of horizontal composition that was offered, presumably independent from a vertical curatorial and institutional area, still re-installed exhibition logics and zoo perspectives, such as with the Occupy staging in the exhibition spaces of the Berliner Kunstwerke by the AG Space Design Occupy Berlin. The group attempted to transfer 'worldwide camp experiences of Occupy' into the institutional spaces.[18] The intention was to 'create a Global Square to connect and interrelate the revolts and thus contribute to the coordination and strengthening of social culture opposed to the arrogance of power'.[19] An anticipation of criticism can be read in the Declaration of Occupy Biennial:

> This is not an art project or a publicity stunt, nor is it a substitute for the occupation of public space. Although we may be in a gallery in Berlin, we are not a static movement on display. We are part of larger actions unfolding across the planet.[20]

11 On this, see the actions of *Occupy Museums*, especially those in the Pergamon Museum in Berlin, http://occupymuseums.org/.
12 http://occupymuseums.org.
13 Artur Żmijewsky, 'Foreword', in *Forget Fear. 7. Berlin Biennale*, ed. Artur Żmijewsky and Joanna Warsza (Cologne: Verlag der Buchhandlung Walther König, 2012), online: www.berlinbiennale.de/blog/en/comments/forget-fear-a-foreword-by-artur-zmijewski-19528.
14 Ibid.
15 Artur Żmijewsky, '7th Berlin Biennale for Contemporary Art', *Pressemappe* from 20 April 2012, www.berlinbiennale.de/blog/wp-content/uploads/2012/04/7BerlinBiennale_Pressemappe.pdf.
16 Joanna Warsza, 'Mit Kunst wirken', *Pressemappe* from 20 April 2012, www.berlinbiennale.de/blog/wp-content/uploads/2012/04/7BerlinBiennale_Pressemappe.pdf, emphasis. I.L.
17 Artur Żmijewsky, '7. Berlin Biennale für zeitgenössische Politik', *Pressemappe* from 20 April 2012, www.berlinbiennale.de/blog/wp-content/uploads/2012/04/7BerlinBiennale_Pressemappe.pdf.
18 http://occupybb7.org/plan.
19 http://occupybb7.org/node.
20 http://occupybb7/declaration.

[redacted]

This position was criticized not only by Occupy Museums, where it is stated on their web site in the context of a 'zoo' action in a branch of the Deutsche Bank in Berlin:

> This human zoo [the seventh Berlin Biennial] financed by the German Government, objectifies and de-politicizes activists who have been exhibited in a room where they have their meetings, discussions, and sleep. However, as people who believe in action, we do not see this situation as a static one. It embodies the problematic nature of many contemporary neoliberal spaces which the Occupy/15M must confront.[21]

Instead of leaving the Biennale, with the slogan 'You cannot curate a movement!', they called for immanent, non-zoologically verticalized, horizontal practices for the entire institution of the Berlin Biennale, probably less to set a lasting horizontal process in motion, but rather to demonstrate the boundaries of a critical art project.[22] Or differently: first steps were invented in the horizontality experiment, for how traditionally vertical structures can be transformed into horizontal practices that must be further developed in other places.

The Declaration of the Occupation

As little as 'experiences in the camps' can simply be transferred to institutionalized spaces, the process of a horizontal constituent power was just as ambiguous during the assemblies and organising in the occupied squares. The process of heterogeneous singularities, which arose in exodus in the occupied squares, signified a break with existing arrangements of space and time, but was still no flight into a realm beyond power and domination relations. Traditional and hegemonic ways of thinking and acting were found in the squares in a sometimes conflictual simultaneity with the testing of alternative socialities and political practices.

One of the first pieces of writing that the Occupy Wall Street movement published was The Declaration of the Occupation of New York City, decreed by consensus on 29 September 2011 in the General Assembly in the occupied Zuccotti Park, renamed Liberty Square, in which some six to seven thousand people took part.[23] The Declaration was treated as a 'living document that will grow and change with time. As democratic, consensus-based decision-making assemblies continue to shape the declaration we will publish new editions accordingly'.[24] This is no immutable declaration, but rather a document that can and must be reformulated and adapted to changed compositions and conditions. In this sense, the Declaration is part of a permanent constituting. At the same time, this preliminary declaration of the whatever many in the occupied Liberty Square begins like a constitution (of which multiple versions are circulating). The printed version starts with 'We, the people, …'.[25] The first words of the Constitution of the United States are thus quoted, but without continuing in the diction of transferring legislative powers to congress and representatives. No legislative power and no other power are transferred, as the

21 http://occupymuseums.org.

22 'The curators spoke of offering resources to the movements but we see a strikingly clear power structure. We propose to move this experiment forward in a totally horizontal and transparent way. For example:
- Erase the hierarchical divisions between the offices, art exhibition, and movement community. All people can sleep anywhere, work anywhere, discuss anywhere.
- All decisions will be made by the assemblea, which includes and embraces former curators, directors, workers and the entire KW community.
- The former curatorial team participates in actions as activists among activists not organizers, observers, or curators.
- All financial decisions pertaining to finance from the German Government will be made by the assemblea and mapped in complete transparency from the beginning of the biennial to the end.'(http://occupymuseums.org/)
At the end of the Biennale, it was agreed to conduct an experiment of horizontality for one week. In the Biennale E-mail newsletter '7th Berlin Biennale is Moving Towards Horizontality' from 15 June 2012, the initiative 'loosening hierarchies' was welcomed, because it was said to be in keeping with the aspirations of the curators. 'This experiment is consciously naive. Movement activists know that horizontality is sometimes messy and inefficient. Employees of the Berlin Biennale have established a functional structure and know that attending extra meetings is likely to mean extra effort. In addition, critics from all sides know that art institutions love to play games with politics, fetishizing activists' language and aesthetics.'

23 Cf. Sitrin, 'The Chills of Popular Power', p. 29. Communication in the assemblies worked without electronic amplification, but rather through the *people's* or *human mic*. In an assembly of this size, it was passed on in up to five waves until it reached the margins of the assembly (cf. idem, p. 32).

24 The NYC General Assembly, *The Declaration of the Occupation of New York City*, ed. The Sparrow Project, 2nd ed. (Washington 2012), p. 3.

25 Ibid., pp. 12-15, here p. 12. It is interesting that The Sparrow Project begins the Declaration on its website with 'As one people, united...' again, unlike the brochure that can be printed out there, in which it says 'We, the people.' www.sparrowmedia.net/declaration/.

[redacted]

further course of the declaration does not involve representation, but rather two blocks of power that are contrasted in a condensed form in the pronouns 'we' and 'they'. This is also the structure of the version of the Declaration of Occupy Wall Street that is found on the Internet. It is also said to have been affirmed by the General Assembly on 29 September. This version does not begin by quoting the US Constitution, but rather condenses the power blocks already with the first unifying words: 'As one people, united, …'.[26] The people are united into one people and contrasted as the 99% governed in the dichotomous separation from the 1% governing. Horizontality is halted and unified. In fact, critics of the movement often object to the slogan, 'We are the 99%', as being both presumptuous and representationist.

In my analysis and interpretation, the Declaration serves a different purpose and a different argumentation. It shows that the process of constituting, which signifies a break with existing relations of domination as well as a breach, opens up a new space of thinking and acting. This does not immediately happen unequivocally, but rather ambivalently at the least. The Declaration presumes constituent constitution-establishing power in the traditional sense, and at the same time, it transgresses the traditional understanding of constituent power, because it does not repeat the juridical logic of legislature. And it is a preliminary, living document, which only shows a segment of an ongoing process of negotiation. A constituent process is always conflictual and is constantly newly composed. The Declaration thus captures a preliminary consensus and hence a conjoining of the heterogeneous voices in the General Assembly, even though the unifying formulation 'as one people, united' makes this invisible again.

If we assume that the slogan 'We are the 99%' is an extremely good PR idea, then the political questions remain, as to how the heterogeneous many of the '99%' are not to be understood as a homogeneous block opposite the rest. How are heterogeneity and inequality dealt with, and how is inclusion practised? Let's take a closer look at the Declaration. In one of the books that has come out of the movement, one of the conflicts about the formulation of the Declaration is made transparent.[27] A debate is described about the basis for discussing the Declaration at the assembly on 29 September. The conflict erupted exactly about the unifying words and because it is not at all possible to presume an equality of all with the term 'the people'. The version that was discussed began with the wording:

> As one people, formerly divided by the color of our skin, gender, sexual orientation, religion, or lack thereof, political party or cultural background, we acknowledge the reality: that there is only one race, the human race, and our survival requires the cooperation of its members.[28]

Several People of Colour protested against the beginning of this formulation 'As one people, formerly divided by'. At that moment they had come together as a group for the first time and demanded a reformulation: the version 'formerly divided' was unrealistic, they stated, and made the history of the oppression of the marginalized invisible. For this reason, it should be replaced by 'despite the divisions of'.[29] The criticism was directed against the assumption, implicit to the formulation 'formerly divided', that a division of 'the people' had been overcome and, with it, structural inequalities and discrimination. The seemingly minor change to 'despite the divisions of' signifies no less than a fundamental turn of the relations of equality and inequality. The change expresses that many differently positioned people come together in horizontal practices in the General Assemblies and thus in the movement, despite the fact that hierarchizing divisions between genders, sexualities, 'races', and religions continue to exist. The change was accepted by the General Assembly.[30]

This story can be seen as exemplifying the many struggles in Occupy Wall Street, which resulted less in people staying

26 www.nycga.net/resources.

27 Hena Ashraf, 'Claiming Space for Diversity at Occupy Wall Street', in *This Changes Everything: Occupy Wall Street and the 99% Movement*, ed. by Sarah van Gelder and the staff of YES! magazine (San Francisco: Berrett-Koehler Publishers, 2011), pp. 33-35; first published one day after the assembly at http://henaashraf.com/2011/09/30/brown-power-at-occupy-wall-street/; see also the website of 'In Front and Center: Critical Voices in the 99%', http://infrontandcenter.wordpress.com/.

28 Ibid., p. 33.

29 Cf. ibid., p. 34f. In addition, the formulation 'the human race' was also found to be problematic - a formulation that can still be read unchanged in every version of the Declaration.

30 However, there were obviously still other changes in the formulation of the beginning of the Declaration, so that the list of relations of inequality was ultimately dropped entirely, and now there are two versions circulating: the unifying version is to be found on the Internet (whereby 'united' can also be read in a non-identitarian understanding of 'conjoined' and 'common'), whereby the printed version contains the ambivalently used constitutional designation, 'We, the people'.

[redacted]

away entirely because they saw no possibility for themselves to be mentioned and to inscribe themselves in the movement. Instead, Occupy Wall Street was increasingly distinguished by inclusive heterogeneity and horizontality, and attention was given at every Assembly to who was speaking and how to mutually treat one another. The people inscribe themselves with their voices, positions, and abilities into the constituent, tendentially horizontal power of the occupations.

Principles of Solidarity

In their common practices, the individuals in the movement do not assume that something unequivocally common already exists simply in their coming together and assembling — even though the gesture of the Declaration is to be interpreted in this direction. If one listens to the participants, though, and pays attention to other stories as well, it quickly becomes clear that the constituent power of the occupation movements, not only in New York, intended to practice a democracy in establishing respectful and responsible mutual social relationships, in which existing logics of domination are immanently suspended. The participants aspired to and also practised horizontality and equality in dealing with one another, but always starting from the knowledge and experience that the social relations, which are fought against and in the midst of which an exodus, a break occurs through the occupation, are always also part of the confrontations and compositions of the constituent power of heterogeneous singularities. Many of the occupiers think governmentally, in the Foucaultian sense, and presume that the relations that are to be radically changed, structure and traverse the subjectivity of each participating person and even the practice of the occupation itself, because they define what it means to suspend existing times and spaces and newly arrange them. Hierarchized inequalities and the concomitant social relations are taken as the starting point for mutual interaction, in order to break through them, to minimize them, and to strive for possibilities of horizontality and equality. Equality in the sense of egality is often established in a first step by listening, by being able to speak and letting others speak, through mutual respect for one another.

The starting point for this way of dealing with one another and the problematization of existing political, economic, social and legal relations are the hierachizations that arise from them, and the differences and heterogeneities of the singularities. The formal recognition of multiplicity is not sufficient for this; it must actually be established in social practice and also borne. The horizontal procedures in the assemblies and the consensus-based 'decisions' can be considered examples of this. What appeared to be difficult, however, was grasping the 'decisions' as actually being processual, rather than as something that had come to an end and had to be implemented exactly in that way. All of this involved a process, which certainly did not always achieve what was aspired to.

In the sense of the horizontal practices that I want to emphasize here, a further document from Occupy Wall Street can be considered exemplary for describing the constituent power of the heterogeneous many, which is rooted in the social. It was already accepted on the first day of the occupation, on 17 September 2011, by an arbitrarily composed General Assembly for the first time. This is another captured moment in an ongoing process of constituting, which does not revert to the logics of a tendentially unifying constitutionalism: the Principles of Solidarity. These social regulations were necessary, especially in terms of the assemblies, because in the beginning, only 'white men' spoke there, and it quickly became clear that continuing this practice would have meant the end of the movement. The Principles of Solidarity formulate the foundations of social intercourse — in the assemblies and in the camp, and also in the actions and the organising that were taking place up to that point in time. It is a matter of mutual respect, personal and collective responsibility, being aware of privileges and the influence they have on all interactions. However, these principles of solidarity also cover the common goal of redefining the value of work, and convictions such as the right to education and protection of the private sphere, as well as the ambition to practice and support broad access to information. At the conclusion of the Principles of Solidarity, it says: 'We are daring to imagine a new socio-political and economic alternative that offers greater possibility of equality.'[31]

What this involved, however, was more than imagining socio-political and economic alternatives. They were already practised in the assemblies and occupations of public and private spaces, in the conversations, debates and mobilization in the neighbour-

31 The NYC General Assembly, Principles of Solidarity, accepted September 17, 2011, www.nycga.net/resources; printed unchanged in The NYC General Assembly 2012, pp. 4-7, here p. 7.

[redacted]

hoods and communities, through a moneyless exchange economy of things and abilities, called 'mutual aid'. The starting point was the respective intelligence, the respective abilities of the whatever many, the ambition and the practice of permanently expanding inclusion in an ongoing process of practices, presentist democracy. It can be read again and again that horizontal relations, consensus, and inclusion are not a programme, not something that the movement demands of itself, but rather can only take place when they are constantly practised anew.[32] In a flyer from Occupy Wall Street, under the heading 'What is the problem we are trying to address?', it says:

> Since we can no longer trust our elected representatives to represent us rather than their large donors, we are creating a microcosm of what democracy really looks like. We do this to inspire one another to speak up. It is a reminder to our representatives and the moneyed interests that direct them: we the people still know our power.[33]

This political movement that challenged existing forms of democracy and broke with them, which was based on the horizontal practices of assembling, talking together, and listening to one another, had a crucial, if not the crucial component in those areas that were traditionally, at least conceptually, banned from democracy as a form of domination, because they were considered hard, if not impossible to govern, components that were repeatedly attributed to revolt and chaos: a circulating and expanding new economy of affects. In a wholly fundamental way, not only the Occupy Movement, but also the 15M movement in Spain brought affects as the foundation of the social — mutual support, respect, paying attention to one another — back into the political and the economical.

Impatience with a Constituent Power

The Occupy Movements signify an exodus from the two complementary figures of direct and representative democracy, an exodus from vertical, unifying institutionalization, because they act in a non-juridical way and practice democracy in a presentist and horizontal way. This is no less than a break with the existing order of 'Western' democracy. The exodus manifests itself in the central public square, in the assembly of the many and in practising new ways of living. This presentist movement is self-organising and instituting, a democratic constituent power, which does not want to repeat the old struggles over the takeover of power but instead seeks to release itself from the juridical logic of representation and sovereignty.

Yet, is not a constituted, institutionalized, vertical power of the occupation movements also necessary, which goes beyond the already developed and changing organising and instituting? Must that which has already been achieved in the process of constituent power and horizontality not become more condensed, vertically organized and institutionalized, in order to strengthen its potentiality and effect lasting, fundamental social changes? Based on a constituted power that is nationally, transnationally and globally networked? Yes and no. A networked constituted power is needed, arising from the movement's critique of representation, starting from the organising that has already taken place in the course of constituent power, horizontal and increasingly decentralized in its actions, in order to intervene in the existing relations of domination at a different level and in a different way, where the dynamics of these relations of domination have already been temporarily and partially suspended through the occupations.[34] New vertical condensations are needed. No traditional representationist or hierarchically organized institutionalization seems suitable for these forms of the vertical. Which forms could be suitable instead, is currently being discussed in many places and in searching practices. There are historical examples for how this kind of alternative organising could be arranged, whether it is the workers or spokes councils — which are not to be mistaken for representation. Whether the practices of the imperative mandate, which can be withdrawn at any time, still provide forms that can be transformed and applied today is something that has to be tried out as

32 Cf., among others, Sitrin, 'Some Issues with Horizontalism', p. 31.

33 Flyer from Occupy Wall Street, 'What is Occupy Wall Street?/Why We Are Here Today Talking?/What is the Problem We Are Trying to Address?', distributed in New York in April 2012.

34 On this theoretical and political movement of exodus and intervention, and the relation between the political and politics, see also Isabell Lorey, *Figuren des Immunen: Elemente einer politischen Theorie* (Zurich: Diaphanes 2011), pp. 307-13.

[redacted]

needed. It appears foreseeable that new institutions of a common that has yet to be produced will not emerge other than starting from the multitude.

In order to avoid repeating traditional patterns of domination, a constituted, vertical power, which has still to be invented, must not interrupt, halt or neutralize the process and the movement of the constituent, tendentially horizontal power. It would have to be a constituted power, in which the ongoing constituent power can be actualized in different ways. The constituent power needs the interrupting exodus as a beginning, which creates a breach at the same time for new, horizontal social and political practices of living together as needed. The exodus and the processually constituent power open up a new, condensed composition of the many, which is continued in the distribution and horizontality of those composed. This is also why the dissolution of the camps is not to be lamented, because the distribution and renewed circulation is just as much a part of the constituent power as the practices that emerged in the phases of the suspending occupation. At this time, the art consists of not pushing the construction of a traditional form of constituted, vertical power out of old, purportedly well-tried patterns of thinking and acting, not accelerating the time of constituent power in horizontality and pouring it into the familiar pattern of efficiency and success. Constituent power must further develop and spread, even at the risk of becoming so scattered that possibilities of concentrating and condensing are missed. The occupation movements involve radical changes in politics, society and economy. A process has been set in motion, which strengthens and can continue to strengthen processes that have existed for some time, and this process may still take a long time. This constituting process allows an exodus of the many and perpetual striving for and engagement with horizontality to become newly necessary again and again. The art consists of keeping this process of a radical change of democracy going, along with its previous economic foundations.

When horizontality is transferred as a tool into vertical logics of exhibition and representation, it is not uncommon for it to turn into a zoo. As a practice of organising, by means of which an institution is to be transformed, it is accompanied by forms of emerging instituting. Horizontality itself does not exist without aspects of verticality. Other forms of verticality emerge in the situativity of constituting. How sustainable and inventive this process can be made, and whether it is possible to invent new forms of verticality in it, must be tried out again and again in many places with tenacity and the exchange of experiences.

[redacted]

Indirect Action
Some Misgivings About Horizontalism

Mark Fisher

Strategy and feedback from action are more significant than detailed planning ('Fire — ready — aim!' as Tom Peters wrote); hierarchies give way to networks; the periphery is as important as the centre; self-interest and competition are balanced by trust and cooperation; initiative and inventiveness are required rather than compliance; smartening up rather than dumbing down.[1]

> The new vision was to be one of fluidity, flexibility, spontaneity and itinerant programming, taking its cue from the model of biennials, fairs and festivals, each of which offered 'a more fluid and decentred model of arts presentation with a focus on new commissions'.[2]

> What the new zeitgeist clashes with are the power relations of the old hierarchical world. And this is the materialist explanation for [the revolts in] 2011: it as much about individuals versus hierarchies as it about rich against poor. The driver of behavioural change has been technology. There's been a revolution in the recording, storing and searchability of information; in the networked availability of information; in the digitization and globalization of commercial transactions; and finally, through, social networking, in the ability to form connections away from the old hierarchical channels of the past. In each technology, the 'node' – or individual – has been empowered at the expense of the hierarchical central core, which is the State or corporation - or even the tribe.[3]

Who is speaking here? The first quotation comes from right wing ideologue Phillip Blond, one of the thinkers behind British Prime Minister David Cameron's concept of the 'Big Society'. The second is a summary, by critic J. J. Charlesworth, of a 'vision document' circulated by the then artistic director of the Institute of Contemporary Arts, Ekow Eshun, in 2009. The third is from the discussion of new social movements in *Why It's Kicking Off Everywhere*, by the BBC's Economics editor, Paul Mason. But the better question would be *what* is speaking here? The congruence in tone and content here suggests that we are in the presence of a pervasive ideology, one that is disseminated in art institutions as well as in government, and one that is shared by the elements of the left as well as by the right. Practically all mainstream political discourse is suspicious of, and sceptical towards, the State, planning and the possibilities of organized political change. 'Is' slides into 'ought', as historical claims about the emergence of a new kind of network society quickly become breathless celebrations of this networked world. To say that this is an ideology is not to say that the material shifts described by these theorists are not real; it is only to acknowledge that the technological changes which these writers identify do not spontaneously give rise to political discourses or perspectives. The appearance of spontaneity is itself an ideological effect. The widespread acceptance of this network ideology — with its conviction that hierarchies have been superseded by networks, and its privileging of flexibility and fluidity over fixity — signals that some arguments originally presented by post-68 theorists such as Lyotard and Deleuze and Guattari have now been absorbed into the mainstream. The ubiquity of concepts such as diversity, plurality and inclusivity, together with the widespread hostility towards the idea that there could be absolute values, means that Lyotard's once-reviled 'postmodernism' now practically constitutes common sense. The success of the network ideology is part of a general crisis of political and cultural authority. Certain left-wing versions of the ideology (especially those circulated within the neo-anarchist currents which have become synonymous with the Occupy Movement) maintain that authority is an intrinsically right-wing concept. Authority is *in itself* bad.

I want to argue here that this rejection of the very concept of authority has been disastrous for the left. It has led to a kind of self-defeating and self-loathing marginalization and to an

1 Phillip Blond, The Ownership State: Restoring Excellence, Innovation and Ethos to the Public Services (London: National Endowment for Science, Technology and the Arts, 2009), p. 11.
2 J. J. Charlesworth, 'Crisis at the ICA: Ekow Eshun's Experiment in De-Institutionalisation', (2010); www.metamute.org/editorial/articles/crisis-ica-ekow-eshuns-experiment-deinstitutionalisation.
3 Paul Mason, Why It's Kicking Off Everywhere: The New Global Revolutions (London: Verso, 2012), p. 133.

[redacted]

unwarranted faith in spontaneity and face-to-face interaction (an emphasis strangely at odds with the technological aspects of network culture, which have downgraded the importance of face-to-face communication). It has contributed to the left's continuing failure to make any hegemonic headway, despite the spectacular discrediting of neoliberalism caused by the financial crisis. Never has the word 'curate' been so widely used in cultural circles, but never has there been less confidence in the validity of the concepts inherent in curatorship: the linking of management with care and authority. In summary, the left's disdaining of authority — and the concomitant embrace of 'horizontalism' — has done little to displace what I have called *capitalist realism:* the belief that capitalism is the only political-economic system that 'works', and that it is impossible even to imagine any alternative to it.[4] In fact, rather than challenging capitalist realism, horizontalism has — at least in some respects — further embedded it.

At this point, it's worth reminding ourselves of something that should be obvious: namely, that the left has not always rejected authority. Doubtless the origin of the left's current difficulties with authority lie, in fact, in the excessive enthusiasm for authority formerly exhibited by certain elements of the left. Now, though, the left is faced with a (non-)choice between cleaving to authoritarian political structures (that, in any case, are no longer viable) or adopting anti-authoritarian forms and strategies which do not work. 'The traditional left (communist and socialist in orientation) typically espoused and defended some version of democratic centralism (in political parties, trade unions, and the like)', David Harvey has recently observed.

> Now, however, principles are frequently advanced - such as 'horizontality' and 'non-hierarchy' - or visions of radical democracy and the governance of the commons, that can work for small groups but are impossible to operationalize at the scale of a metropolitan region, let alone for the seven billion people who now inhabit planet earth. Programmatic priorities are dogmatically articulated, such as the abolition of the state, as if no alternative form of territorial governance would ever be necessary or valuable.[5]

However, it would be a mistake to lapse into nostalgia for democratic centralist political organizations, and for the conditions that made them possible. The task now is to resist the false choice between obsolete authoritarianism and impotent anti-authoritarianism. There is no returning to the authoritarian organizations of the twentieth century, and we should not mourn their disappearance. The leftist critique of authoritarianism that coalesced during the 1960s was crucial. But we must recognise that the renewal of the left promised by these anti-authoritarian movements never fully happened, and part of the reason that it stalled was the turning away from the question of authority. Authoritarianism is the abuse of authority; it is therefore to be opposed, not by a wholesale rejection of authority, but by the conceptualization and constitution of proper authority. Before we turn to this question, however, it is worth reviewing network ideology, and some of the problems with it.

Adam Curtis's 2011 BBC television series *All Watched Over by Machines of Loving Grace* was an attempt to investigate the way network theory fitted into a broader ideological mosaic that also includes evolutionary psychology. Curtis focused in particular on the discourses of self-organization which have become so popular amongst certain strands of neo-anarchism. (For this reason, the series faced a great deal of criticism from neo-anarchists.) What Curtis analysed was the way in which the network thinking, with its emphasis on horizontalism, and the biologization of culture, via Dawkins's selfish gene theory, have gone hand-in-hand. Curtis identified what at first glance appeared to be a paradoxical mixture of biological fatalism (DNA means that nothing much will ever change) and can-do dynamism (individuals are a boundless reservoir of creativity). But this is only apparently paradoxical — the view that nothing can change at the level of political system is actually perfectly compatible with the belief in the 'creativity' of individuals and small groups. What Curtis's series explored was the way in which hostility to the State can become hostility to politics as such.

As an indication of how easily this can happen, I offer an anecdote. When I spoke to a fringe meeting after a protest organized

4 See Mark Fisher, Capitalist Realism: Is There No Alternative? (Winchester: Zero Books, 2009)
5 David Harvey, Rebel Cities: From the Right to the City to the Urban Revolution (London and New York: Verso, 2012), p. 125.

[redacted]

by the Trades Union Congress (TUC) against the UK coalition government's cuts, a small group in the audience started mildly dissenting. What they were objecting to what my claim that what we must seek to do now, in the moment when neoliberalism is in crisis, is impose a new orthodoxy. As far as I could tell, the dissenters didn't belong to any kind of political organization —rather, they expressed a weary contempt for political organization as such. There was little point participating in existing political processes, or in competing for hegemony in the media, they said. Their problem was not with a particular hegemonic formation — neoliberalism — but with the very concept of hegemony. Furthermore, they maintained, trade unions were 'bureaucratic', (but, as I suggested to them, wasn't the 'bureaucratic' structure of the TUC what enabled it to get half a million people *including them* onto the streets of London?). All that you could do, they maintained, was withdraw as far as possible from the structures of the State; maybe it would be possible to influence some of the people with whom you immediately came into contact. They seemed to believe that a widespread spiritual renewal was more likely than even modest change achieved through organized politics. What was striking about these views — coming from people who would presumably consider themselves far to the left of mainstream politics — was their remarkable congruence with the 'Big Society' rhetoric pushed by David Cameron. Just like Cameron, they argued that *top-down control*, *government*, *hierarchy* and *bureaucracy* are all *old*, *inefficient* and *oppressive*.

The kind of quietism I encountered on that day in Hyde Park might appear to be a particularly extreme kind of disengagement, and quite far from the networked (hyper)activism celebrated in Paul Mason's *Why It's Kicking Off Everywhere*, with its frenzy of communicative action ('I Tweet In My Dreams' is the title of the chapter devoted to the 'network individual'). But it is neither. Scepticism about the possibilities of political agency is in fact so widespread that we might say it constitutes one face of dominant ideology. Yet this withdrawal from parliamentary politics and from struggle over media hegemony is also recommended by the neo-anarchism operative in the Occupy Movement, which similarly disdains what it sees as the outmoded and impotent State form, as well as the decadent structures of mainstream media (or MSM). The difference between the two — and this, clearly, is by not an insignificant difference — is that while the former favours withdrawal into the private sphere, the latter is about collective (self)organization. But these collectives pointedly do not seek to take over the State. What, then, is the aim of something like an Occupy encampment?

I must make two disclaimers here. The first disclaimer concerns the problems of making any kind of general statement about Occupy. The level of disagreement within Occupy, together with its refusal to produce a clear programme, means that it is irreducibly heterogeneous, and this heterogeneity is necessarily betrayed whenever a determinate statement is made about the movement. The second disclaimer is that scepticism about aspects of the Occupy Movement should not be taken to mean that I oppose it. But celebrating Occupy does not mean accepting it on the terms of its own (unofficial) ideology.

Even to pose the question of what Occupy's aims are is to risk the contempt of many involved in the movement, who argue that for Occupy to pose 'demands' is in itself a mistake.[6] But if Occupy does not aim — at least at some point — to influence government policy or — at least at some point — to influence hegemony via MSM, what are its hopes? In its deployment of horizontalism, Occupy aims to be prefigurative: it wants to anticipate future forms of (post-hierarchical) political organization. The question, then, is how — in the lack of the organs of the State or the mass media — are these forms of political organization to propagate? The idea must be a kind of *contagious withdrawal* from the structures of the State, capital and the media, which will spread through lateral networks rather than via the 'arborescent' structures of mass media and parliamentary politics. If the aim is not to take over or even influence the State, then there must be a faith in the practical sufficiency of the movement itself. The point is not to direct demands towards, or protest against, an Other, but for the movement to constitute itself as an immediately effective collectivity. Yet, this faith in immediate — which is to say, unmediated — action betrays a lack of faith in the efficacy of *indirect* action. As Maurizio Lazzarato, drawing on the work of Gabriel Tarde, has argued, such 'action at a distance' has been a defining characteristic of politics since the emergence of tele-technological communicative systems (the telegraph and the telephone) in the nineteenth

6 See, for instance, Karen McVeigh, 'Wall Street Protesters Divided over Occupy Movement's Demands', *The Guardian*, 19 October 2011; www.guardian.co.uk/world/2011/oct/19/occupy-wall-street-protesters-divided.

[redacted]

century.[7] Systemic change necessarily entails action at a distance, since it requires shifts in economic organization, hegemony, ideology, infrastructure, as well as the practices of everyday life. The emphasis on immediacy, however, militates against belief in a system as such, since we do not directly experience anything like the 'capitalist system', and, crucially, cannot immediately or directly act against it either. The danger is that this focus on the immediate will lead to what Nick Srnicek and Alex Williams call 'folk politics', a politics which takes its form and its vision from poor analogies with everyday experience. The challenge, for Srnicek and Williams, is to construct a politics that can contest capital on its own — abstract — level.[8]

The ultimate importance of Occupy may, however, turn out to be precisely its *indirect* impact, its contribution to a shift in the ideological atmosphere. The floating of the concept of the 99% (versus the 1%) suspends questions of identity in the name of antagonism, and Occupy has given a voice to the post-2008 discontent which it otherwise would not have had. The movement's experiments with horizontalism are best treated as just that — experiments which may yield new modes of political participation, but which could equally well be impasses or atavistic throwbacks. By now, there is nothing especially 'new' about discourses of anti-hierarchy and self-organization. Some of us first encountered them via cyberculture in the 1990s. In 1995, the *Wired* editor Kevin Kelly's *Out of Control* laid out the then latest version of network theory, making exactly the connections between biology and network thinking that Adam Curtis recently explored in *All Watched Over by Machines of Loving Grace.* As Curtis showed in his series, these ideas have a lineage which can be traced back from 1960s communes, to postwar cybernetics and to the early days of the ecology movement. All of this is important, because neoliberalism's triumph depended upon the imposition of a temporality which defined hierarchy, the State and organizational discipline as *old* and the network, rhizomatic distribution and individual creativity as *new.*

The question has to be: why has the rhetoric of horizontalism been allowed to propagate so readily under neoliberal hegemony? At the moment, it is the right that has done better out of the shift into the network paradigm. The uncomfortable fact is that, while the 'old' 'hierarchical' and 'bureaucratic' labour movement forced capital into conceding a welfare state, groups espousing 'self-organization' have tended to fail in their stated aims. Occupy has so far caused capital very few serious problems (although this is not to say that it will not do so in the future). The UK student campaign against increased fees of 2010 is another example of a new movement which made some extravagant claims about its anti-hierarchical quality, but which failed to achieve its objectives. Gilles Deleuze's essay 'Postscript on Societies of Control' is a highly prescient account of the way in which the move into network culture would affect politics. Deleuze's claim was not, however, that networks would be inherently liberating; they would, rather, be the new terrain over which power struggles were fought. As Deleuze wrote,

> It's not a question of asking whether the old or new system is harsher or more bearable, because there's a conflict in each between the ways they free and enslave us. With the breakdown of the hospital as a site of confinement, for instance, community psychiatry, day hospitals, and home care initially presented new freedoms, while at the same time contributing to mechanisms of control as rigorous as the harshest confinement. It's not a question of worrying or of hoping for the best, but of finding new weapons.[9]

The switch into Deleuze's 'control societies' can be correlated with the decline of the so-called Fordist regime of economic organization. The arrival of computerization, precarious labour and globalization spelled the end of the 'disciplinary' social models that had taken shape in the nineteenth century. Just as there is nothing inherently liberatory about network society, neither is there anything intrinsically hostile to workers in post-Fordism, either. We can no longer be in any doubt that the conditions which gave rise to the 'old left' have collapsed in the global North, but we must

7 Maurizio Lazzarato, 'The Concepts of Life and the Living in the Societies of Control', in *Deleuze and the Social*, ed. Martin Fuglsang and Bent Meier Sørensen (Edinburgh: Edinburgh University Press, 2006).
8 See Nick Srnicek and Alex Williams, *Folk Politics*, forthcoming on ZerO Books.
9 Gilles Deleuze, 'Postscript on Societies of Control', in *Negotiations: 1972-1990*, trans. Martin Joughin (New York and Chichester: Columbia University Press, 1995), p. 178.

[redacted]

have the courage not to be nostalgic for this lost Fordist world of boring factory work and a labour movement dominated by male industrial workers. The shift into so-called 'cognitive' labour has been overstated — just because work involves talking doesn't make it 'cognitive'; the labour of a call centre worker mechanically repeating the same rote phrases all day is no more 'cognitive' than that of someone on a production line. Even so, the liberation from repetitive industrial labour remains a victory. Antonio Negri and the Italian autonomist tendency from which he comes have always argued that capital was forced into post-Fordism because of the workers' movement. It wasn't the arrival of post-Fordism alone that led to the disintegration of that movement; it was the hegemonizing of post-Fordism by neoliberalism which transformed post-Fordism into a workers' dystopia — a dystopia, moreover, which was built out of workers' desires themselves. Capital became like a genie which granted workers' wishes but in a way that was very different from what they wanted or expected. The desire to be freed from boredom was met — but with the stripping away of the social and existential security that had been provided by the social democratic state. The consequence is a condition of permanent anxiety that arises from a mandatory entrepreneurialism which demands that everyone should always be selling themselves.

It's important to recognize, then, that Post-Fordist capitalism and neoliberalism are a *capturing* of workers' desires. The problem is not desire itself — as opposed, let's say to the ascetic rigour of the disciplined militant — but the way in which capital has been better able than the left to absorb and instrumentalize the desires that erupted in the 1960s. The right has been able to profit from identifying the left with an allegedly superseded 'top down' version of politics which is all about blocking or containing desire.

It should be noted here that whilst the language of self-organization has propagated, neoliberalism itself used every single thing it wants the left to believe is outmoded: top-down control, government, leaders, hierarchy and bureaucracy. Neoliberalism was as top-down as you like: originating in think-tanks, its ideas were then propagated via government and influential party leaders. It's impossible to imagine neoliberalism without Deng Xiaoping, Reagan and Thatcher. As Jodi Dean points out in a trenchant critique, while the left was naively ingenuous in its critique of the State, the right spouted an anti-State rhetoric while making sure it controlled the State:

> Even as various elements on the right developed strategies for funding and winning electoral campaigns, interpreting the Constitution, and rewriting laws, even as corporate and business interests steadily increased their political investments, the left failed adequately to defend what had long ago been won, namely, the notion that the most fundamental role of the state is ensuring a minimal standard beneath which no one is allowed to fall. Indeed, many dismissed the state as useless and outmoded, preferring to theorize instead a politics beyond the state (a move which left an open field for conservative strategists).[10]

Furthermore, neoliberal power shows that there is no necessary opposition between the top-down and the decentralized: instead, neoliberal managerialism combines the two. Deleuze understood very well the Kafkaesque form that neoliberal power would assume. 'Postscript on Societies of Control' describes a power that is both top-down (management must be obeyed) and decentralized via systems such as 'continuous professional development'. The worker ends up performing their own self-surveillance. None other than *Red Tory* ideologue Phillip Blond notes a paradox that I also discuss in *Capitalist Realism*: that, rather than eliminating bureaucracy, as it promised to, neoliberalism has led to its proliferation. Since public services can never function as 'proper' markets, the imposition of the 'market solution' in healthcare and education 'generates a huge and costly bureaucracy of accountants, examiners, inspectors, assessors and auditors, all concerned with assuring quality and asserting control that hinder innovation and experiment and lock in high cost'.[11] Or, as J. J. Charlesworth observes in relation to arts policy,

> There is of course another term to describe the process occurring in this new 'decentred' art

10 **Jodi Dean,** Democracy and Other Neoliberal Fantasies: Communicative Capitalism and Left Politics **(Durham, NC: Duke University Press, 2009), p. 35.**
11 **Blond, op. cit., p. 10.**

[redacted]

> centre. It is 'de-skilling'. The vision of a fluid, flexible, temporary institution is, ironically, entirely concomitant with a general trend towards bureaucratisation and the abolition of expertise in organisational structures that mediate between cultural practitioners and arts policy.[12]

Horizontalism is easier to espouse than to practice. In any case, power and hierarchy cannot be abolished by fiat. When formal power disappears, a more oppressive informal power structure can appear in its stead. What we can be then be faced with, as Adam Curtis showed in *All Watched Over by Machines of Loving Grace*, is a worst of all worlds situation — in which the most manipulative, vocal or passively aggressive dominate, but in which decision-making is slow and cumbersome. One of the reasons that the student movement in the UK flared up and then disappeared might be that it lacked the institutional robustness which could allow its antagonism to be sustained after the initial outpourings of affect had waned. There were all sorts of claims made within the movement about its anti-hierarchicalism, yet there seemed to be something of an informal hierarchy within the movement itself. Many of the hubs were the elite Russell Group universities, and some of those pushing the idea that hierarchy was dead were privately Oxbridge graduates. One of the pernicious effects of the emphasis on hierarchy (and horizontalism), in fact, is that it obfuscates questions of class.

The achievement of horizontal social structures should always be a goal of leftist political practice, but that is not to say that immediately adopting a supposedly horizontal form will allow the left to achieve its aims. It could be, in fact, that adopting horizontalism might be counterproductive for leftist groups. UK Uncut, one of the most successful of the anti-cuts groups which emerged in the UK at the end of 2010, made much of its horizontalism. But its success might have had far less to do with its much-vaunted network openness and much more to do with the fact that it was organized around a simple dogmatic message — if tax-avoiders paid more, then there would be no need for cuts in services.

Conclusion

The upshot of all this is not that we should return to what the neoliberals called the 'old' politics, even supposing that were possible. This would confirm rather than challenge the temporality neoliberalism has imposed. We have to believe that the currently collapsing neoliberal reality system is not the only possible modernity; that, on the contrary, it is a cybergothic form of barbarism, which uses the latest technology to reinforce the power of the oldest elites. It is possible for technology and work to be arranged in completely different ways than how they are configured now. This belief in the future is our advantage over the right. Phillip Blond's networked institutions may have a cybernetic sheen, but he argues that they must be situated in a social setting which is re-dedicated to 'traditional values' coming from religion and the family. By strong contrast, we must celebrate the disintegration of these 'values' as the necessary precondition for new kinds of solidarity. This solidarity won't emerge automatically. It will need the invention of new kinds of institutions, as well as the transformation of older bodies, such as trade unions. As Deleuze wrote in the 'Control' essay,

> One of the most important questions will concern the ineptitude of the unions: tied to the whole of their history of struggle against the disciplines or within the spaces of enclosure, will they be able to adapt themselves or will they give way to new forms of resistance against the societies of control? Can we already grasp the rough outlines of the coming forms, capable of threatening the joys of marketing?[13]

The trade union movement is evidently still capable of mobilising hundreds of thousands of people. Occupy and groups like UK Uncut, meanwhile, have energies, concepts and strategies which the trade unions lack. A synthesis of these two approaches would yield something that was genuinely new.

Much of the leftist discourse around horizontalism stems from a time when Stalinism was a clear and present danger; to say the least, it doesn't pose such a danger any more. It isn't a case of having to choose between an 'old', discredited Stalinism and a

12 Charlesworth, op. cit.
13 Deleuze op. cit., p. 182.

[redacted]

'new' networked post-leftism. Rather, we can learn from what the neoliberals did, and use an ensemble of strategies. The spectre of Stalinism is one of neoliberalism's most powerful weapons, and it continues to suck resolve from the left. We must cease to confuse authoritarianism with authority. As leftists involved in public services or curatorial cultural practice, we are already engaged in positions of authority — the aim should not be to dissolve this authority, but to struggle to find ways to constitute it in a more democratic and collective fashion. The primary challenges we now face no longer concern the critique of ossified structures, but the creation of new organizations and concepts. The time of de-institutionalization is past — now we must have the courage to invent new institutions, institutions that will have both the flexibility and the robustness to combat capital. Similarly, rather than being confined by a too-rigid set of ideological dogmas, the problem is a set of ideas that are too loose and vague to pose a challenge to the neoliberal orthodoxies which continue to dominate our workplaces, our public services and the media.

[redacted]

Bartleby's Tragic Aporia

Sonja Lavaert

[redacted]

'I want to destroy the structures that make millions the slaves of few and make these few the slaves of their own power, their own wealth.'[1] These words — not by Marx, Bakounin or some obscure Italian anarchist but by Wagner — are at the heart of *C(h)oeurs*, the latest production by Alain Platel and Les Ballets C de la B.[2] The title (in French, 'coeur' means 'heart' and 'choeur' means 'choir') refers to the hearts of revolution and the choirs of exiles. They are the voices, the words, the screams, the open mouths, the ferocious and instinctive gasping for the love of the crowd. *C(h)oeurs* stages the battle between reason and emotion. Dancers move against the flow, choir members appear in front of the footlights, the consolation offered by many becomes an uncomfortable spasm. The piece displays the tragedy of human ability. It is a fearful warning, unsettling like the tormented sculptures by Berlinde De Bruyckere, an indictment of the order of military uniforms and the hysteria of agitated masses. It is revolutionary art demonstrating that art is revolution. Still, it takes institutions such as the Teatro Real Madrid, Ludwigsburger Schlossfestspiele, numerous festivals, concert halls and government subsidies to realize a piece like *C(h)oeurs*. Just like Weiwei's installations or paintings by Kiefer or Richter only come into their own, regardless of their critical content, when they are displayed and seen in the galleries, museums and biennials on which they depend. Institutions, politics and art are intertwined. Institutions enable art to take place, even though the characteristic activity of art is an indictment of and rebellion against the same institutions.

Aporia

Social institutions are projects that are being realized, imagination that is being tested in reality. In that sense they are a lot like the works of art they accommodate. But there are always rules that are imposed. Institutions — both the concrete organizations with their buildings, funds, directors and budgets, and the regimes with their value systems and procedures — create a general space for the benefit of private subjects. The notion of 'institution' presupposes general rules, but these rules are always invented, made and imposed by people, which is precisely where they differ from natural laws. At one time they originated in the brain of an individual; they have not always been there. This is why, paradoxically, the structure of social institutions also presupposes the possibility of negation, change and disobedience. Rules are challenged, ignored, circumvented, disputed, changed or eliminated. If not, they deteriorate into coercion or violence. Social institutions therefore navigate, to the rhythm of time, between general validity and the specificity of their origin, between equality and individual differences, between unity and the multitude of the people.

There is something wrong with current institutions, but this is not because we live in a flat world of networks.[3] The problem is rather the reverse: institutions can only be established and questioned in an open, enlightened, horizontal, democratic space. And although the world of networks is a precondition, it offers no guarantees. It is in this ambiguous tension that the western history of philosophical dogmas and democratic institutions has unfolded ever since the Renaissance. It is difficult to invent rules that suit everyone, in light of the many conflicting interests of individuals, but one must base them on the multitude, because that's what rules are about. The stalemate that results from the tension between the singularity of a general rule and the widespread multitude of self-willed individuals often suggests a quantitative solution because of its quantitative nature. Ever since the realization of dreams came within reach of reason, in other words since the Enlightenment, the quantitative approach has gradually evolved into institutions; and we have now reached the point where quantifiable institutions are regarded as pre-eminently democratic.[4] The tension is resolved in relationships that are based on numbers and majorities — especially now, in the flexible globalized world of networks and knowledge. Social issues are counted and measured, redirected to administrative levels and the calculation of data that lend themselves to that. Democratic political institutions are identified with structures of representation, ownership, monopolies,

1 Richard Wagner, 'Die Revolution', *Volksblätter*, April 8, 1949. Quoted in the programme of *C(h)oeurs*, 12.06.12-14.06.12. Concertgebouw Brugge, Belgium.

2 Concept, direction and set design of *C(h)oeurs* by Alain Platel, produced by the Teatro Real Madrid, executive producer of Les Ballets C de la B. Collaborators: Holland Festival, Concert Hall Brugge, Ludwigsburger Schlossfestspiele, the City of Madrid, the Spanish Ministry of Culture, the City of Ghent, the Province of East Flanders, the Flemish government, Berlinde De Bruyckere (and other visual artists) and 107 volunteers in Ghent during four winter months in 2011/2012.

3 The general proposition of this book, for instance in Pascal Gielen, 'Institutional Imagination. Instituting Contemporary Art Minus the "Contemporary"'.

4 As in Michael Hardt and Antonio Negri, *Multitude: War and Democracy in the Age of Empire* (New York: Penguin Press, 2004).

[redacted]

competitions, territories and all kinds of calculable entities (be it often only allegedly, as with languages and peoples). In short, the old institutions from before the revolutionary Enlightenment are in fact still occupying the space. Based on measuring the returns it is decided what knowledge and art is produced and communicated when, where, how and by whom, and who has access to it how, where and when.

In fact, the problem of institutions arises in Western thinking since the early Renaissance, i.e. when the problem of politics arises and from the moment that politics is regarded as art.[5] That is why one stumbles upon the problem of art when designing a political theory and is confronted with political issues when thinking about art. As always when events coincide in time, the one event will legitimize the other and they become each other's allies. Their internal logic is also related: art, politics and institutions, both in form and content, are about problematic freedom or the relationship between design and realization. They are about the aporia of thinking and acting, the tragedy of the human condition. Therefore we can focus on art in order to learn how to organize society or to decide which institutions or art institutions we need nowadays.

For what is an institution, both in its concrete form and as a general cultural phenomenon? If we make abstractions of specific vehicles — in the case of art — and of existing expressions — in the case of politics — an institution is a relationship that binds the subject to society through collective historical forms of agreement that are made possible by a space-time dimension that in turn has been put into motion by language. The subject is not an impenetrable free-floating cell. It is social and always already connected to structures that are also social. Contemplating this leads to the condition for access itself, which is language. Language is the most elementary institution, and this clarifies the following: a problem with institutions is that we are not exclusively dealing with an actual reality but always also with a 'could be', a force or power that carries its own contradiction and negation with it. Each 'can' also implies a 'cannot'.

The aporia resulting from the verb 'can' is aptly illustrated by many experiences of art. It is however also a quite common experience for everyone, which makes it tragic and explains why it is such a recurrent theme in the repertoire of art production, no matter in which medium, place, time, language or culture.

The tragic aporia thus is both what takes place in the art experience itself and the content of the art production, that which is expressed by it. Linguistically speaking, the tragic aporia is both object and subject. According to the French philosopher Merleau-Ponty, language-based art, because it uses language as a vehicle, is the only art that tries to understand itself.[6] We can speak about speaking but we cannot paint about painting or make music about making music. In the light of the problematics of the institution, it is important to note that Merleau-Ponty, however intelligent his statements on language are, is mistaken in the exception that he makes. All art, regardless of its medium, takes place at a primary level and at a meta level at the same time. All art thinks itself, just like politics and languages do. The tragic aporia is precisely intensified by this layered movement of self-reflection to the rhythm of a geometric series.

An interesting elaboration of the questions relating to institutions, art and power, which is in tune with these intuitive thoughts, can be found with the Italian philosopher Paolo Virno. Even though he has written next to nothing about art as such, Virno is quite popular among art theorists. By his own account, this is primarily because of the images that he uses to interpret contemporary social phenomena, such as virtuosity.[7] According to Virno, the experience of the performing virtuoso artist — Glenn Gould playing a Bach sonata, the actor or dancer on a stage — is characteristic of contemporary political action, Post-Fordist labour and also of that typically human form of activity that precedes all other activities and is of all times: language. Post-Fordist labour changed into virtuosity at the moment it became linguistic and communicative or when general abilities were applied economically and historically. Virno's appeal for art theorists comes from a lot more than attractive metaphors and has to do with the core themes in his work. He connects the dissemination of art, which nowadays starts with the very process of production — art is everywhere — to two theories that are interesting within the context of this essay: a theory about creativity and a political theory about institutions. By analysing creativity, it must be possible

5 Jacob Burckhardt, *La civiltà del Rinascimento in Italia* (Florence: Sansoni, 1980), pp. 7-14.
6 Maurice Merleau-Ponty, *Signes* (Paris: Gallimard, 1960), p. 100.
7 Paolo Virno in Pascal Gielen and Sonja Lavaert, 'The Dismeasure of Art: An Interview with Paolo Virno', *Open: Cahier on Art and the Public Domain* 17 (2009), p. 17.

[redacted]

to understand what exactly is going on socially — in industry, economics, politics — and to look ahead for a possible way out of the malaise, an *exodus*. The theory about institutions fits very well with the openness and ambiguity of human nature and offers a suggestion for a remedying action: the *katechon*. I will dwell upon these two topics in Virno's thinking.

Political Institutions and Human Nature

The essay 'Il cosidetto "male" e la critica dello Stato', a chapter in Virno's most recent work, *E così via, all'infinito*, had already been published in an issue of *Forme di vita*, a magazine dedicated to the study of human nature.[8] The issue's title, *L'animale pericoloso: natura umana e istituzioni politiche*, indicates the direction of the authors' thinking: man is a dangerous animal. That is why political institutions are a necessity, at least according to Carl Schmitt, who is often mentioned and quoted in the various contributions. The coercion and discipline of institutions is a necessary protection against the blackness of the human soul. Schmitt identifies institutions with sovereign national institutions of state and coercive one-way traffic. Anyone who begs to differ — liberals as well as anarchists and communists — is naïvely and wrongly assuming that man is by nature good. Chomsky is illustrative of such a naive critique of state institutions, and what is remarkable is that Virno reads Schmitt as a critique of Chomsky. If man is a dangerous, unstable and self-destructive creature, then it is necessary to establish a political body of unity that has the monopoly on political decisions. According to Virno, we cannot simply dismiss this proposition as the authoritarian tendency of a conservative and outmoded author, as it contains an anthropological truth that is supported by the insights 'of the enlightened Freud'.[9] People are not good. With Freud, Virno also finds an argument against Schmitt's one-way traffic: it is a form of compulsive repetition. Since Freud, we know that people are driven by two opposite impulses: sometimes they are inclined to expend themselves and lose sight of reality — there are no rules! — while at other times they are repressed by external dangers and the rules take over. Institutions lay down the rules that tell us what should be done and how, where and when it should be done. They regulate the economy of the to and fro between these two impulses. So in itself there is nothing wrong with rules that keep people from self-destruction, but it does become problematic when the rules take over and deteriorate into pathological com-

pulsive repetition. According to Virno, Schmitt's pessimism about human nature is justified, but the political propositions that he derives from it must be reversed. On the other hand, Chomsky's faith in the goodness of people is wrong, but the disobedience of his radical thinking must be defended, precisely on the basis of the 'riskfull instability of the human animal'.[10] The so-called badness of people does not at all imply sovereignty of the State, on the contrary. To radically opposed the State and capitalistic production means to acknowledge the unstable nature of the human animal. Sovereign institutions of state that have the monopoly on political decisions and whose rules function as compulsory repetition must be criticized precisely because people are not good by nature.
Virno takes the arguments for his proposition about our natural badness from anthropologists such as Gehlen and Plessner. He takes from them that people are problematic creatures because they don't have a specific environment. Besides, culture is also ambivalent in that it wards off dangers but also multiplies risks. Culture protects humans from their own nature by shielding them from their malleability and indefiniteness but at the same time it is the most important expression of that malleability and indefiniteness and so encourages the development of those characteristics. Again, this is based on Freud. In *Das Unheimliche* (The 'Uncanny'), a text generally regarded as an essay on art, Freud explores the terrain of the, terrifying that has to do with what has gradually become familiar and known. In an etymological analysis, he demonstrates the semantic movement of the German word '*heimliche*' from 'the familiar, harmonious, agreeable, homely' to 'hidden from the eyes of strangers, stealthy, secret, furtive' as something that gradually becomes more and more ambiguous and finally coincides with its negation.[11] Moreover, the '*Unheimliche*' is also often associated with unintentional repetition: the thing that is innocent in other circumstances may become *unheimlich* by repetition. Freud sees the explanation for this emotion in the mental life of the child and in

8 Paolo Virno, 'Il cosidetto "male" e la critica dello Stato' [So-called 'Evil' and the Critique of the State] in E cosí via, all'infinito: Logica e antropologia [And So Forth, into Eternity], (Turin: Bollati Boringhieri, 2010); Forme di vita. L'animale pericoloso: natura umana e istituzioni politiche [Forms of Life. The Dangerous Animal: Human Nature and Political Institutions], (Rome: Derive Approdi, 2005).
9 Virno, 'Il cosidetto "male" e la critica dello Stato', p. 153.
10 Ibid., p. 154.
11 Sigmund Freud, 'Het "Unheimliche"', in Cultuur en religie 2 (Amsterdam and Meppel: Boom, 1983).

[redacted]

compulsory repetition. The *Unheimliche*, then, is something that was repressed that keeps surfacing as it resists repression. Looking for something that fits the bill, Freud finds thoughts or feelings about death. Throughout the ages, thoughts about death have always been difficult. There is little room in the subconscious for the idea of our own mortality. At the same time, the longing for the womb, the very first beginning, the state of tranquillity where nothing is demanded of us and everything is taken care of, has also been a constant throughout the ages. Ultimately, the absolute security of the pre-natal state cannot be distinguished from the condition that follows death. This is how Freud explains that the *Unheimliche* is in fact the *Heimliche*, or the familiar thing that was first repressed but later freed itself from this repression.

Problematic human nature can also be described by making use of the three characteristics of verbal language practice: negation, modality of possibility, infinite regress. These fundamental characteristics of language — they can be found in all languages — evoke the memory of the emotional situation of the human animal without an environment and they offer a structure for an analysis of emotions. Pain, sympathy, desire, fear and aggression — the emotions we share with other animals — are shaped by negation, possibility and infinite regression. Besides these, there are emotions such as boredom and angst, which are caused directly by the linguistic structures. The analogy with logic and language philosophy allows Virno to translate Freud's anthropological insights into categorical, neutral terms and analyse Schmitt's theory to the bone. It shows how both good and evil presume a deficit of instinctive orientation and how they feed on the uncertainty regarding that which could be something other than it is. Contingency is the distinguishing characteristic of the practice of mankind and it shows that logical aporias, the oscillation between yes and no, and the paradox of the *Unheimliche* are only all too human. Political theories become weak or dangerous the more they cherish the illusion of being able avoid the paradox. Or, to put it in a positive way: the problem of political institutions can be defined much more efficiently if we face the paradox of the *Unheimliche* and do not deny the simultaneous occurrence of danger and protection. It allows for the unmasking of institutions that provoke aggression in the name of protection and it also suggests a criterion:

> Institutions offer real protection only and exclusively if they use the same secondary conditions that also fuel a threat, if they keep feeding on their openness to the world and the ability of negation, infinite regress and modality of possibility, and, finally, if they demonstrate at all times that they belong to the domain of that which could be something other than it is.[12]

Instead of discarding the negative or pretending it doesn't exist, we should develop a different understanding of it based on ambiguity, oscillation and alarm. In fact, the problem of aggression arises mainly where the modern centralized state is in crisis. According to Virno, the production processes that are based on abstract knowledge and linguistic communication as well as the social struggle of the 1960s and 1970s, which led to a culture of disobedience, are to blame for the current crisis.[13] The question we are facing today is therefore what political institutions are possible outside of the apparatus of the State. Virno's answer to this is the political-theological model of the Jewish *exodus*. Rather than submitting to the Pharaoh of Egypt or rebelling against his regime, the Israelites left the country. They undermined the monopoly of the Pharaoh's decision by a 'resourceful withdrawal'.[14] Crucial in the story of the exodus is the importance of discord and protest, the grumbling in the desert. This importance excludes the possibility that the resourceful withdrawal could be based on the — illusory or not — goodness of mankind.

The questions that Schmitt was struggling with, such as that of the relationship between a civil and natural condition, are still with us. Virno believes it is useful to return to the seventeenth-century version of the problem definition and the strict formulation, 'why obey?'[15] This, after all, remains the most important question in a theory of political institutions. The answer 'because it is the law' leads to an infinite regress, which Hobbes cuts short with the theory that obedience is legitimized by the transition from a natural to a civil condition. But does a clean break between

12 Virno, 'Il cosidetto "male" e la critica dello Stato', p. 159.
13 Paolo Virno, *Antropologia e teoria delle istituzioni* [Anthropology and the Theory of Institutions] (http://eipcp.net/transversal0407/virno/it, 2007), p. 3.
14 Ibid., p. 4.
15 Virno, 'Il cosidetto "male" e la critica dello Stato', p. 162.

[redacted]

the natural and the civil condition really exist? Can the highly contrasting multiplicity of natural life be restrained by the political singular body, and, what's more, if this were possible, in whose interest would it be? Virno subjects the problem to a logical analysis and finds that Hobbes' reasoning is flawed in several ways that reveal his true motive. As he sees it, the obligation to obey is both cause and effect of the institution of the State. In the natural condition, human behaviour is controlled by the alternatives of pleasure and pain, as is the case with animals that have no language. In the human animal, these alternatives are reorganized in pairs of useful/harmful and correct/incorrect, which are both unthinkable outside of linguistic thinking. Hobbes often points out that the dangers of the natural condition are not caused by the *absence* of linguistic thinking, but are in fact linked to it. So the contrast natural-civil does not coincide with the contrast animal-man, either for Virno (because man is an animal) or for Hobbes (because animals are not ambiguous, like people are). Nonhuman animals do not have the ability to present evil as being something good; they cannot pretend, deceive, lie or cheat. It is precisely this typical human ability of secrecy, linked to the verbal use of language, that threatens the peace. In contrast, says Hobbes, the systematic application of rules silences any alarming ambiguity.[16] The natural state demonstrates an ambiguous, oscillating, alarming openness to the world, whereas the civil state puts that openness in parentheses and creates an artificial environment where unambiguous, repetitive behaviour prevails. Hobbes' motive for the definitive and complete submission of nature is the uncontrollability of what is ambiguous. Ambiguity must therefore be eliminated.

The natural condition manifests itself in politics in two cases: when the people become a multitude of individuals who no longer obey, or when the sovereign suspends the law and declares a state of emergency.[17] The rioting multitude corresponds with the state of emergency in reverse: in both cases the law becomes a matter of facts and the distinction between the rules and the facts to which the rules are applied becomes blurred. The entire issue is about following rules and regularity. Beyond the rules there is a preceding regularity that forms the backdrop of any positive attitude. This regularity consists of the linguistic human animal's unchanging behaviours, which — although intrinsically without content and indeterminate — take a different form in concrete situations, places, moments and when faced with different events.

The theory of institutions should express the three levels of human practice, which are regularity, the invention of a particular rule and the contingent application of that rule. None of these levels is immune to the 'so-called evil'.

Virno not only recognizes the destructive urges of mankind, he also believes that these are not dealt with by putting decisions in the hands of a sovereign and neither by relying on democratic institutions that are linked to the traditional sovereignty of the State. In fact, every institution that wishes to permanently banish naturalness is overtaken by the very danger it sought to overcome. In the final part of his essay *Il cosidetto 'male' e la critica dello Stato*, Virno examines how institutions that do not do this, institutions of the multitude, may look like.[18] He does so by focusing on two anthropological phenomena, language and ritual, and introduces the concept of '*katechon*'. What is interesting about this method is that it still leans on the argumentation by both Schmitt and Hobbes but reverses their perspective. He uses their arguments in favour of a radically opposite political stance: pro multitude, communism/ democracy, protests and disobedience.[19] This reversal also allows him to demonstrate the similarity between pre-modern thinking and modern thinking that sought to discard the pre-modern but failed. *Katechon*, or the 'force that impedes' is the political equivalent of the ritual and the mirror concept of the resourceful withdrawal of the *exodus*.[20] Whereas the sovereignty of the State is based on obedience and the unambiguous exit from a natural condition, *katechon* is aimed at the paradoxical domain in between the natural condition and the regulated condition — the force that impedes swings between the positive and the negative and back again without permanently establishing the positive and without permanently banning the negative: it only perpetuates the swinging itself. *Katechon* is a republican institution that tries to contain the risks of instability in a provisional manner; for example, the leagues, councils or assemblies that are established by the multitude during unstable transitional periods and crisises. *Katechon* is associated with circumstances and occasions. That is why in a state

16 Ibid., pp. 164-65.
17 Ibid., pp. 166-67.
18 Ibid., p. 177.
19 Communism and democracy are synonyms to Virno, as they are to Antonio Negri. He also speaks of 'democracy of the multitude' and 'democracy of the commons': these are all synonyms.
20 Virno, 'Il cosidetto "male" e la critica dello Stato', p. 191.

[redacted]

of emergency the rules have to be established time and again and why you can't in general say much about it before and outside of the actual situation. Except that these rules must include the possibility of their own negation, which is a useful recommendation for today's art institutes.

Creativity and Natural History

Even though Virno hasn't written that much about art, his theoretical and political reflections are based on assumptions and sources that are related to aesthetics. In his recently republished debut *Convenzione e materialismo*, he continues Walter Benjamin's attempts to develop a theory of art that in no way could be used by fascism. Benjamin found what he was looking for in the technical reproducibility that led to mass use: he stripped art of its aura and uniqueness. Virno too wants to lose the aura but links this to historic singularity, which is a workable idea in regard to politics and institutions. With uniqueness without aura, the special and individual become susceptible to generality; even more, the special is regarded as having always been social. Within this perspective, politics can be regarded as an ethical community of specialties and it becomes possible to think of institutions of the multitude and multiplicity. In view of the fact that Virno rarely explains his assumptions — including the importance of Agamben, for instance, a matter I will return to later — his essay *Per una storia naturale della creatività*, written as an introduction to the reissue of 2010 of Emilio Garroni's *Creatività*, arouses curiosity.

The inflation of the word 'creativity' over the past few decades is a sign of a radical shift in mentality. Creativity has become a public interest since we have become so familiar with the unexpected. Virno wonders how people act, think and communicate in situations where contingency is overemphasized and uncertainty rules. He believes we should reverse the order of the discourse and also take as our starting point a strict theory of creativity on the basis of which human existence can be distinguished from the existence of other animals in order to understand from this theory what is happening today.

The contrast that we see between creativity on the one hand and discursive knowledge, the vernacular, causality or science on the other — which often results in regarding creativity as an activity that isn't subject to any conditions — is the heritage of a romantic-idealistic philosophy. The Italian aesthetician Emilio

Garroni discards this heritage and the theological remnants that control it once and for all by identifying creativity with adaptation to the environment. By saying that the specifically human ability to change behaviours and representations is not the prerogative of exceptional geniuses but coincides with the instinct of self-preservation, his only option is to extend the concept of this preservation instinct and acknowledge its complexity. Garroni's naturalistic position on creativity demands a reversal of the issue.[21] If creativity means an adaptation to the environment, this adaptation in turn requires categories of aesthetics in order to be adequately defined. The idea of creativity as a procedure of adaptation is important because of what it excludes rather than because of what it says in a positive sense. That is, it excludes the existence of a domain of intellectual, ethical or artistic freedom beyond the primary life context where we seek answers to the stimuli from our environment. According to Garroni, creativity is inherent in the way in which we apply a rule in a particular case, or the way in which we specify a natural law in relation to certain contingent phenomena, or the way in which we use an intellectual principle with universal validity in a unique situation that cannot be repeated. The assertion that application is the actual locus of innovative behaviour is founded on the following two assumptions: that nothing new can be thought of unless it is forged from a dense network of rules and laws, and that not a single rule conclusively states how it must be used in a specific case.[22] While the central role of the moment of application is a recurring theme in philosophical, judicial and theological traditions, the step that Garroni takes from reading Kant's *Critique of Judgement* by cross-linking application and creativity is historic, for he reduces the procedures that allow customs and paradigms of knowledge to change to the manifold routes one can take or construct when applying a rule in special circumstances.[23] Creativity consists of navigating the no man's land that stretches between the import of a norm and what people do or say when the norm is applied. With human beings, adaptation to the environment is not guaranteed by operational schemes or by rules as such, but by a contingent application of the rules, which

21 Paolo Virno, 'Prefazione: Per una storia naturale della creatività' [For a Natural History of Creativity] in Emilio Garroni, *Creatività* (Macerata: Quodlibet, 2010), p. 10.

22 Ibid., pp. 15-16.

23 The theme of the central role of the moment of application can be found with Aristotle, Paul, Schmitt, Wittgenstein: Virno, 'Prefazione', pp. 16-17.

[redacted]

is by definition susceptible to unexpected variations. The typical human creativity expressed in the application coincides with adaptation and is therefore part of its regular functioning. It is unique and at the same time universal. Garroni also attempts to clarify the relationship between the unvarying and varying aspects of the human experience through his naturalism: there are unvarying, genetic, innate conditions that not only allow for greater cultural and historical variation (i.e. creativity) but also impose them — a statement that drives both adherents of the hermeneutic tradition and cognitive scientists up the wall.

Verbal language clearly demonstrates the intertwining of creativity and rules. Twentieth-century linguistics, which focused on the arbitrariness of the sign, has contributed a lot to explaining the innovative variation of human linguistic usage. The names that are often mentioned by both Garroni and Virno are those of Saussure, Peirce, Jacobson and Benveniste, and especially Chomsky, who distinguished between rule-governed and rule-changing creativity.[24] Initially, Garroni uses the words rule, law, norm or principle as synonyms but gradually he makes a distinction between rules and patterns (what Virno calls 'regularity') of the intellect. The most radical rule-changing creativity is a varied specification of the regularity of the intellect, in other words, in the never unequivocal, always ambiguous transition from undefined regularity to a complex of empirical rules.[25] The rule-changing creativity is thus also reduced to an application, finding its roots in the typically human activity of placing and specifying. The innovative application coincides with what Kant calls a 'reflective judgement' and which is characterized by bringing together a multitude of sensory phenomena through the free play of the imagination. The reflective judgement is an aesthetic judgement. The reason why a discourse is innovative must be found in something else than the rules that govern it; something, however, that is not outside of these rules but 'underneath' them (which is exactly what Dante and Agamben say, and a matter that I will return to later).[26] Innovation is possible thanks to the play of the imagination, which in special cases allows for norms to be applied. The ability to interpret, recognize and change actual situations is subject to, but not the same as, the rules. Creativity that is governed by rules, just like creativity that changes them, is based on the ability to judge, which makes possible an infinite use of finite means. Reflective judgement intervenes in both the establishing of a new game and in the unexpected move within the known game. Eventually, rule-changing and rule-governed creativity amount to the same thing: changing the rules only occurs during their application; and vice versa, there can be no application of rules that does not foresee them changing. For institutions, the consequences of this proposition are downright revolutionary.

So, for Garroni, creativity is adaptation to the environment. This adaptation runs parallel to the diversification of varying cultural rules and unvarying innate categories of thinking. Application requires the free play of the imagination, with which reflective judgement feeds itself. The moment of application, in which biological adaptation and historical innovation meet, is therefore aesthetic in nature. This means that aesthetics have a far wider range of application than art in the narrow sense of the word. The traditional identification of the part with the whole not only does injustice to the whole but also to the part one sought to elevate. To deny the presence of aesthetic judgement in the most varied kinds of actions and discourses is to deny the typical, not-to-be-generalized characteristics of works of art. Garroni dwells on the relationship between art and the aesthetic function in general, precisely because the latter cannot be reduced simply to specialized art. He calls art the non-knowledge-based specialization of something that is a condition of knowledge in general; this something is the ability to judge, or the skill and practice to apply the universal principles of the intellect in varying ways.[27] This skill, which is exercised in any practical-intellectual activity, is clearly expressed in the work of art. The artistic specialization of the moment of application is a non-knowledge-based specialization because of its meta-historical collocation. In poetry and music, *a priori* categories are applied and the functioning of the ability to judge is expressed as such. Works of art are empirical objects with a spatial-temporal reality in which the condition for experience becomes materialized and perceptible. Art is non-knowledge-based because it lends a phenomenal aspect to the mental requirement that enables us to distinguish phenomena and bring them together. The borderline between disseminated and specialized creativity is therefore uncertain and varying. What we have here is more like an enclave

24 Ibid, p. 20.
25 Ibid., pp. 22-23.
26 Ibid., p. 25.
27 Ibid., p. 28.

[redacted]

where distributed creative activities take on the poetic, painterly or musical form without necessarily already being poetry, painting or music. This enclave is precisely where aesthetics must focus. To understand painting means to gain insight in the game of similarities and differences that link it to industrial design or children's drawings. To understand poetry means to gain insight into the poetic function of the vernacular, campaign slogans, newspaper headlines or advertising copy. If Garroni would be the head of a Master's programme in theatre, he would tell his students about the theatrical structure of general human usage first.

So, we could say that adapting universal rules in contingent circumstances is the way in which people adapt to their environment and that art is the non-knowledge-based specialization of creativity that is present in each application of rules. Artistic expressions, including installations, video, literature, cinema or the performing arts, present an image of the sources that we rely upon to keep ourselves alive. What's more, human adaptation is never complete and definitive. The familiarity of the world that surrounds us can change into an *unheimliche*, disturbing forlornness any second. Art also plays a role in this: it does not limit itself to a specialized expression of adaptation procedures but also offers compensation for their tentativeness and incompleteness. Art enables us to develop a familiarity with the unexpected and the disturbing.

As far as I know, there is no text by Virno in which he clearly indicates the analogy of his considerations with those of Agamben, or where he explicitly names him as a source. In the late 1980s and early 1990s, they both worked for the magazine *Luogo commune*. They were friends, neighbours, shared the same mission, fought the same battle, read the same books and had mutual friends that inspired them, such as Antonio Negri. I do not intend to elaborate here on the various aspects of their connection and collaboration, nor do I wish to speculate about who influenced who the most. I will dwell on three instances in Agamben's thinking that coincide with the theories that Virno has set forth, to thereby shared an extra light on the issues discussed here. Unlike Virno, Agamben has written extensively about art. In his debut, *L'uomo senza contenuto*, he writes about the original structure of the art work, which he links to human nature — man is an emptiness — and later, in the essay *L'opera dell'uomo*, to the typically human activity — man's work. Agamben illustrates and/or looks for the formula of creativity or typically human activity — which we can turn into political advantage — in performances by Vanessa Beecroft, poems by Dante or stories by Melville. He finds this formula in *Bartleby, the Scrivener.*

Bartleby, an Exercise in Contingency

In Melville's novella, thinking as the pre-eminent figure of Western philosophical tradition appears dressed as a humble clerk or in the shape of the activity of writing. Agamben links the character of Bartleby with the image of the desk upon which nothing is written, the *tabula rasa* of Locke and Aristotle, thinking as a blank, pure potentiality. With Aristotle, the possibility to be or to do is always also the possibility not to be or not to do. This possibility to not-to is the hidden linchpin of his doctrine. In his essay *Bartleby o della contingenza* (1993), Agamben tells the story of the enlightened Arabic philosophy and its debate with orthodox Sunnites in order to illustrate the various aspects of intellect as a potentiality. What laws govern the transition of the possible to the real? Who moves the writer's hand? Contrary to Sunnite theologians, the *falasafa* consider these questions, in the assumption that the possible can either realize itself in creative activity or not. By contrast, orthodox Sunnites make any statement about possibility versus necessity pointless because they regard the activity of creation as a continual immediate production of miraculous events that absolutely do not interact and are therefore not subject to any law or causal relation. This is not just about the difference in opinion between theologians and philosophers; the theologians want to break Aristotle's writing desk once and for all and do away with the experience of possibility. If potentiality would only mean the positive ability to do or to be, then we could never experience it as such, as it would only exist in the activity in which it is being realized. The experience of potentiality is always also the negative potentiality not to be or not to do. Aristotle tries to escape this aporia via self-reflexive thinking. A thinking which thinks itself does not think an object nor does it think a nothingness. However, the aporia appears again immediately in the question of how one can think a pure potentiality. How can a blank writing desk address itself?

Agamben's essay becomes interesting when he effectively links these Aristotelian Arabian reflections with the character Bartleby in Melville's novella. Bartleby is the extreme figure of the nothing from which all creation springs, the pure potentiality. Our ethical tradition has often attempted to circumvent the problem of poten-

[redacted]

tiality by reducing it to will and necessity: not what you are capable of, but what you want or should do, is the prevailing theme in ethics. This is what the Lawyer in the novella constantly reminds Bartleby of. When Bartleby is asked to go to the post office and he gives his customary reply, 'I would prefer not to', the Lawyer interprets this as 'You will not?', to which Bartleby responds, more precisely, with a variation of his standard reply: 'I prefer not'. He renounces the conditional mood, according to Agamben, to eliminate all traces of the verb 'to will'.[28] Potentiality is not the same thing as the will. To think that the will has power over potentiality and that the transition to deeds is the result of a decision that terminates the ambiguity of potentiality, is the eternal illusion of morality.[29] Bartleby 'can' without 'willing'. It is not that he does or does not want to transcribe the text or leave the office — he would prefer not to. The formula that is repeated so meticulously time and again destroys any possible link between will and potentiality. 'I prefer not' is the formula of potentiality. Deleuze underlines the linguistic ungrammaticality of this expression that disconnects words from things, acts or language event.[30] Bartleby's formula disconnects the use of language from all references.

According to Agamben, experiments are not the prerogative of the exact sciences. In poetry and philosophy there is also a lot of experimentation, although, unlike with scientific experiments, the issue is not verifying or falsifying a hypothesis. Experiments in art and philosophy have no verity because they question 'being' itself, as in Melville's *Bartleby, the Scrivener.* In this type of experiment, the question is not whether something is effective or not (which can be checked). Rather, it is an exploration of potentiality. To the extent that potentiality can be and not be, it is exempt from the conditions of verity and the principle of non-contradiction. A 'being' that can at the same time be and not be is called 'contingent' in philosophy. Bartleby's experiment is an exercise in contingency. In Leibniz's scheme — 'possible' is what can be, 'impossible' is what cannot be, 'necessary' is what cannot not be, 'contingent' is what can and cannot be — the figure of contingency coincides with the extent of human freedom.[31]

In his essay *L'opera dell'uomo* (2004), Agamben expresses Virno's question of what it means to be human in Aristotelian terms as well. He wonders whether there is such a thing as typical human work. The work of man is closely linked to 'being at work' and is the opposite of potentiality. Agamben refers to Aristotle's controversial proposition that human intellect is nothing but an intellectual potentiality. In Western culture, this proposition first led to indignation, seen from a Christian standpoint, and later to aporias, from the perspective of the Enlightenment. Nevertheless an enlightened reading is possible that does not end in aporias, and Agamben finds an example of this in Dante's work. In *De Monarchia*, Dante searches for the principle of a just form of government. He wants to develop a theory about empire, the domain of things that are measured in time, in other words a theory about institutions, especially political institutions. Dante also asks the question whether there is a general human activity, an 'end goal at which the potentiality of mankind as a whole is aimed'.[32] This end goal cannot lie in the fact that man exists (because elements exist too), or in his complex nature (minerals are complex too), or in the fact that man is alive (so are plants) or has understanding (this we share with animals). Dante thinks that the general task of man lies in his specific understanding 'that stems from his possible intellect'.[33] The difference with the intellect of animals or angels, who both understand in a continuous manner, is that human beings do not always understand. Dante underlines the fact that human understanding is not continuous — the intellectual potentiality — to then posit the multitude. It is not possible, after all, that potentiality is completely and at one time actualized through one human being and 'that is why mankind has to be a multitude, so that its total potentiality can be actualized'.[34] In the same way, there must be a multitude of things which can be generated so that the whole potentiality of prime matter 'lies under the act' (sub actu),[35] otherwise there would be a separate potentiality, which is impossible.[36] This is not a very clear passage, but what strikes

28 Giorgio Agamben, 'Bartleby o della contingenza' [Bartleby, or On Contingency], in Gilles Deleuze and Giorgio Agamben, *Bartleby: La formula della creazione* [Bartleby, the Formula of Creation] (Macerata: Quodlibet, 1993), p. 43-85, here p. 64.

29 Ibid., p. 65.

30 Ibid., p. 66.

31 Ibid., p. 74.

32 Giorgio Agamben, 'L'opera dell'uomo' [The Work of Man], in *Forme di vita: La natura umana* [Forms of Life: Human Nature] (Roma: Derive Approdi, 2004), here p. 122; also published in *La potenza del pensiero: Saggi e conferenze* [The Faculty of Thought] (Vicenza: Neri Pozza, 2005); Dante Alighieri, *Monarchia* in *Tutte le opere* (Florence: Sansoni, 1965), pp. 250-51.

33 Dante, *Monarchia*, p. 251.

34 Ibid., p. 252.

35 Ibid., p. 252; Agamben, 'L'opera dell'uomo', p. 122.

36 Dante literally says: as Averroës has demonstrated in his commentary to Aristotle's *De Anima*: *Monarchia*, p. 252.

[redacted]

me is that the exact same formulation can be found with Virno and Garroni in their exposition of creativity, innovation and rules (see above). If we make abstractions of the concrete content in the relevant passages with Virno/Garrone and Agamben/Dante and compare both argumentations as if they were purely formal mathematical formulas, we can deduce the following: The typically human activity consists of the constant actualization of the full potentiality of the possible intellect. As human thinking is exposed to the possibility of not happening or not working and is, in other words, potentiality and can only become activity through the play of the imagination, it presupposes and requires a multitude. In Virno's interpretation, this proposition of Dante's is revolutionary: thinking presupposes the multitudes of the crowd, the imagination and disobedience.

In his 1970 debut *L'uomo senza contenuto*, Agamben speaks of art as 'the most disturbing' of all things, a fact that regrettably has been forgotten by modern man.[37] Art is dangerous, not only for those who make it but for the whole of society. At the same time, art is a gift. This has to do with its meaning in relation to time. The original structure of a work of art is its rhythm, and rhythm is what goes, flows, changes and resumes itself over time.[38] Rhythm is both within time and interrupts it. When faced with a work of art, we become aware of time standing still, of an interruption, as if we suddenly find ourselves in a dimension on a primary level, outside of time. The work of art belongs to an essential dimension because, time and again, it grants humanity access to its original place in history and time. Therefore art is no luxury, it is not superfluous or just decorative. Even more, the question about the importance of art is beside the point, because art is essential to mankind: it is the typically human activity as described by Dante, which actualizes general potentiality in an incomplete, tentative manner. In music and poetry, we observe rhythm as something that avoids the continuous flight of moments, as a manifestation of timelessness within time. Visual art, architecture and narrative prose too give mankind access to its original time dimension and the space of its belonging to the world. Art gives people a place, a shelter in which they can determine the benchmarks of their stay on Earth and find their own truth (rhythm) in the unstoppable flow of linear time. As rhythm, art stops time and beats time. It is the gift of a place of one's own. That is why all art, regardless of its medium, is architecture. And that is also why all art, regardless of its content, is disturbing and revolutionary.

Exercises in Exodus

The analogy between Agamben's considerations and Virno's theories is striking. Bartleby's passive resistance is reminiscent of the disobedience of leaving and ignoring. The 'prefer not to', the negation and the searching for a — different — place are exercises in contingency, to use Agamben's terminology, or in exodus, to use Virno's image. To Virno as well, contingency is the main characteristic of human practice, institutions are incomplete and provisional, and art gives mankind a place in time, enabling us to acquire familiarity with the disturbing. But art too is disturbing, and an exercise in exodus. It is a 'dismeasure' that challenges benchmarks.[39] The biblical image of the exodus has been used for centuries as a metaphor for liberation and revolution. It is a paradigm for revolutionary politics, according to Michael Walzer in *Exodus and Revolution* (1985). *Exodus* is a story that is embedded in our collective memory, a judicial-theological text intended for analogous application, an example of an act of resistance to 'try at home', a realistic presentation.[40] The image of the exodus reminds Virno of this revolutionary practice, and vice versa: because of his experiences in the movement of 1968-77, he recognizes what Walzer says. The exodus also reminds him of how Marx described, in *Das Kapital*, the early stages of North-American capitalism when frontier man left wage labour in droves and headed west, and vice versa: the practice of the frontiers may serve as an example of disobeying the laws of the capitalist labour market.[41]

Virno's reflections, in the wake of Garroni and Agamben, shed some light on the current situation. They revoke the romantic notions and compel us invert the questions. Is there still something to be learned from this? Creativity is the central concept in current labour processes, which are based on knowledge and verbal communication. Creativity takes place in the application of the rules. It is adaptation to the environment, but this means that human adaptation to the environment, such as creativity, is by definition incomplete and tentative. The rules are being changed

37 Giorgio Agamben, *L'uomo senza contenuto* [Man without Content] (Macerata: Quodlibet, 1994/1970), p. 9.
38 Ibid., p. 150.
39 Paolo Virno in Gielen and Lavaert, op. cit., p. 18.
40 Michael Walzer, *Esodo e rivoluzione*, trans. M. D'Alessandro (Milan: Feltrinelli, 1986/1985), pp. 13-14.
41 Paolo Virno, *Esercizi di esodo* [Exercises in Exodus] (Verona: Ombre Corte, 2002), pp. 177-82; Karl Marx, *Das Kapital: Kritik der politschen Ökonomie: Erster Band* (Berlin, 1987/1867), pp. 792-802.

[redacted]

in the course of the application, but this means that there is no application of rules that does not foresee this changing. Art is the non-knowledge-based specialization of creativity that coincides with the typically human potentiality, which therefore belongs to everyone. Art belongs to everyone. This of course has consequences for institutions. We can apply Les Ballets C de la B's motto here: 'This dance belongs to the world and the world belongs to everyone'.[42] Fully aware of contingency and even for the sake of contingency, the tragic aporia, ambiguity, instability and the danger of the multitude, for everyone's sake therefore, Virno makes a plea for institutions — political institutions, but by extension also art institutions — that are open to their own negation as forces that impede. This means that they do not suppress the fight against them, the disobedience, the unruly imagination or the tendency to change them. It means that they become stronger and serve their purpose better — offering a space — as they no longer suppress opposition and make room for the confrontation with themselves, thereby enabling themselves to change. In opposition to the institutions are we, the people, the multitude, the makers of art, everyone. And for us it's the other way around: we are called to arms, to resistance, imagination, autonomy, rebellion, disobedience, innovation, appropriation and change. We are called upon to enterprisingly withdraw ourselves from the institutions that make many the slaves of few and make these few the slaves of themselves and their own illusions.

42 Quoted in the programme of C(h)oeurs, 12.06.12 - 14.06.12. Concertgebouw Brugge.

[redacted]

Institutionality as Enlightenment

Blake Stimson

If men wish to be free, it is precisely sovereignty they must renounce.
– Hannah Arendt

Institutionality as Power

There is a tender spot, it might be said, for many of us who work with institutions of art, a spot that is not always given its full due. When we are being tough-minded — rigorously analytical, detached from the sympathies of our day-to-day intercourse with familiar people and things, and self-reflexive about the larger social and political conditions of our enterprise — suspicions about our institutions often exceed our appreciation. In this state of mind, many of us are inclined to view archives, libraries, Internet repositories, museums, galleries, auction houses, personal collections, academic organizations, and even our precious institution of art itself, with Pierre Bourdieu, say, or particularly with Michel Foucault and the broad sweep of his influence, as nodes within a 'general system'. When we see art institutions in this systemic way, they take on a life beyond any individual repository and the peculiarities of its people and things. In so doing, the measure of their institutionality shifts from the vertical rule of theological or philosophical understanding, ceremonial sites or sacred things, and meaningful personal relationships or moving aesthetic experience, to the horizontal jurisdiction of complex systems.

'The archive', as this *corpus mysticum* is sometimes referred to generically, is understood to be a mix of social structure and cultural form that organizes knowledge in a manner that governs, delimits and directs the kind of insights we gather and pleasures we enjoy, and all largely below the level of our cognition, or at least below the level we admit to publicly. Regardless of whether we are referring to the economy of art, its bureaucracy, epistemology or cultural value, the foundational metaphor for such horizontalist accounts is Adam Smith's invisible hand.[1] In this way, art and its institutions are gauged by disembodied technical and systemic criteria that promote ends outside of any individual intention and at a remove from any particular use, ends at a remove from the vertical authority of theology and philosophy, ceremony and sacred sites, human bonds and aesthetic experience.

When we are thinking like Bourdieu or Foucault, in other words, the archive is first and foremost a distinctly modern ideological tool used to exercise power and accumulate wealth and we understand it in the larger socio-symbolic and socio-affective ways that Foucault intended with terms like *discourse*, or *governmentality* or, of course, *archive* itself. The general system of file cabinets and file folders, databases and search engines, objects and definitions, auctions and appraisals, etc. serves to route the horizon of possible understanding from desire to 'thingliness', from the root condition of subjects to that of objects.[2] The archive, this line of thought assumes, is a kind of imagined community of things and understanding beyond the horizon of our direct cognition and it polices its own boundaries and controls access to authority in all the ways that any secret society does, that is, not only through procedural means of enforcement but also by less structured, less conscious cultural means.

To call on one example that suggests this general delimiting effect on our experience, we might agree to Allan Sekula's simple but expressive phrasing when he wrote of the archive's 'dry compartmentalization'.[3] Or we might call to mind any tawdry nineteenth-century image of police files, museum storehouses, or any of the sundry typologies of scientists, philosophers, or medical researchers, and say that the dryness of these forms of organization is itself illustrative of a general and comprehensive system of understanding both conscious and unconscious, that is, of an 'episteme' in Foucault's capacious sense, or of 'doxa' in Bourdieu's. The Assyrian scribes' careful tally of severed heads in can serve to illustrate the pre-history of this institutionalized knowledge and its taste. Their record-keeping is prehistorical and premodern for our purposes only because it is still visible as power, still done at the decree of a political leader and thus is not yet elemental enough to fall below the horizon of the political proper and function simply as knowledge, or in Foucault's terminology 'power/knowledge'.

1 That is, in Smith's wording, a factor 'which was no part of [human] intention'. Adam Smith, *An Inquiry into the Nature and Causes of the Wealth of Nations*, ed. R.H. Campbell, Andrew S. Skinner and W.B. Todd (Oxford: Oxford University Press, 1976), p. 456.

2 '[W]e have in the density of discursive practices, systems that establish statements as events (with their own conditions and domain of appearance) and things (with their own possibility and field of use). They are all these systems of statements (whether events or things) that I propose to call *archive*.' (Michel Foucault, *The Archaeology of Knowledge & The Discourse on Language* [New York: Vintage, 1982], p. 128). For one comprehensive historical investigation into these limits, see Thomas Richards, *The Imperial Archive: Knowledge and the Fantasy of Empire* (New York: Verso, 1993).

3 Allan Sekula, 'Between the Net and the Deep Blue Sea (Rethinking the Traffic in Photographs)', *October* 102 (Fall 2002), pp. 3-34, here p. 24.

[redacted]

Indeed, I think we can further say that when it comes to theorizing the archive (if not, as I will argue below, when it comes to working in it) some variety of this tough-minded Bourdieuianism or Foucauldianism, explicit or otherwise, is not only ingrained in us as critics and scholars but even holds true as a naive but nonetheless fully habituated knee-jerk response for most of our students. Such classroom reaction may be just one more garden variety of the best sort of sophomoricism — no different in kind from knee-jerk connoisseurship, say, or knee-jerk identity politics, or knee-jerk philosophizing — but that makes it no less symptomatic. Think, for example, of how a typical undergraduate student might respond if asked to explain why one art work deserves to be in a museum and another does not: part of her may be itching to invoke justifications like 'masterpiece', 'genius', and 'creativity', but if my experience holds true what will come out instead is some intuitive version of the Foucauldean conjoining of knowledge and power or a naïve but nonetheless fully workable version of the one-upmanship argument laid out by Bourdieu in his 1979 *Distinction*. Understandably enough, my students have occasionally brought this argument to bear by asking about the role that professionals like us play in the amassing of wealth, power, and prestige by our superiors.

The organization of objects and information in archives, as in museums, as in any institution, such students would invariably say if the vocabulary were available to them, in other words, is a function of a 'habitus' or a '"regime" of truth' and, like any regime, it has its rulers and its ruled, its structure of power and its domination, exploitation and exclusion. It is a system of organization driven by the pursuit of its own perpetuity and it is precisely its 'dry compartmentalization' — into periods and isms, into media and movements, into artists' names and their influences and legacies, into good art and bad, into our taste and theirs — that empowers it. Taste, they would certainly say even if they don't really want to believe it, is a top-down organizing system dictated by collectors and curators, critics and scholars, and institutions like museums, universities, libraries, archives, galleries and private collections, or it is a matter of posing oneself against that system. It is professionals like us who endow taste with its social value, not anything intrinsic to the art work itself much less intrinsic to the aesthetic experience it offers.[4] Beyond this regime of truth and the battles against it, they might say if pressed to find a nonconstructionist value for taste, all that remains is that beauty which resides in the eye of the beholder, the delectation of personal preference, 'taste' in its most banal, consumerist sense: Manet over Monet, say, or abstraction over figuration, or, for that matter, latte over cappuccino — you the art appreciator, momentarily divorced from your workaday role as tough-minded critical historian, sophomoric cynic, or heartless banker-cum-arts-patron, decide which better strikes your leisurely mood or shopaday fancy.

Such, we might risk, has been the institution of art's default theory of institutionality for a long time now, at least when it is asked to actively characterize such a theory or even when it more passively assumes one. What makes it particularly appealing to scholars, however, is something greater still, or at least closer to home: the archive for our purposes is less some '"regime" of truth' out there — in government buildings, say, that we abide from a distance — as it is a regime in here, in museums, or research institutes, or art magazines, or art history lecture halls and textbooks. As the generic undergraduate response would suggest, our Foucauldean theory of the archive and our Bourdieuian theory of taste also define a limit condition for our scholarship, a moment when its capacity to understand is reduced to all the abject poverty and brute, instrumental authority of 'dry compartmentalization'. To put this in more common parlance, the threshold of art history and related humanistic forms of study is the moment they are reduced to 'thinking in boxes', the moment they are reduced to the form of thinking of the bureaucrat rather than the leader, the form of thinking that aims at ensuring the continuity of the institution that endows him or her with an authority that has nothing to do with the object in question. So it is that this limit has little to do with the content of any specific piece of the archive but instead mostly with the way in which knowledge is organized, the way in which thoughts or statements relate to each other, the way in which art history's periods and isms and all the rest of it function as a self-reproducing, self-justifying system of relations; the way, in other words, that our knowledge is our power.

But such Foucauldean or Bourdieuian worries and temptations really only represent half of any art-oriented scholarly relation to the archive — the theoretical half, we might call it, the

4 **Michel Foucault,** Power/Knowledge: Selected Interviews and Other Writings, 1972-1977 **(New York: Vintage, 1980), p. 133.**

[redacted]

workaday or shopaday half, the mind half rather than the body half, the half that thinks in terms of social systems and marketplace calculations rather than in terms of the fullness of human sensuous experience. We can also consider how we have used the archive rather than how we have conceptualized it, how we engage with it as practitioners rather than as theorists. Foucault himself, for example, was never one to simply document conquest, never one to simply use archival knowledge as an index and agent of power, even balefully. Instead, like many of his contemporaries who came of age with the 1960s, he saw the information he gathered from the archive as a means of contesting power, a means of challenging the system of thinking in boxes and its role reproducing and entrenching the powers that be. Indeed, if the slogan drawn from Foucault's *theory* of the archive is 'knowledge as power' (or, in the more constricted form already introduced that makes clear the fully intractable, systemic character of the relation, 'power/knowledge'), then the slogan drawn from Foucault's archival *practice* as a historian would be better given as something very different, something more like 'speaking truth to power'. Something similar, of course, could be said about Bourdieu.

This second slogan makes sense immediately to any reader of Foucault, I think it is fair to say, but it poses a problem for his theory insofar as it gives autonomy to truth, insofar as it gives some breathing room by which it can separate itself from power, by which it can make itself an actor in its own right. This, we might say, is simply a slippage in Foucault's account, a slippage between his theory and his practice and a slippage between the sense of control over the object world that 'knowledge' indicates and the sense of grounded conviction that the term 'truth' conveys. For example, we can see this slippage when he said that his goal was 'not a matter of emancipating truth from every system of power (which would be a chimera, for truth is already power)', stoutly reaffirming the power/knowledge (cum power/truth) doctrine in the first half of his sentence, 'but', continuing in the second, it is a matter 'of detaching the power of truth from the forms of hegemony, social, economic and cultural, within which it operates'.[5]

It is this 'power of truth' detachable from the power proper of 'the forms of hegemony', the moment in which the tight power/knowledge nexus that Foucault postulates is sundered and a space opens up between hegemony and some emergent counter-hegemony, between a 'regime of truth' and truth proper, the moment of the possibility of speaking truth to power before that truth is realigned, that will concern me in what follows. That is, it is here in that split nexus that we might find what I am calling 'the tender spot' of art history's relation to the archive.

The Tender Spot

To get at this distinction between truth in the form knowledge/power and truth as a form of knowledge separable from power, we might focus first on the term 'archive' itself. There are two commonly used meanings — one that carries forward from antiquity and the other that has its roots in the Enlightenment. The older meaning, 'archive' in its noun form, is, generally, the referent when we use the term in its Foucauldian sense as I have been describing it here. Most minimally conceived it is no different from any database, any rational ordering system, any self-enclosed systematic form of knowledge or value, any thinking in boxes. The later meaning, 'archive' in its verb form, is different: on the one hand, of course, it means simply to place an object in an archive but, more importantly, on the other hand, it also indicates a change of status for the object, a movement from an active database to an inactive one, a downgrading of importance, a movement from the category of the present to the category of the past, a movement into attic or basement or offsite where the object is preserved for some indeterminate future use. This idea was first developed in the national archive established in Paris in 1789 and then formalized further in 1796 after debate about whether to keep the records of the old regime or destroy them; but the modern idea of the archive as a public repository of the nation's past maintained for future reinterpretation is inconceivable without the concept of progress as it had already been developed prior to the revolution in the Enlightenment.[6]

To recall what this idea meant for the emerging concept of the archive, we can look to Marquis de Condorcet, writing just prior to the revolution: 'No one has ever believed that the mind can gain knowledge of all the facts of nature', he wrote, arguing that we do, however, make great advances in understanding by learning how to classify them and to subsume them under more general

5 Ibid., p. 133.
6 See Ernst Posner, 'Some Aspects of Archival Development Since the French Revolution', in *Archives and the Public Interest: Selected Essays by Ernst Posner*, ed. Ken Munden (Washington D.C.: Public Affairs Press, 1967), pp. 23-35.

[redacted]

facts. This gain does not result from an evolution of physiological capacity — the development of bigger or more elastic brains, say — but instead through the development of social systems: the 'strength and limits of man's intelligence may remain unaltered', he continued, but the 'language that fixes and determines his ideas will acquire greater breadth and precision'.[7] This, we might say, is a notion of the compartmentalization of knowledge that pledges not to become dry or static, that pledges not to become institutionalized as such, an understanding of knowledge, in other words, that pledges to retain its humanity. The prophylactic warding off of the implicitly anticipated problem of dryness, the problem of thinking in boxes, the problem of power realized through the stasis of epistemes, was thus given in the Enlightenment ideal of progress, in the idea that the method of compartmentalization — that is, of knowledge itself or fixing and determining meaning in order to master it — would change or open out to be ever more refined, more nuanced and generative of understanding. In the future, it was assumed, we will be better able to understand the past and so holding on to raw data — archiving it — serves as an investment in this promise, as an investment in the idea that the meaning of any given archival object can, in principle, forever be contested, revised, expanded upon, and better understood.

'Archive' in its verb form, thus, refers not to the process of fixing and determining meaning, of enacting the connection of truth and power in Foucault's sense, but instead the opposite, that is, to the process and the promise of *un*fixing meaning, of detaching truth from power. This is the tender spot we hold for the archive and it is something we experience all the time: it was made available when the more sober forces of the French revolutionary government preserved the documents of the old regime and made them public and it is what happens when a government document now becomes declassified or a private document is given over to a public archive.[8] 'To archive' in its Enlightenment sense, thus, is inextricably linked to the promise of detaching truth from the exclusive domain of power by moving it from the realm of private discretion into the realm of public judgment, where it invites reexamination and reinterpretation, where it waits to take on a new attachment to power, in significant measure through the work of scholars like us. Of course, this detachment is itself something that is granted by power but it is done so for a reason — that is, it speaks of a moment where the archival document is no longer of immediate use and concern to power, or the moment when the document has become obsolete, the moment it has become history in its yet-to-be written sense. This does not mean that it will not take up a relation to power again as it enters into history books and the like, but for the moment it has all the potential of the 'power of truth', as Foucault termed it, and not what we Foucauldians might call the truth of power.

Such an archive-specific status for a piece of information in between its life and its afterlife, in between its original attachment to power in business or politics or museology and its later attachment in emergent historical understanding, as an expression of the politics of the author or publisher or reader, can also be said to be evident in the *form* of the archive. The archival organization of knowledge has a distinct structure. It is typically given little or no narrative or other instrumental organization — it may be roughly chronological or may be not, correspondence may be separated from manuscripts and business documents or may be not: it doesn't really matter — and instead is organized mostly by simple accretion. The archive lines up one scrap of information after another, after another, with no single part valorized over any other. As such, any given piece of information is at base a serial form, an equivalent form, and remains so until extracted, revalorized and elevated to the status of historical consequence. The smoking gun is not pre-given by the archival form — it is not framed, or placed on a pedestal, or put at the centre of a narrative reconstruction of events — but instead is there only to be discovered as such.

This active, extractive role made possible by the archive was summed up nicely in 1971 by Noam Chomsky as he debated and distinguished himself from Foucault for Dutch television:

> I'm looking at history not as an antiquarian, who is interested in finding out and giving a precisely accurate account of what the thinking of the seventeenth century was – I don't mean to demean that activity, it's just not mine – but rather from the point of view of, let's say, an art

7 From his 'Sketch for a Historical Picture of the Progress of the Human Mind', in *Condorcet: Political Writings*, ed. Steven Lukes, Nadia Urbinati (Cambridge, MA: Cambridge University Press, 2012), p. 134.

8 Posner, 'Some Aspects of Archival Development Since the French Revolution', p. 26.

[redacted]

> lover, who wants to look at the seventeenth century to find in it things that are of particular value, and that obtain part of their value in part because of the perspective with which he approaches them. And I think that, without objecting to the other approach, my approach is legitimate; that is, I think it is perfectly possible to go back to earlier stages of scientific thinking on the basis of our present understanding, and to perceive how great thinkers were, within the limitations of their time, groping toward concepts and ideas and insights that they themselves could not be clearly aware of.[9]

The archive is not simply a record and process of enforcing the will to power, it is also a record and process open to that desire which speaks truth to power. In this regard, the archive of Foucault's own writings could itself be taken to be a repository of such desire — 'connecting together modes of veridiction, techniques of governmentality, and practices of the self is basically what I have always been trying to do', as he himself put it — even if, with Chomsky, they stand for a desire necessarily understood to be bound by the limitations of its time, a desire unable to fully channel the point of view of the art lover because of its investment in 'finding out and giving a precisely accurate account' of the past.[10]

One way to further consider the value of the art lover's desire for art history is to look to the archive as a concern for art practice. There have been a variety of different ways that art has taken on the archive as a method but, generally, we might speak of just two: first, there is the aim to articulate and preserve a certain relation to the world, such as we might see in the work of Karl Blossfeldt. This function is different from documenting the world, reporting on it or commenting on it — instead, it seeks to preserve a connection to the world through a process of making aesthetic judgments. Witness, for example, his manifesto: 'The plant', he said famously, 'must be valued as a totally artistic and architectural structure'. The particular mix of aims at issue here — preserving and knowing realized through a process of idealization — is crucial: this is what makes it art and not something else. Its valorization is drawn not through simple cognition but instead through a process of lingering over the object, spending time with it, savouring the nuance and character of its 'totally artistic and architectural' form, seeing it as an object of love or desire, and preserving it for later gratification.

Something like this is always true for art, at least when it is functioning as art qua art and not serving some other role: it makes its claim on the beholder as attachment, not as reason. This is patent when we look at photographs like Blossfeldt's that contain some ambivalence about their status as art, photographs that easily cut either way, asking us, on the one hand, to read them as if we were plant scientists of one variety or another, or, on the other hand, to indulge in them for the purpose of visual pleasure, to relish the perfection of their formal resolution as if they were themselves art or architecture. Blossfeldt's planned but never-completed archive was to be a kind of treasure-chest of jewels, a selection of the best and the brightest. In the sense that I have been using it here, thus, 'archive' is really not the right word — the word 'collection' might be better, or maybe even 'museum'.

The second and more fitting general way in which we might consider the archive as a basis for artistic form and the art lover's desire, a way more proper to the notion of the archive as it is used here, is to consider the objects contained as not being special, not being the best and brightest of their type. What is loved in this use of the archive as artistic ideal is not the exceptional status of the archival objects but instead their generic quality, their equivalence from one to the next and the next and the next. The question that this poses to us is *why*, or, rather, *what*? What is the appeal of serial form when the units are not laid out in a progressive narrative order or in a system of comparison for distinguishing good from bad, ideal from less ideal, but instead are allowed their full equivalence as undifferentiated units within a larger structure? There is a kind of default answer to this question assumed in the literature, one that is certainly correct — that is, that the aesthetic charge of serial form draws on the power of mechanical reproduction, or, even more so, draws on the commodity form to work against an

9 Noam Chomsky, 'Human Nature: Justice vs. Power: A Debate Between Noam Chomsky and Michel Foucault' (1971) in Noam Chomsky and Michel Foucault, *The Chomsky-Foucault Debate: On Human Nature* (New York: The New Press, 2006), pp. 1-67, here pp. 10-11.

10 Michel Foucault, *The Courage of Truth: The Government of Self and Others II: Lectures at the Collège de France 1983-1984* (New York: Palgrave Macmillan, 2011), p. 8.

[redacted]

older notion of art as the experience of ideal form. Seriality in this industrial and capitalist sense is anti-aestheticist, but that does not make it without aesthetic power or consequence of its own.

To appreciate that power and consequence, we can look back to the nineteenth-century's continuation (rather than its corruption or falsification) of the Enlightenment and consider the 'secret', as Marx called it, of the 'universal equivalent form' or the 'value-form of the commodity'. Marx's invocation of secrecy, like the invisibility of Adam Smith's invisible hand, was a way to say that labour had been rendered disembodied and systemic by the market's calculus of exchange and thereby detached or alienated from the labourer. Marx's account is the root form of our own tough thinking, just as it is for Foucault and Bourdieu, but it is also different in that he owns up to — and incorporates into his theory — a tender spot, or, to sharpen my metaphor with something even more fleshy, a soft underbelly. Marx insisted that the reducibility of labour to the universality of the commodity — its becoming discursive, dryly compartmentalized, nothing more than power/knowledge — is inseparable from the cultural development of the abstract universal concept of 'human equality', a concept that, for our purposes, was formalized in theory by the Enlightenment and, in a limited political sense, in practice by the French revolution. What we experience in the seriality of the commodity, in other words, is not just alienation but also enlightenment in the abstract form of equivalence, the abstract form of universality, carrying its own substantial aesthetic charge.

This is an ideal very different from the exquisite perfection of Blossfeldt's plant photographs. Both approaches abstract from particulars, but instead of that abstraction essentializing through synthesis or distillation in Blossfeldt's quasi-scientific manner, the commodity abstracts into generic equivalence. The soft underbelly of the commodity form, the Enlightenment promise that human equality is realizable through the production of knowledge and understanding, through the power of reason, that is, through the work of art historians and others like us, is, in this way, the appeal of the archive. This is its beauty — it must be called — the beauty that inheres in its form. We might refer to it as the 'archival ideal' and situate it opposite to, dialectically or otherwise, Foucault's account of archival control. The tender spot for art history, thus, resides in that moment of meaningfulness embodied in the archive that has not yet attained determination, the moment in which meaningfulness might still be found in any one or another of an archive's boxes or bins or folders or in any one or another of a museum's many objects. It is that moment in which truth is still detached from power, waiting to take on new social authority, the moment of epistemological innocence, the moment when the dream of progress in all its original Enlightenment glory becomes available through the thoughtful inquiry of scholars like Foucault or Chomsky or us.

Institutionality as Enlightenment

Generally speaking, modern art and art historical inquiry alike have always been about this tender spot. But when it is only that — just the soft underbelly of the commodity form, the point at which the commodity glimpses its unalienated humanity, the moment that it feels the presence of another possible world — then it is only unrealized potential. In this sense, modern art has almost always been largely horizontal even if it has been organized around a distant and forever unrealized dream of verticality, always an anarchism that dreams of socialism, always an art that yearns to become life, always a form of ad hoc sociality pinned to a misty fantasy of institutional form that would rescue it from the glittering but dreary asociality of the market.

When we allow ourselves to experience the fraught distance between desire and its object that this horizontality conjures, as one deep-feeling, critically-minded art lover reports, the emotional consequence can be intense:

> The disenchantment of the world is horrible, intolerable. Any mass movement or cult figure that promises a way out of it will be clung to like grim death. Better even fascism than technocracy: there is a social id in most of us that goes on being tempted by that proposition.[11]

11 **T.J. Clark,** *Farewell to an Idea: Episodes from a History of Modernism* **(New Haven and London: Yale University Press, 2001), p. 7. He goes on to describe the terror: 'the true terror of this new order has to do with its being ruled - and obscurely felt to be ruled - by sheer concatenation of profit and loss, bids and bargains: that is, by a system without any focusing purpose to it, or any compelling image or ritualization of that purpose' (p. 8).**

[redacted]

This is just to say what we've always known: capitalism produces alienation — it represses the social id that resides in most (but perhaps not all) of us — when it does not find overt expression in a corresponding political ideal such as democracy or fascism and instead exercises its authority on the technocratic level of social management that Foucault and Bourdieu detailed.

The history of modern art is largely a history of manifesting that alienation as a symptom, just as the history of modern art history has often been a matter of finding purpose in that symptom as art. The fundamental critical question is really to what degree this repressed social id might realize itself, not in the rootedness of identity as clan, nation, mob, or *Übermensch*, but instead with the extensity of transparent and universal algorithms in an anti-technocratic system. At the moments when this desire is allowed to arise as a design problem, it moves from the dingy archives back into the open air of public life. Modernist artistic programmes that brought the social id to the surface as a design problem rather than a symptom — think of the Bauhaus, for example, or Constructivism and De Stijl — and social programmes that realize such designs — like universal suffrage, healthcare, pension, and education — have their limits, for sure, but they do bring to the fore the great promise of abstraction. The only alternative to approaching the world in such a formal, forward-looking, institutionally-minded way is to leave the sociality of desire to spontaneous or ad hoc origination, the kind of social being that first emerges as micropolitical sovereignty but eventually cements itself in the habituated prejudices of identity and place. Without the institutionalized abstraction of universality, social design sinks below the horizon of visibility into a fetid private dominion of elders, experts, and the economy's invisible hand casting the rest of us into a circumscribed and epiphenomenal public sphere of culture.

Putting the same concern differently, we might ask to what degree is our social id allowed to realize its aims as Chomsky's art lover? That is, to what degree are we permitted to address the world at large in ways that our desire recognizes itself in a higher purpose — justice, say, or freedom, or belonging, or beauty, or truth — and to what degree are we forced to turn that desire back in on itself where it finds expression only as simple desublimation, simple refusal, simple retreat from a world defined by power/knowledge, into the restricted immediacy of individual embodiment, cultures of taste, and temporary local evasions of the power/knowledge nexus?

The threat of system — of discourse, governmentality, and episteme, say, or of field, habitus, and doxa, or of all that falls under the broad sweep of technocracy — has always stood over and against individual, embodied autonomy, and local cultural formations. Modern art has routinely responded in kind not only with critique but also with one version or another of bodily superabundance aimed at exceeding its threat or giving expression to that threat as symptom. Those that have described, analyzed, and expressed that threat are legion — Foucault and Bourdieu not the least among them — but here is another that brings our current epoch of computer conventions to the fore:

> The world is totally confused — everyone uses the word 'technology' for PACKAGES AND CONVENTIONS — like email, Windows, Facebook, the World Wide Web. These all use technologies but are themselves just collections of design decisions somebody made without asking you. I see humanity as unknowing prisoners in systems of invisible walls — specific conventions created by hidden tekkies, sometimes long ago and never questioned since, by anybody.[12]

This is an insider's rant — from Ted Nelson, the designer best known for coining the terms 'hypertext' and 'hypermedia' in 1963 — but its concern with hidden, systemic, technocratic control is consistent with modern criticality as a whole. A Nelson acolyte puts a finer point on this critique by taking it down to a rudimentary design principle: 'The file' — by which he means the convention of storing data in separate packages or, as Nelson put it, within a system of invisible walls — 'is a set of philosophical ideas made into eternal flesh', made into discourse or episteme, habitus or doxa.[13]

Given the rudimentary critical premise that such structures control our patterns of thought, experience, and desire and thus limit our sovereignty, the question is how to respond: Should we attempt to tear down the system's invisible walls or try to make them visible and plastic? Put differently, the question is really a philosophical one about the nature of freedom: Is freedom itself

12 Ted Nelson, *Possiplex* (San Francisco: Mindful Press, 2011), excerpted here: http://hyperland.com/possiplex/Excerpts.htm.
13 Jaron Lanier, *You Are Not a Gadget: A Manifesto* (New York: Knopf, 2010), p. 12.

[redacted]

social or individual, vertical or horizontal, ideal or material, free as in speech or free as in beer?[14]

The consequences of freedom are inevitably and necessarily material, of course, but freedom itself is a capacity to act, not a thing to possess, and that capacity is always both a function of and definition of its limits. Fons Elders, the Dutch philosopher moderating the televised 1971 Foucault/Chomsky discussion, summed up this distinction neatly for our purposes: 'I have the impression that for Mr. Chomsky, rules and freedom are not opposed to each other, but more or less imply each other', on the one hand, he said; but, on the other, 'I get the impression that it is just the reverse for you, Mr. Foucault.'[15] Indeed, Chomsky's art lover might be said to be a lover of rules — not of rules per se but instead of getting the rules right — the rules of composition, say, or colour, or harmony, on the one hand, and the rules of justice, freedom, and truth, on the other. Any specific instance of such rules — those of the Bauhaus, Constructivism, or De Stijl as artistic programmes, for example, or of universal suffrage, healthcare, pension, and education as social programmes — is by definition flawed, inadequate, overdetermined by its historical context, but it can still be a bearer of truth and speak meaningfully to our desire when, as Chomsky put it, 'the structure of our mind and the structure of some aspect of [its] reality coincide sufficiently' and that coincidence takes on intelligible form.[16] In Foucault's analysis, by contrast, beauty exists only in the moment of exceeding those structures, the moment when the invisible walls are bypassed, the moment when the Bauhaus or universal suffrage are perceived as untruths, as forms of power/knowledge.

This debate about the role of openly articulated rules — that is, the role of institutions — for the realization of freedom has a long history, of course, but in the present context of rapidly expanding public disenfranchisement though cutbacks in social spending and the massive upwards redistribution of wealth on the one hand, and the stirrings of popular revolt against that redistribution on the other, it is particularly relevant. It is sometimes cast as a battle between 'verticals' and 'horizontals', as anthropologist and activist David Graeber put it recently. On the one hand, there are 'the sort of people whose idea of political action is to march around with signs under the control of one or another top-down protest movement' and, on the other, there are those who refuse 'to work with or through the government or other institutions which ultimately rely on the threat of force, and a dedication to horizontal democracy, to treating each other as we believe free men and women in a genuinely free society would treat each other'.[17] A more liberal version has the horizontalist critique this way: 'We need to starve the beast' — western democratic governments — 'of our personal investment and energy'. Instead of democracy ('government for the horseback age'), we need 'adhocracy', an extra-institutional social process 'as common as negotiating where to go for dinner or seat swaps on an airplane'.[18]

By definition, institutions, like any form of power, are backed by the threat of force. This is as true of the claim for the cultural value of the Bauhaus as it is for the ethical claim made by universal suffrage, even if in both of these cases the level of force is relatively weak. Feeding such beasts by participating in their value systems is a form of complicity with that force. One critical response, thus, is simple withdrawal from any universalizing institutionality into localizing adhocratic sociality.

As insightful as they can be about the institutional operation of power, critics like Foucault and Bourdieu, Nelson and Graeber often gloss over two questions: first, the rudimentary ethical distinction between good power and bad, just power and unjust, public power and private, and, second, the qualitative distinction between discursive power and market power or the cultivated political, social and cultural power of institutions, on the one hand, and the raw, asocial, extracultural, economic power of the invisible hand, on the other. This is not always the case, of course — think, for example, of Bourdieu's call to 'never forget that institutions of cultural freedom are social conquests, no less so than Social Security or the minimum wage', or his simple but incisive characterization of neoliberalism as a 'programme for destroying collective structures which may impede the pure mar-

14 See Richard Stallman's distinction between libre and gratis, e.g.: "free software' is a matter of liberty, not price. To understand the concept, you should think of 'free' as in 'free speech', not as in 'free beer'.' https://www.gnu.org/philosophy/free-sw.html

15 Chomsky, op. cit., p. 25.

16 Ibid., pp. 27-28.

17 David Graeber, 'On Playing By The Rules: The Strange Success of #OccupyWallStreet', www.nakedcapitalism.com/2011/10/david-graeber-on-playing-by-the-rules-%e2%80%93-the-strange-success-of-occupy-wall-street.html#B0vfAllpvwq2hKpm.99. www.nakedcapitalism.com/2011/10/david-graeber-on-playing-by-the-rules-%e2%80%93-the-strange-success-of-occupy-wall-street.html.

18 Peter Fein, 'Democracy is Obsolete', Techpresident (June 12, 2012), http://techpresident.com/news/22332/op-ed-peter-fein-pdf12-democracy-obsolete.

[redacted]

ket logic' — but it is the case often enough in their writing and is certainly so in the broad sweep of their influence.[19] Because these writers and those that have followed them have focused so extensively on institutional critique, there has often been a passive, and sometimes active, critical sympathy for what Foucault late in his career called 'the market's role' as a 'test' that 'pinpoint[s] the effects of excessive governmentality', or more broadly, as a test that makes visible the effects of excessive institutionality.[20]

The market does indeed do its critical work pinpointing and excising excesses and more in institutions of all sorts — familial, cultural, religious, governmental, and, with particular vengeance of late, educational: all that is solid melts into air, all that is holy is profaned, as the Communist Manifesto had it famously. We need only think of its consequences for the many examples of corrupt state socialism, or the overbearing authority of corrupt forms of political theology, or even its consequences for our modest cultural domain of art and its sometimes imperious sense of its own good taste, to acknowledge that capitalism has the power to liberate individuals from the tyranny of institutions. Neoliberals are right that the market serves as an effective check and balance for institutions — that much is clear — but what serves to check and balance the excesses of the market?

Critical theory, like anything else, has a history; and its tasks arise and fade from view in the march of time even if they inevitably live on as foundations or sites of repression for future projects. To illustrate this, we need think only of Marx's inaugural two-part claim that, first, 'the criticism of religion has been essentially completed', and, second, 'the criticism of religion is the prerequisite [or foundation] of all criticism'.[21] The discursive criticism of institutions developed by Foucault, Bourdieu, and others played a crucial role during the Cold War, just as the historical criticism of religion did in the work of Friedrich Schleiermacher and his followers in the wake of the French Revolution, but it too has been essentially completed. Of course, this does not mean in either instance that there is not more critique to be accomplished, more abuses of institutional authority to be uncovered, more discursive confabulations to be decoded, but instead only that the method or framework for criticizing institutions is firmly in place.

So too, just as Marx recognized the origin and engine of the criticism of religion in the triumph of the bourgeoisie, we must also see the foundation of our criticism of institutions arising from our period's victorious consumer society. As one historian of that origin has put it: 'Everyone discovered that culture had been mass produced like Ford's cars: the masses had a culture and culture had a mass. Culture was everywhere, no longer the property of the cultured or cultivated.'[22] Everyone discovered that culture was a discourse, a habitus, a function of power, and each of us came to want his or her own piece of the cultural pie. We no longer had patience for dreaming of universal ideals, or imagining and designing their implementation, and instead left that to the closed-door labours of technicians and the invisible hand of an increasingly unregulated economy.

The critical insight into institutions signalled by theoretical terms such as 'discourse' and 'habitus' inaugurated half a century ago in the midst of the Cold War was unquestionably liberating, and in many ways, just as the ongoing exercise of this critical project, like the ongoing critique of religion inaugurated two centuries ago in the wake of the French Revolution, will certainly continue to be. It is a project, however, that has been essentially completed, as Marx put it, and one that cannot be fully extricated from the very powerful, very effective critique of institutions given to us by neoliberalism.[23] As one critical observer has put it, critical theory's emphasis on the critique of institutions rather than on seeing them as agents of freedom (as, for example, was the case with the old figure of the citizen) has inadvertently 'delivered strong systems and weak subjects' and, as a result, has unintentionally 'recapitulated the model of strong markets advanced by the culture wars'.[24] Put differently, it leaves the domain of freedom largely in the dusty cloister of the archive. Our question, thus, must become one about looking at institutions anew — not to roll back the critique that has been essentially completed but instead to move beyond it to

19 Pierre Bourdieu and Loïc J.D. Wacquant, *An Invitation to Relexive Sociology* (Chicago, IL: University of Chicago Press, 1992), p. 198; Pierre Bourdieu, 'The Essence of Neoliberalism', *Le Monde diplomatique*, December 1998, available in English at http://mondediplo.com/1998/12/08bourdieu.

20 Michel Foucault, *The Birth of Biopolitics: Lectures at the Collège de France, 1978-1979* (New York: Palgrave Macmillan, 2008), p. 320.

21 Karl Marx, 'Toward a Critique of Hegel's "Philosophy of Right"', *Selected Writings*, ed. Lawrence H. Simon (Indianapolis, IN: Hackett, 1994), p. 28.

22 Michael Denning, *Culture in the Age of Three Worlds* (London and New York: Verso, 2004), p. 1.

23 As argued, for example, in Luc Boltanski and Eve Chiapello, *The New Spirit of Capitalism* (London: Verso, 2006).

24 Christopher New×eld, *Unmaking the Public University: The Forty-Year Assault on the Middle Class* (Cambridge, MA: Harvard University Press, 2008), p. 157.

[redacted]

the critical tasks of our own day.

One option that is available to us is to reappraise institutions in the manner of Chomsky's art lover. Can archives, systems, and rules be beautiful? Is it possible 'to perceive how great' our institutions once were 'within the limitations of their time, groping toward concepts and ideas and insights that they themselves could not be clearly aware of?' Can dry compartmentalism be reclaimed as a design project for living, vivid human freedom? What about the force backing such institutions — the rule of law, say, or even the rule of taste? Such an enterprise was once central to modern art, as much as it was to its critical appreciation. By and large that project has been absent from our cherished institution for decades now, but like anything else, we do not work in a vacuum and there are glimmers of its rebirth all around us — in various artistic enterprises, political organizing efforts, and in many battles being waged on the technological front (the software-based delegated voting system Liquid Feedback developed and advocated for the Pirate Party is a case in point).

Such a concern with the promise of institutions has been put in negative ethical terms by Slavoj Žižek: 'Do we have the right to remain at a distance from state power', he writes, 'when state power is itself disintegrating, turning into an obscene exercise of violence so as to mask its own impotence?'[25] There is no question that our half-century of institutional critique has been on target: institutions are invariably abusive; they represent congealed power that cannot but be taken advantage of by the innate human tendency toward prejudice and corruption. There is also no question that institutional critique has been effective, largely by cultural means, turning us all into Foucauldeans and defining the authority of our institution in self-reflexive, self-contradictory anti-institutional terms just as the institutional authority of the State has come to define itself evermore through a form of anti-governmentality.

The time is ripe to resuscitate and rethink the historical promise of institutional power as an agent of enlightenment. When power is registered vertically through hierarchical structures and rules backed by force in institutions such as governments, museums, or universities it will inevitably be abused, for sure, but it is also relatively available to be held accountable to the public interest. When it resides in the horizontal domain of the economy, or technology, or our postmodern notions of disaggregated culture and micropolitics, it remains largely invisible and below the horizon of political challenges. The tender spot that marks the institutional desire of our social id cannot subsist as mere potential or in the cloistered immediacy of dinner negotiations or seat swaps on planes. As we 'jump scales', so David Harvey has put it, 'the whole nature of the commons problem and the prospects of finding a solution change dramatically'. Indeed, he complains, a 'fetishism of organizational preference (pure horizontality, for example) all too often stands in the way of exploring appropriate and effective solutions'.[26]

Institutionality is first and foremost a question of scale. As its scale approaches sovereignty — i.e. sufficiently large to defend itself from threats and exploit the energies of its constituents — it nears the capacity for ugliness and barbarism; as its scale approaches universality — large enough to be representative and accountable to all — it nears the capacity for beauty and enlightenment. No institution is perfect, of course, but insofar as it reaches beyond the simple horizontality of the commodity form that originally gave rise to it and toward the vertical ideal of enlightenment universality, it nourishes the great democratic promise of enfranchisement. This has been the standard that has driven modern art from the beginning, through its many isms, and up into contemporary art. That not all artists and critics working with institutional form fully appreciate its history and drive is understandable — like any other ideal it is conflicted and routinely compromised — but that impurity makes it no less the motor of freedom.

'If men wish to be free', Hannah Arendt insisted, 'it is precisely sovereignty they must renounce.'[27] If we wish to be free then there is nothing better we can do than insist upon systems, rules, enclosures, and institutions that redirect the unbridled sovereignty of politicians, bankers, and ourselves. Freedom from domination — particularly, at this moment in much of the world, freedom from the ruthless domination of the market — depends on such institutionality. Early twentieth-century artistic programmes like the Bauhaus and social programmes like universal suffrage were,

25 Slavoj Žižek, 'Foreword: The Dark Matter of Violence, Or, Putting Terror in Perspective', in Sophie Wahnich, *In Defence of the Terror: Liberty or Death in The French Revolution* (London: Verso, 2012), xi-xxvii, here xxiii.
26 David Harvey, *Rebel Cities: From the Right to the City to the Urban Revolution* (London: Verso, 2012), p. 68.
27 Hannah Arendt, 'What is Freedom?' in *Between Past and Future: Eight Exercises in Political Thought* (New York: Meridian Books, 1963), p. 163.

[redacted]

for sure, limited institutions thick with the exercise of power/knowledge, but from the vantage of a Chomskyean art lover looking back on them now they are nothing short of beautiful. Love of this sort is just the most conventional form of art appreciation — it is the love of objects that take on the shimmering penumbra of aesthetic value as they deteriorate into ruins. For some of us latter-day verticals, that makes their beauty all the more soul-stirring, all the more an experience of newly enflamed desire arising from the unrealized yearnings of the past.

[redacted]

Part III
Instituting in a Flat World

Flatness Rules
Instituent Practices and Institutions of the Common in a Flat World

Gerald Raunig

> All multiplicities are flat, in the sense that they fill or occupy all of their dimensions; we will therefore speak of a plane of consistency of multiplicities.
> (Gilles Deleuze, Félix Guattari, Mille Plateaux)

Flatness Instead of Depth

The earth is a flat disk, the world a plane of consistency of flat multiplicities, and these multiplicities haunt the surfaces. Everything happens on the surface, nothing below it. Everything is flat and that is good. When the lack of depth in contemporary thinking is brought up in the art industry or magazines, this usually involves an old topos. The recurrent complaint about how superficial the world is, which facilitates a tendency to mediocrity, is nothing other than the dull repetition of a cultural-pessimistic figure, which persistently affirms the old elite or desires new elites. Yet there is no depth of the soul, no depth of the State anymore, and the dichotomous certainties of bourgeois society are becoming diffuse. The autonomous individual wallows in self-enslavement and machinic subservience, the State becomes an economic tool in an invisible global hand. The distinction between private and public melts away in our hands, wherever and whenever we try to get hold of it. In the era of social media, privacy is a dangerous threat and comparable to self-chosen social death. And even though more and more new political theories assert attributions of the public as being plural, agonistic or conflictual, this interpellation just as frequently fades away unheard. Since the early 1990s, Post-Operaist philosophy has been pointing out that the sphere of the public is increasingly moving from the political into the realm of production, thereby becoming 'depoliticized' in a specific sense. It is production that now assumes the structure of the public sphere by increasingly taking over the modulation of social cooperation. Social cooperation, coordination and communication become central moments of valorization specifically in production processes. Whereas collaboration, negotiating common concerns, exposing oneself to the eyes of others, now tend to take place only in the area of work, the dimension of the public sphere is vanishing as a civil sphere of political agency.

In this situation of the implosion of the public sphere, the merging of private and public, the question that meaningfully moves us is not how to teach 'postmodernism' the depth that it lacks, how to return heights and sublimity to the old public sphere, or how to re-establish verticality in a purported world of homogenization and relativism. Instead, we are faced with the problem of how horizontality can assume an emancipatory form again, against the background of the ways in which Post-Fordist production functions. If we are really dealing with a 'communism of capital' today, as Paolo Virno, Christian Marazzi or Antonio Negri emphasize, how can this perverted form of 'communism' be turned into a new *commonism*? Especially in the terrain of Post-Fordist production, which centres around co-opting and valorizing cooperation and sociality, the currents of social cooperation on the surfaces have to be *differently* reterritorialized, not as the concept of the public sphere suggests; at the same time differently from the way that the compulsions of contemporary production specify: not as occupying a homogeneous space, not as regaining sovereignty in the form of an old community or a territorial state, but rather as the flat re-composition of the common. Flatness instead of depth. Becoming-common instead of public sphere.

One more effort, progressive professionals of the art institutions, if you would become common!

But what does 'common' mean here? As Antonio Negri and Michael Hardt write in their preface to *Common Wealth*, the common is, on the one hand, 'the common wealth of the material world — the air, the water, the fruits of the soil, and all nature's bounty — which in classical European political texts is often claimed to be the inheritance of humanity as a whole' (p. viii). On the other hand, and this is the aspect stressed by Hardt and Negri, the common encompasses 'those results of social production that are necessary for social interaction and further production, such as knowledge, languages, codes, information, affects, and so forth' (p. viii). In terms of the latter, the common hence means the practices of interaction, of care, of living together in a common world. These are practices that do not consider humanity as being separate from nature, neither in the logic of exploitation nor in that of protection.

Both aspects of the common, however, are not to be understood simply as something that naturally exists, which needs only to be cultivated and managed, but rather as a constantly present production of the common. In this context, a third aspect can

[redacted]

be inferred in addition to the conventional basic aspects of the common listed in the preface to *Common Wealth.* This third aspect centres around the question of the concatenation of singular currents, of the re-composition of multiplicity: the common as the self-organization of social cooperation. The self-organization meant here is not at all a simple empirical fact or even a seemingly natural automatism, but rather the political project of instituting the common. Instituting the common implies that the common cannot be understood as a being-common, but rather only as a becoming-common, as a constant production of the common.

In this essay, I intend to propose two complementary ways of instituting the common, primarily from the perspective of the cultural field. One starts more from the machinic instituting of micro-political artistic practices and social movement — their conceptual framework is given in my term *instituent practice.* Along with Antonio Negri, I call the other, which involves the transformation and re-invention of state apparatuses, the 'institution of the common'.

To begin with the latter: What would become of institutions in the art field, if they become institutions of the common? They are by no means art institutions of the common, to the extent that they are institutions that solely preserve and administer the archives and collections entrusted to them as *remainders* of a 'common heritage' for an educated class. Yet they would also not be institutions of the common if they only prepared and conveyed these treasures of a past 'common' to as many people as possible. The common is not a quantity of 'cultural assets' accumulated in the past, which is either reserved for the few or foisted onto the broad masses through education by experts from cultural history and museum pedagogy. Gone are the days not only of exclusive cultural connoisseurship, but also of the participation imperative in its populist form.

Public access to high culture for as many classes of the population as possible, access in the sense of the material accessibility of 'cultural treasures' and access in the sense of conveying know-how, in order to achieve immaterial access: all of that sounds good, but it has been tainted in art institutions in recent decades by neoliberalism. In the age of neoliberal transformation, the social-democratic museum as a public service has turned into a *modulating museum.* First of all, this clearly implicates a development that turns the demand for 'culture for all' into a simple logic of increasing the number of museum visitors. However, it is not simply a matter of quantities, but rather of the instrumentalizing mixture of striating measures and self-deformation, of modularization and modulating. Whereas the time and space are organized, striated and gridded in small structures for those working in the museum, and increasingly for the visitors as well, so that the modularization of all participants is taken to an extreme, the modulating state of cultural education never ends. In the new mode of modulation, people never stop starting, yet at the same time, they are never finished with forming the self.

The Post-Fordist imperative of creativity implies a double interpellation to modulation: an interpellation to measuring modularization, an appeal to layer, striate and count all circumstances, the whole of life, and at the same time it is an appeal to be prepared to constantly change, adapt, vary oneself. Modulation is determined by this double interpellation; it is based on the interplay of a clean temporal and spatial separation and striation of the modules with the inseparability of endless variations and boundless modulations. Whereas in one case modulation means restraint, using a standard measure, bringing every single module into form, in the other it requires the ability to glide from one register to another, to translate into as yet unknown languages, to interlock every possible level. If the definition of modulation consists on the one hand in forming modules, on the other it demands a constant self-(de-)formation, a tendency to permanently modify the form, transformation, even formlessness.

In modulation mode, 'culture for all' implies that art institutions have a culture-political obligation to push quantity and marketing in a populist-spectacular way, and 'culture from all', in its perverted neoliberal form, indicates an all-encompassing (self-) obligation to be creative. On the side of the institution as well as on the side of reception, modulation becomes the focal point: striating and measuring mass culture consumption on the one hand; the modulating interpellation of creativity and cooperation, participation and activation on the other. These once social-democratic concepts, which have dominated and impelled European cultural policies in the last four decades in more or less progressive formations, have successively been wholly divested of their originally emancipatory aims. Today they have become cornerstones of the neoliberal modulating museum.

Against the backdrop of the modulation of the museum, the call for the end of flatness in art, for the deepening of the

[redacted]

conservative-conserving museum, is to be seen as a defensive and backward-looking strategy: back to the bosom of the canon, of art historical tradition, of aesthetic rules. It seems as though the only alternative to modulation is to be found solely in a return to the obsolete mechanisms of national and colonial institutions. Yet we can still reject the choice between Scylla and Charybdis, between neoliberal or reactionary, between a modulating or exclusionary positioning of the art institution: there is a possibility for disobedience to the alternatives of adapting to the neoliberal mainstream or returning to an elitist figure of verticality. Here it is important that the art institution is regarded neither solely as an appendage to the State or the art market nor as a heterotopia that could function by itself as being completely other than the State and the market. Constructing a deviation from the false choice between a neoliberal or a reactionary form means, in the best case, seeing the art institution as indeed being part of a state apparatus in the late welfare state. However, the art institution is capable of transforming the State apparatus from the inside, specifically to the extent that the art institution becomes a potential component of an instituent machine and accomplice to instituent practices.

Especially in the multiple crises we have experienced in recent years, it cannot simply be a matter of an orderly retreat of progressive forces, of the businesslike management of dwindling cultural budgets, of docilely helping to carry out the austerity policies of European governments. The crisis is not a purely economical one. As far as art institutions are concerned, the crisis affects not only budgets: it produces a rupture in the familiar continuum of cuts and practical constraints, forcing the institutions to think about an altered function in relation to other social actors.

It is exactly at the crisis-related rupture of the art institution that an offensive becomes imaginable, which consciously impels the transformation from 'public institutions' to 'institutions of the common'. Especially where there are remainders of the welfare state, these are not to be just compliantly fed into the modulating machine of neoliberal capitalism. Instead, they are to be used for experiments of the transition into institutions of the common. The point is to reorganize remainders of the civil public sphere and of society conceived as social-democratic, in order to redirect the manifold currents of the modulating institutions and to transform the public into the common. In a certain way, this implies no less than newly inventing the State, specifically because and while it still rudimentarily functions. Or rather: it implies inventing a new form of state apparatus while the old one still exists. This re-invention of the State apparatus from below can only succeed as re-territorializing the institution, if it is tried out from many different sides, in small contexts, in a micro-measure, and in radical openness to questions of organization.

Perhaps it seems far-fetched to expect art institutions to re-invent the State. This expectation may not meet with success either, but in comparison with other state institutions, such as institutions of education, science or research, the art field certainly has advantages. An odd mixture of claims of autonomy, frequently an experimental orientation, the self-evident expectation of critical stances and attention to political topics enhances the potential for free spaces and turns art institutions into exceptional cases in comparison with other state institutions or those (partly) funded by the State. In the art field, it is also possible to build on the concrete experiences of progressive art institutions in Europe: while the otherwise neoliberal policies of New Institutionalism undermined institutions in the 1990s and 2000s, a minoritarian line of radical cultural policies was developed in the critical art field, which is already to be interpreted, in certain aspects, in the direction of institutions of the common.[1]

From this perspective, an institution of the common does not mean simply the administration and preservation of 'public' 'cultural treasures'. In the increasingly constrained situation of the cultural field, a limitation to the stance of cultural functionaries is not an option. The institution of the common goes beyond establishing and preserving general accessibility, but rather makes the possibility conditions for becoming-common available. 'Becoming-common' does not refer to a better future someday when pigs fly, but rather has aspects of actualizing the past, aspects of an expanded present becoming, aspects of the potentiality of an archaeology of the future. To concretize an art institution of the common, which opposes the modulating museum, there are largely three complexes of orientation.

1 Examples of this radical turn toward supporting discursive and activist practices, which are quite different in size and degree of institutionalization, were and are the Shedhalle in Zurich, the MACBA in Barcelona, the Van Abbemuseum in Eindhoven, the NIFCA, the Rooseum in Malmö, the Reina Sofia in Madrid, but also the curatorial practices of the Croatian collective WHW or the German artists Alice Creischer and Andreas Siekmann.

[redacted]

First of all, there is the orientation in terms of content: the art institution of the common need not reproduce the traditional canon, but it also need not exceed it with alternative canons. It need not play along in the competition of the latest hypes of artists, their objects and discourses. It is much more important to launch projects outside the realm of canonization and spectacle, which enable long-term effects and political-aesthetic experiments. Turning away from fetishizing the objects and from a short-term attention economy in this way also makes it easier to let go of disreputable 'acquisitions' — such as colonial spoils. The art institution of the common has a responsibility to investigate its colonial and neo-colonial entanglements, to deconstruct them and try out a practice of decolonization. Here 'common' means no practice of exhibiting (neo-)colonial objects under the banner of the 'universal' or 'world cultures', but rather an earnest exchange beyond times and geographies, a practice of translating that takes histories of domination and different geopolitical contexts into consideration.

At the level of modes of production, the art institution of the common must primarily question the rigid time management in the cultural field, break through it, enable time for taking a deep breath, and reterritorialize time. Elements of the rupture, the break, and the strike are necessary for addressing the precarization of working conditions in one's own context. Instead of precarization being seen only in the vertical logic of labour struggles on a small scale, it has to be made visible in its complexity and differentiated hierarchization. This would reveal what there is in common, or at least what the connection is, between the curator burned out by the extreme time regime of the exhibition business and the outsourced security person, between the museum director worn down by political turf wars and the cleaner with no residence permit, between the underpaid head of collections and the gallery educator constantly on stand-by. Starting from these transversal internal connections, it is also possible to discuss the economic intertwining of funding sources far beyond the simple dichotomization of state or private sponsors. Without hope of a position of purity and clean money, the flows of money must still be laid open, contextualized and discussed in terms of ethical aspects.

Finally, in a machinic understanding of the art institution of the common, all models of the participation and activation of the audience must be reconsidered ambivalent processes in the Post-Fordist participation imperative. Instead of the paternalist perspective that asks how (ever new) audiences can be included and activated in the museum, the material and immaterial resources of the art institution are to be made available for the production and treatment of political-aesthetic problem complexes, transcending the logic of integration and incorporation. At precisely this point, the art institution becomes an exemplary institution that tests the transition from public institutions to institutions of the common.

The Two Temporalities of Instituent Practice

The turn from a policy of audience integration and activation toward a micro-political machine emerging in the in-between spaces and intersections between the institution and instituent practice gains special significance in the connection of production in the art field with that in social movements. Here too, it is possible to take recourse to the experiences of the late 1990s and 2000s, to an expanded scene of transversal practices between political activism, art production and progressive art institutions.[2] These experiences, however, are nothing other than delicate beginnings, prototypes of a future practice, which must construct their abstract machine in light of the multiple crises and the new Occupy Movements.

2 Since I purposely dispense with examples in the main text, I would like to refer here in a longer footnote to various practices from the context discussed, to the extent that I have dealt with them. There is certainly no claim here to typology, completeness or the development of a canon. On the early interventionist practice of the group WochenKlausur, cf. Gerald Raunig, *Charon: Eine Ästhetik der Grenzüberschreitung* (Vienna: Passagen, 1999), and Gerald Raunig, 'De- and Reterritorializing the Class-Room and the Arts: WochenKlausur at School', in *Magic Moments: Collaboration between Artists and Young People*, ed. Anna Harding (London: Black Dog, 2005), pp. 112-15; on the exemplary instituent practice of the Hamburg desire machine Park Fiction, cf. 'Instituent Practices, No. 2: Institutional Critique, Constituent Power, and the Persistence of Instituting', in: *Art and Contemporary Critical Practice: Reinventing Institutional Critique*, ed. Gerald Raunig and Gene Ray (London: MayFfly Books, 2009), pp. 173-86; on the fight-specific practice of the Isola Art Center in Milan, cf. the relevant chapter in Gerald Raunig, *Industrien der Kreativität: Streifen und Glätten 2* (Zurich and Berlin: diaphanes 2012); on the mixed artistic-activist-theoretical practice of the Russian work group Chto Delat, cf. Dmitry Vilensky and Gerald Raunig, 'An Issue of Organisation: Chto Delat?: Dmitry Vilensky in conversation with Gerald Raunig', *Afterall* 19 (Autumn/Winter 2008), pp. 5-19; on the cooperation of the Universidad Nomada with the MACBA in Barcelona and with various social movements, cf. www.universidadnomada.net/; on the activist art practice of the PublixTheatreCaravan, cf. Gerald Raunig, *Art and Revolution: Transversal Activism in the Long Twentieth Century*, trans. Aileen Derieg (New York and Los Angeles: Semiotext(e), 2007); on the Continental Drifts of the 16 Beaver Group and Brian Holmes in New York, the Midwest of the USA and elsewhere, cf. http://brianholmes.wordpress.com/; on the 'errorist' movement of the Argentinian grupo etcetera, cf. http://grupoetcetera.wordpress.com/.

[redacted]

What is then the function of artistic production in these new transversal overlaps? Institutional critique in the narrower sense, in other words the critique of production conditions in the cultural field and critique of concrete institutions, will be conducted in the best case by the institution of the common itself. This does not mean that artists will be excluded from it, but their central critical activity does not remain limited to the critique of their art-institutional surroundings. This implies that an especially unproductive variation of artistic institutional critique is eliminated: narcissistically circling around oneself, institutional critique as self-critique, which illuminates being trapped in the art field in a thousand facets and denies every transgression, every shift of the boundaries of the field.

Nevertheless, there are two aspects of artistic institutional critique that still remain relevant: one aspect is thematizing and problematizing social and political conditions, and especially proposals for a good life, suggestions for possible new worlds, machinic-dividual production of desire, and the involvement in its actualization. This is where critical artistic practice also moves from the critique of the institution in the direction of instituting; it becomes an *instituent practice*.

When I talk about an 'instituent practice', this actualization of the future in a current becoming is not the opposite of institution in the way that a utopia, for instance, is the opposite of bad reality. Nor is it necessarily to be understood in its relation to institutedness. Instituent practice as a process and concatenation of instituent events is instead an absolute concept beyond the opposite of institution: it does not *oppose* the institution, but it does flee institutionalization.

This understanding of instituent practice further develops the ideas with which Antonio Negri established his concept of constituent power. In his book *Insurgencies*, Negri primarily pursues the question of how a constituent power could be imagined, which does not produce constitutions separated from itself, but rather *constitutes itself*: 'con-stituent' power as a 'com-position' that constitutes itself in a machinic process. Starting from this terminological genealogy, instituent power is also to be understood as self-instituting. In this, it goes through two temporalities that also make up its two components: on the one hand, the component of what is evental in the instituting; on the other, the component of sustainability, of insisting, of always newly starting again.

Multiplicity extends into all dimensions of instituting, as far as possible, into all the folds of the spatial surfaces and temporal continua: there is the multiplicity dispersed over a plane, which is condensed and composed in the moment of instituting (event, incision, break), and there is the continual multiplication of instituting along a timeline (stream, process, persistence).

As for the first component, the temporality of the event, the break, the incision, the first time: instituting as the installation of a new arrangement enables questioning the connection between constituent power and instituent practice, of composition and installation. This raises problems of the form of concatenation, problems of inclusion and problems of authority in a double sense: authority as decisive instance, which installs itself implicitly or explicitly as a hierarchical position, but also 'authority' as a singular 'origin' of instituting, as machinic-dividual authorship (*auctoritas*). If instituent practice can be understood as stream *and* as incision, then it is the event of instituting, in which the preliminary decision is made about how cooperation, collectivity and participation develop, how the 'con-' in constituent power (as a sign of the common) relates to the mode of instituting.

The discourse about 'the author' of instituting occurs here in two different and decisive modes: on the one hand as 'authoritarian' subject imposing its form on the object of instituting; on the other as instituent machine, the 'authorship' of which does not depend on an individual or collective. Transposed to artistic practice, this terminological bifurcation of au(c)thority recalls the distinction between the paternalist artist, on the one hand, who identifies a community and chooses it as her/his object, predicting and preceding it, and the arbitrary artistic singularity, on the other, who enters into the machinic stream that leads to instituting, where sometimes more, sometimes less artistic skill is needed. In this second mode there is no talk of avant-garde, of the artist predicting or even preceding, but rather of becoming-common as experimenting with forms of social organization, with the installation and composition of singularities. The mode of installing is therefore not only symbolically effective, but its tendency toward either an authoritarian positing or a com-position of the singular is also crucial for its later potential as insisting, instituent practice and for the ongoing impulses for machinic-dividual production of desire.

[redacted]

As for the second temporality of instituent practice, the process, the stream, the insistence: these mutually interlinked main components of instituent practice centre around the properties of long duration, persistence and repetition, which are only seemingly opposite to the event. The instituting, the first, repeats itself, but not as an origin — strictly speaking, there is no strong first time in the flux of instituting. Instituent practice does not stop with instituting a break, an incision, but is instead distinguished by ever-new instances of instituting, the first time of which is actualized in a non-linear way in potentially endless variations.

Multiplying and perpetuating the event of instituting allows a change in the quality of participation: specifically, the concatenation of the many, ongoing and differently composed instances of instituting forestalls an authoritarian mode of installation, turning against the closing (in) of the institution at the same time. Manifold ensembles of self-organization promote a broad and changing participation in the instituting when it is newly composed as constituent power again and again. It is only when there are as few essentialist references as possible, for instance to a myth of origins or a certain community, that these new constituencies can emerge. The multiplication of instances of instituting shifts the composition of the multiplicity distributed over a plane with every new event of instituting.

Overlaps, interactions, mutual reinforcements of instituent practices and institutions of the common sometimes occur. How, in which form, in which mode, to what extent, and even whether the instances of a machinic instituting of artistic micro-politics and social movements can and should concatenate with the transformations and reinventions of state apparatuses, remains a question of the situative appraisal. The 'political project' of instituting the common, however, can be impelled starting from both poles — in conflictual complementarity, in the creation of a plane of consistence of flat multiplicities, more with a view to immanent horizons than in anticipation of a vertical oriented to a focal point, a unity, an author.

This text revisits and further develops discussions of the eipcp project 'transform', which can be read especially in the following issues of the web journal *transversal*: http://eipcp.net/transversal/0106, http://eipcp.net/transversal/0407, http://eipcp.net/transversal/0507, http://eipcp.net/transversal/0707, and http://eipcp.net/transversal/1007.

Institutions with an Attitude, and Networks

Toward a Republic of Arts in a Spiked World and toward World Art History

Marc Jacobs

> One answer is the need for critical selfconsciousness. To be constantly open to alternatives, to hold dear the aim of acting thoughtfully. An academic, professional and enlightenment ideal perhaps. And it has to be said that, for some, theory has become an end in itself. Some do seem to let their enthusiasm for intellectual fashions show a little too much, with slogans and soundbites, postures and superficiality.... Hence for me it is an issue of attitude. Suspicion of easy answers, of neat schemes for partitioning the world which put things in their place, grand all-encompassing theories which purport to explain everything. A suspicion of comforting familiarity. The attitude is about debunking, retaining a sense of humility, constantly reflecting on what we do.... To think critically.[1]

Reframing: that is what this contribution is about. The main title and subtitle of Thomas Friedman's 2005 book *The World Is Flat: A Brief History of the Twenty-First Century* pose two challenges. The witty one-liner '*maps lie flat, therefore flat maps lie*' speaks volumes. Another metaphor would be welcome, one that better captures reality or recent evolutions. The world is bumpy and spiky. And why should we opt for a *brief* history, if a long history is possible? If planetary warming, global economics, empire, multitudes and worldwide networks are really considered appropriate and adequate frames of reference and of argumentation in discussions about contemporary arts and their institutions in Europe, why should the protagonists then be contented with a mere decade, if we can mobilize half a millennium (or more)?

In a path-breaking book, where historiography meets pragmatic theory with scholars like Luc Boltanski or Bruno Latour, the French historian Jacques Revel distinguishes three types of (historical) research about institutions. The first is focussing on the institution as a legal-political reality or entity (e.g. an administration or a museum). The second deals with organizations (the family, school, museum, hospital…) functioning in broader societies according to more or less explicit rules and responding to a collective demand. The third considers institutions as every form of social organization that links roles, values, norms, models of relations and behaviour, and shows a certain regularity.[2] It makes a huge difference to (also) consider institutions from the last point of view, to see them in their historical and above all social evolution and development. The divide between institutions and thick and hybrid networks can be evacuated as a false problem, as it might block ways of progressing and finding new solutions. I claim we need a detour, in history, to enrich the available toolbox and to move on.

If you read the publications by Negri, Hardt, Virno, and other gurus, references to the Early Modern period in European history abound. However, they usually do not refer to artists, collections, museums and so on, but to forces that are more handy on the battlefields and barricades, like rebellious peasants, warlords and armies. A clue for the hyperlink to the past, I propose, is readily available in the URL of one of the major discussion platforms where the ideas, challenges, dreams and constructions mentioned above were nurtured and tested in the previous decade. Please do savour the original address: www.republicart.net/ (followed by http://transform.eipcp.net/ and http://eipcp.net/). We propose to glance at the Early Modern formula of the Republic of Letters, appropriate and translate it, and strategically relaunch it, not as a stay-behind network but as an active and multistranded platform of connections. The old formula functioned over large parts of Early Modern Europe, thanks to the relay postal system and the bandwidth of messages and the contents of envelopes. Next to ideals, erudite strategies and win-win, cultural brokerage and keeping open the lines for communication and reflection were important. Today, the e-post and by extension several layers of the World Wide Web, offer new possibilities. In practice, this can connect with recent policy developments, by expanding the spatial and temporal scales. And yes, empires and similar topics will come into the picture, but with the awareness that each of these phenomena

1. Mike Pearson and Michael Shanks, *Theatre/Archaeology: Disciplinary Dialogues* (London: Routledge, 2001), p. 8.
2. 'toute forme de l'organisation sociale qui lie des valeurs, des normes, des modèles de relations et de conduites, des rôles; en ce sens, toute forme sociale qui présente une certaine régularité peut relever d'une analyse institutionelle': Jacques Revel, 'L'institution et le social', in *Les formes de l'expérience: Une autre histoire sociale*, ed. Bernard Lepetit (Paris: Albin Michel, 1995) pp. 63-84, p. 64.

[redacted]

have a history and keep on evolving. So there are hope and futures, even for artists, art institutions and what they (re)produce: 'art'.

From sieges to forts and from trenches to trenches?

The last few years, a set of contemporary arts institutions and affiliated thinkers and fans have been cultivating a progressive discourse about their functions in and relations with 'the world' and how to change it, represent it, chastise it, undermine it and/or save it. This is connected to the perception of a (largely, in the P. Bourdieu sense of the word, 'field specific') movement of 'institutional critique'. It came in three subsequent waves in this cultural subfield, involving generations of artists and curators, agitating 'against' and then eventually operating or being supported from within institutions, like forts in the Old Wild West. This is how Sheikh summarized it concisely:

> In the first wave of institutional critique from the late 1960s and early 1970s – long since celebrated and relegated by art history – ... the critical method was an artistic practice, and the institution in question was the art institution, mainly the art museum, but also galleries and collections. Institutional critique thus took on many forms, such as artistic works and interventions, critical writings or (art-)political activism. However, in the so-called second wave, from the 1980s, the institutional framework became somewhat expanded to include the artist's role (the subject performing the critique) as institutionalized, as well as an investigation into other institutional spaces (and practices) besides the art space.... In contrast, the current institutional-critical discussions seem predominantly propagated by curators and directors of the very same institutions, and they are usually opting for rather than against them. That is, they are not an effort to oppose or even destroy the institution, but rather to modify and solidify it.[3]

Critically operating from an outside position seems to have been subsumed (for the moment) by critical discourse from the inside of institutions. This could lead to bad forms of verticality, digging trenches for static warfare in a flat battlefield instead of trenches of archaeology, research and development.

Unexpected and unlikely new allies for museums and institutions for contemporary arts, organizations with often (openly or in practice demonstrated or misrecognized) exclusive or elitist aspirations and affiliations, are the philosophical engineers or gurus of the Operai movement (Paolo Virno, Michael Hardt, Toni Negri...). For outsiders, like me, this is a strange match within a zone of the Western cultural sector and related academic discourse, flirting with the alternative/antiglobalization movements or remnants of Marxist agitation. As Virno emphasizes himself, these thinkers are not really into arts or arts institutions, nor do they grant it a high priority (except perhaps for poetry). Listen to what Virno said:

> That always embarrasses me a little, as if there has been some mistake, because my knowledge of modern art is actually very limited. I think that people involved in art being interested in my work has something to do with a concept I use, namely 'virtuosity'.
>
> Even more telling is the honest confession and subsequent statements:
>
> The only art of which I have more than superficial knowledge is modern and contemporary poetry.... With regard to the crisis of measure, art is a lot like communism.[4]

3 Simon Sheikh, Notes on Institutional Critique, http://transform.eipcp.net/transversal/0106/sheikh/en (01/2006), accessed 1/10/2012 (just like all the other URLs mentioned in the following notes)

4 Sonja Lavaert and Pascal Gielen, 'The Dismeasure of Art: An Interview with Paolo Virno', in *Being an Artist in Post-Fordist Times*, ed. Pascal Gielen and Paul De Bruyne (Rotterdam: NAi Publishers, 2009), pp. 17-44, p. 17 and p. 18.

[redacted]

From categories to references, compromises and interaction?

A number of links seem to have been skipped or just hyperlinked in flat dreamspace, when aligning (art curator), artist, artisan and *Arbeiter*. How serious should one take suggestions like 'intellectual, artistic workers are the most important component of the new working class'.[5] It is interesting that indeed in a recent reflection about art, very compatible arguments were developed by entrepreneurs and capitalists reflecting on contemporary arts, together with contemporary artists.[6] Theories of Boltanski and Thévenot are useful to make the story and vantage points more complex and varied, and to focus on situations and pragmatism: there are many commonwealths, value systems and forms of 'grandeur' (in the third sense of the concept of institution, see the discussion of Jacques Revel). An author like Luc Boltanski has been mobilized via his work together with Chiapello. But here again the long-term perspective is more interesting and sustainable: like for instance, the toolbox constructed in the magnum opus that Boltanski delivered together with Laurent Thévenot. It was an attempt to develop and think through a critique of critique(s) and to escape discourses built on e.g. class and other categories, by focussing on situated interaction and on attempts to make sustainable constructions (e.g. institutions) and contexts for exchange. These references already belong to the citation network of this literature.[7] Also the more recent books by Luc Boltanski, (like *De la critique*) do merit being used … pragmatically.[8]

Republic of Multitude? And Art Institutions? How? Why?

'Comrades' like Virno ask penetrating questions, develop interesting metaphors but also cherish extreme points of view. Astonishing is the constant flirt, sometimes interesting, sometimes painful (if one thinks about the victims of the Egyptian plagues) with Old Testament scenarios and references, including the Exodus.[9] We could try to read very selectively, turning a blind eye to many blindspots and try to harvest eclectically, when exploring ideas like:

> Exodus is the foundation of a Republic. The very idea of 'republic', however, requires a taking leave

> of State judicature: if Republic, then no longer State. The political action of the Exodus consists, therefore, in an engaged withdrawal. Only those who open a way of exit for themselves can do the founding; but, by the opposite token, only those who do the founding will succeed in finding the parting of the waters by which they will be able to leave Egypt.[10]

This is a bridge too far for me. Why not stay, react and opt for a multilayered solution, avoiding disasters and killings of first-born children? I do not wish to follow all the suggestions and constructions and reject debate-killing power statements like we find on the same website:

> It goes without saying, however, that an opposition to this course of events, if conducted in the name of values of representation, is pathetic and pointless – as useful as preaching chastity to sparrows. Democracy today has to be framed in terms of the construction and experimentation of forms of nonrepresentative and extraparliamentary democracy. All the rest is vacant chitchat.

In a recent book published by Gielen and De Bruyne, Virno sings a different, more pragmatic tune and even accepts to land in subsidiarity models. Savour his answer to the question 'Is the European practice of governing on different levels,

5 Ibid., 38: 'Some entrepreneurs have this cunning mentality and say "Me, too".'

6 See Marc Ruyters' [and Marc Jacobs], 'Kunst en economie zijn slechts onderdelen van een groter geheel dat de simpele tweedeling overstijgt', in *Kunstenaars & ondernemers: Een nieuwe relatie* (Tielt: Lannoo, 2007), pp. 105-16, where Luc Boltanski and Laurent Thévenot, *De la justification: Les économies de la justification* (Paris: Gallimard, 1991), was mobilized.

7 Rudi Laermans, 'Artistic Autonomy as Value and Practice', in *Being an Artist in Post-Fordist Times*, ed. Pascal Gielen and Paul De Bruyne (Rotterdam: NAi Publishers, 2009), pp. 125-37.

8 Luc Boltanski, *De la critique: Précis de sociologie de l'émancipation* (Paris: Gallimard, 2009).

9 Paolo Virno, 'Virtuosity and Revolution: The Political Theory of Exodus', in *Radical Thought in Italy: A Potential Politics*, ed. Michael Hardt and Paulo Virno, trans. Ed Emory (Minneapolis, MN: University of Minnesota, 1996), p. 13-37; www.generation-online.org/c/fcmultitude2.html.

10 See for a critique of the exit strategy, http://transform.eipcp.net/transversal/0808/mouffe/en#redir.

as couched in the subsidiary principle an example of non-representative democracy, too?':

> Absolutely, that is the track I'm on – in a galaxy of foundations, a network of institutes, a dissemination of decision-making locations. Let me repeat, the point at issue is to appropriate intelligence and to create autonomous positions for that intelligence and communication.[11]

The use of the tainted word 'soviets' might trigger alarm bells, especially for people with some awareness of and critical perspectives on twentieth-century history, but we can try to ignore these thorns and attempt to transform an exclusive attitude and an 'or-or' dichotomy in an inclusive 'and-and' approach:

The Soviets of the Multitude interfere conflictually with the State's administrative apparatuses, with a view to eating away at its prerogatives and absorbing its functions. They translate into republican praxis, in other words, into a care for common affairs, those same basic resources — knowledge, communication, a relationship with the 'presence of others' — that are the order of the day in Post-Fordist production. They emancipate virtuosic cooperation from its present connection with waged labor, showing with positive actions how the one goes beyond the other.

Not replacing but adding: then it becomes interesting to start considering some suggestions and start taking these constructions of/for the contemporary art world as serious and plausible. In an 'and-and' perspective (and in defence of representative democracy), I can consider the proposal to '*experiment with and construct new non-representative and extraparliamentary forms of democracy*': to found a(n additional) Republic, a 'non-state public sphere'. It is then possible to selectively and pragmatically quote and appropriate fragments of the guru's texts to make them operational for twenty-first-century arts institutions:

> Because the Exodus is a committed withdrawal, the recourse to force is no longer gauged in terms of the conquest of State power in the land of the

> pharaohs, but in relation to the safeguarding of the forms of life and communitarian relations experienced en route. What deserve to be defended at all costs are the works of 'friendship'.[12]

In order to fully explore the problem and potential, we should create some mental space, not limiting it to a decade but taking into consideration at least half a millennium.

The Republic of Letters

The Early Modern era (1492/1500-1789/1800) was a transition period characterized by emerging state-formation processes in Europe, the breakthrough of (commercial) capitalism and the global proliferation of instruments 'for exerting power at a distance' like the printing press (J. Law, B. Latour...). In that period, a network of scholars, writers, 'museums', libraries and other collections functioned across political and religious borders: the so-called Republic of Letters. The emergence and functioning of this system were closely connected to communication revolutions like the printing press or the fast postal system via relay: the early modern forerunner of the e-mail. The first known occurrence of the concept *Respublica litteraria*, dates July 6th, 1417, in a letter by Francesco Barbaro to Paggio Bracciolini, thanking him for the efforts '*pro commune utilitate*'.[13] The correspondence of erudites, intellectuals and authors during the next three centuries had a large bandwidth and largely functioned as a gift economy. It often involved forms of friendship and mutual assistance in solving problems. It was in that constant flow of information on all kind of topics that critical reflections could be voiced: an epistolary space for critique that crossed frontiers, even in enemy states.

Also in real life, those who invested in the system could count on help and hospitality. Anthony Grafton published an interesting state-of-the-art article about the Republic of the Arts and their citizens, claiming that they:

11 Lavaert and Gielen, op. cit., p. 39.
12 Virno, op. cit.
13 Hans Bots and Françoise Waquet, La République des Lettres (Paris; Berlin; Brussels: De Boeck, 1997) with an excellent bibliography.

[redacted]

> ...for all their idiosyncrasies, offer what seem still to be powerful models for the conduct of intellectuals. They devised ways to conduct research with rigor, even when its results were uncomfortable; to publicize their results, without fear or favor; and, again and again, to rise above their prejudices without losing their convictions... when they maintained friendships that spanned ideological and political borders. And they also both collaborated, to spectacular effect, with artists.... They still, I now believe, have much to teach us about the forgotten premodern intellectual worlds that they inhabited and explored, and also, perhaps, about how modern intellectuals could and should serve the public good in our own poisoned public sphere.[14]

Is a specific urban network cluster needed as a fruitful soil for these kinds of interactions in a Republic of Letters? Anthony Grafton emphasized the importance of tolerant cities:

> The stars that glittered most brightly across distance were usually cities. The Republicans often had to spend time and provide services at courts. But they liked cities that enjoyed a certain measure of autonomy, and whose governors did not share the general belief that torture and execution were the appropriate tools for reducing religious and intellectual dissidents to order and submission. The citizens of the Republic also needed to perch near certain urban institutions: libraries, for example, and the printing presses that gave men and women of letters their only power, that of publicity.... Yet this local world... was closely connected, by contacts made in travel and correspondence networks that passed through the Low Countries to the rest of Europe, with a vast range of impressive foreign contacts,

> who appreciated its lively, fertile culture.... If this state had no maps, no administrative officials, and no borders, how do we know it existed at all?... The Republicans of Letters created many local communities of savants, dedicated to the search for religious or secular truths, or both at once.... They made clear that intellectual life needed a social foundation - and needed it all the more as Europe's age of religious war progressed. And they helped to create the epistolary networks that gave the Republic its true circulatory system.[15]

The Republic of Letters was connected to the emergence of the 'public sphere' in the eighteenth century (and in particular the preludes of that sphere in the seventeenth and even sixteenth century), to the process of increasing autonomy of artistic and disciplinary fields (in particular in the eighteenth and nineteenth centuries), and the struggle for relative autonomy in scholarly and artistic endeavours, that reached its peak (and institutional crystallization) in the nineteenth century.[16] It seems interesting to appropriate some of these evolutions, mutatis mutandis, in a long-term history and perspective on contemporary and future developments, of connecting art institutions in a spiky and divided world.

Republic of Arts, with Museums

Some of the ideas, codes and network dynamics that characterized that Republic of Letters are still, or more than ever, relevant today for what may be called a Republic of Arts, with or without institutions. In the nineteenth century, the national state apparatus, commercial and industrial capitalism but also

14 **Anthony Grafton,** Worlds Made by Words: Scholarship and Community in the Modern West **(Cambridge, MA: Harvard University Press, 2009), p. 16.**

15 **Anthony Grafton, 'A Sketch Map of a Lost Continent: The Republic of Letters',** Republics of Letters: A Journal for the Study of Knowledge, Politics, and the Arts **1, no. 1 (May 1, 2009); http://rol.stanford.edu/node/34.**

16 **See the fascinating story of the Musée de Monsieur in the 1780s, in Dena Goodman,** The Republic of Letters: A Cultural History of the French Enlightenment **(Ithaca, NY: Cornell University Press, 1994), pp. 259-76 and passim; Susan Dalton,** Engendering the Republic of Letters: Reconnecting Public and Private Spheres **(Montreal: McGill-Queen's University Press, 2003).**

[redacted]

new representation techniques, both in the sense of gradations of democratic voting and representation, and of power houses (conceptualized as classic temples, just as other houses of government) like museums and archives, reached another level of sophistication, effect and impact. A museum became an official instrument for exerting power at a distance (both in time and space).[17] In the twentieth and twenty-first centuries, these processes evolved deeper and generated institutional and artistic reactions (like avant-garde and eventually New Institutionalism). The recent communication revolutions (like that of the Internet) and the changing power relations (empowerment of users and other social groups, customers/visitors/taxpayers that take the role of kings/Maecenas, stronger networks of expertise...) have a distinct impact on these processes.

The last fifty years, in particular in contemporary art institutions, other forms and potential have emerged, like the new expectations towards museums. (Should they be networked? Open? A forum?...) The breakthrough of new and faster means of communication and exchanges, more communication/media bandwidth and dialogue did have an influence. It might be interesting to reconsider some of the older ideas implicit in the early modern Republic of Letters (but in the modern situation including those institutions as power houses and tools), in relation to the evolving art fields and to see how compatible they are with modern ideas about (post) New Institutionalism. Models of checks and balances between bureaucracies, firms and experts, between media, corporate life and social movements make this more complex.

Et alors?

There are serious anchor or connecting points in the existing literature to explore this idea. On the *republicarts* and *transform* platforms, reflections that seem compatible have been developed, e.g. in discussions about New Institutionalism. Nina Möntmann ended up with a network as institutional format:

> This conceivable critical institution could, for example, take on the form of an internationally operating 'organized network', which strengthens various smaller, independent institutions and

> activities – be they alternative, artist-run, or research-based – and could also set up temporary platforms within bigger institutions.... the potential of 'organized networks' for superseding modern institutions that are just 'rebooted into the digital age' by 'reconciling their hierarchical structures of organization with the flexible, partially decentralized and transnational flows of culture, finance and labor.' The advantage of 'organized networks' instead is the way they function as 'social-technical forms that co-emerge with the development of digital information and communication technologies.[18]

This coincides with debates about the evolution of the role of museums in general and art museums and institutions in the digital age in particular. In museum studies, the fact that the museum as a form or an instrument is considered being 'in crisis' in a network society has been on the agenda since many years. A broader look beyond the arts makes it clear that a number of general tendencies can be traced in other domains since 2000, e.g. in heritage studies and domains, both in regions as well as on a global scale (the breakthrough and official recognition by UNESCO of the paradigm of 'the intangible', sensitivity for ecology and sustainable development or reflexivity, are now also on the agenda there).[19] The question then is what makes contemporary arts institutions *different*, or how they deal in other ways with those paradigmatic changes, that can be seen as reactions to globalization, risk society, political organization

17 See the deconstruction in Bruno Latour, *Science in Action: How to Follow Scientists and Engineers through Society* (Cambridge, MA: Harvard University Press, 1987).

18 Nina Möntmann, 'The Rise and Fall of New Institutionalism: Perspectives on a Possible Future'; http://transform.eipcp.net/transversal/0407/moentmann/en (August 2007).

19 See for instance the analysis of how the Smithsonian Folklife Festival on the 'holy Museum ground' of the Smithsonian Institution evolved and showed the switch from old Fordist models of resource extraction or preservation to network society and Post-Fordism: Emily Satterwhite, 'Imagining Home, Nation, World: Appalachia on the Mall', *Journal of American Folklore* 121 (2008), no. 479, pp. 10-34. Not only contemporary arts museums claim to be in the front(ier) zone; ethnological and anthropological institutions do too.

[redacted]

shifts, social movements, economic and ecological evolutions (including the Post-Fordist). Here it will be interesting to combine the just-mentioned transferable models from an analysis of the globalized use of electronic media with a transferable but enhanced model of collaboration, knowledge accumulation and cultural brokerage from the Early Modern past, in order to examine the practices of crossing all kinds of borders and thresholds (religious, political, economic...), in particular of individuals, and now institutions, of the Republic of Letters, '*République des Lettres*' and '*Respublica litteraria*'.

The hypothesis that is put forward here is that these contemporary arts institutions share common characteristics (if they function optimally) or goals. First, they can be seen as institutes 'with an attitude': this might be crucial for their impact. Second, and connected to this, they function in a transnational network, in ways that are similar to a Republic of Letters, generating discourses and representations in relative autonomy. Thirdly, they can broadcast, by using institutional tools, voices and products of a Republic of the Arts, the international and interconnected world of contemporary arts as it processes internal and external dynamics and experiences. Fourth, they can work with images, sounds, and other stimulants of the senses to provide new experiences. They have the potential to function as hubs, facilitators and brokers, to provide eye-opening experiences and help deal with complexities.

Intermediaries and Networks

One of the most interesting results of studies on how the Republic of Letters functioned in the sixteenth, seventeenth and eighteenth centuries concerns the importance of cultural brokerage.[20] One of the significant evolutions that began in the eighteenth, century and continued in the nineteenth and twentieth centuries concerns the rise of institutions, which also started to cultivate communication with each other. In the eighteenth century, academies, journals, literary societies, publishers, etc. took over or dominated some of the roles, functions and networking of individuals, but moved toward more autonomous fields rather than cultivating brokerage in several domains of life. Scholarly journals played an important role in facilitating a transatlantic Republic of Letters. In the nineteenth century, museums were strongly advancing institutions. They were excellent in drawing in actor-networks in the processes of scholarly translation (cfr. Bruno Latour), but not particularly in reinforcing or emphasizing (what Mark Granovetter called) 'the strength of weak ties'.[21] In discussions about classic institutes like museums, one of the biggest risks today is that a notion like 'verticality', which is put forward in this book as a key issue, could also just be used as an euphemism or flimsy decoy for what is actually meant and what it — at the end of the day — may turn out to be in practice: hierarchy and a singular voice of authority, legitimated by references to grandeur, dignity, canon, science, tradition. Silence in the Temple! The Director/Curator/Artist/Critic/High Priest speaks! No, thank you. Not anymore in this new twenty-first century. It is: And Institutions And Networks And People (And Objects, Performances, Collections And Repertoires). The number of visitors, customers or anonymous consumers, the size of the audience or turnover, does not tell an adequate story at all. What about participation and participants? Different forms of impact? Sustainable development? All sorts of values? Public good(s)?

There is a fast-growing literature about adjectives and noun modifiers connected to museums, that (should) have effect on the concept of the art museum. Hopefully to put pressure on time-honoured hierarchies, traditions, elites, canons and received — not permanently earned — forms of grandeur. Let me just refer to pamphlets like the 'disruptive museum' by Arnoud Odding and the programmes of 'the participatory museum' inspired by Nina Simon, inviting institutions to be more than just content providers, but also to assume roles as platform providers.[22] Art and heritage museums are actively invited by policy-makers to consider international developments in museum studies and take the challenges to heart.

Let me give the example of a recent piece of legislation in Flanders that directly affects museums, including those of the contemporary arts. In the Council of Europe Framework

20 **Anne Goldgar,** Impolite Learning: Conduct and Community in the Republic of Letters. 1680-1750 **(New Haven and London: Yale University Press, 1995).**

21 **Mark Granovetter, 'The Strength of Weak Ties',** American Journal of Sociology **78 (1973), pp. 1360-80.**

22 **Susanne Gesser, Martin Handschin, and Angela Jannelli,** Das partizipative Museum: Zwischen Teilhabe und User Generated Content: Neue Anforderungen an kulturhistorische Ausstellungen **(Bielefeld: Transcript, 2012); www.participatorymuseum.org/; Arnoud Odding, Het disruptieve museum (The Hague: O dubbel d, 2011).**

[redacted]

Convention on the Value of Cultural Heritage for Society (CETS No. 199), one of the central concepts is defined as follows: 'A heritage community consists of people who value specific aspects of cultural heritage which they wish, within the framework of public action, to sustain and transmit to future generations.' In the Council of Europe's explanatory report, the authors explain that:

> A heritage community is thus defined as a variable geometry without reference to ethnicity or other rigid communities. Such a community may have a geographical foundation linked to a language or religion, or indeed shared humanist values or past historical links. But equally, it may arise out of a common interest of another type.[23]

The brilliant move by the Flemish government was to copy the European definition but add two words: 'A heritage community consists of people *and organisations* who value specific aspects of cultural heritage which they wish, within the framework of public action, to sustain and transmit to future generations.' Archives and museums are some of the most important examples of 'organisations'. The network metaphor is used in the invitation for action and museums, for instance, are required to take responsibility and an active role for a 'heritage community'. This forces a back door for participation, interaction and … critical stakeholders, shareholders and other persons and organizations. They can give the museum institution a run for their money. And vice-versa, hopefully.

From Flat to Spiky, Inter-Imperial Brokerage and Art History

To avoid inward-bound strategies in art institutions and networks, which might be legitimated by 'brief histories' or 'flat world views', it is preferable to go for (long) 'world art histories' and worlds with peaks and valleys. Richard Florida's counterproposal, the metaphor of the 'spiky world' seems a more realistic or useful perspective than that of the flat world that supposedly is emerging:

> On the contrary, our world is amazingly 'spiky'. In terms of both sheer economic horsepower and cutting-edge innovation, surprisingly few regions truly matter in today's global economy. What's more, the tallest peaks – the cities and regions that drive the world economy – are growing ever higher, while the valleys mostly languish.[24]

Measures like population density, urbanization, the number of patented innovations, the residences of the 1,200 most heavily cited scientists in leading fields show images with many spikes, hills and vertical concentrations. Particularly in the field of contemporary arts, this is a crucial insight:

> Concentrations of creative and talented people are particularly important for innovation.... Ideas flow more freely, are honed more sharply, and can be put into practice more quickly when large numbers of innovators, implementers, and financial backers are in constant contact with one another, both in and out of the office. Creative people cluster not simply because they like to be around one another or they prefer cosmopolitan centers with lots of amenities, though both those things count. They and their companies also cluster because of the powerful productivity advantages, economies of scale, and knowledge spillovers such density brings.[25]

Of course, Florida has a specific agenda in promoting contexts for creativity and economic success, but in particular in discussions about art institutions and networks, what he calls the '*global creative class*' is a crucial population. Florida refers to a group of

23 http://conventions.coe.int/Treaty/en/Reports/Html/199.htm.

24 Richard Florida, 'The World is Spiky', The Atlantic Monthly (October 2005), pp. 48-51; http://isites.harvard.edu/fs/docs/icb.topic30774.files/2-2_Florida.pdf; www.creativeclass.com/rfcgdb/articles/other-2005-The%20World%20is%20Spiky.pdf, p. 48.

25 Ibid, p. 50.

[redacted]

'about 150 million people' who are very mobile and interconnect at the highest peaks. Next to the high peaks concentrated in cities, where for instance the MoMA and the MET, the Louvre and the Tates are based, Florida refers to a much larger group of city regions that are far more locally oriented. Here again, very layered images, zones of very different speeds, local contexts and possibilities emerge. Important in this regard are cultural brokers, mediators and translators that can connect these layers. The existing electronic networks are not the only platforms and contact zones. Arts institutions can play this role, interconnecting, intertwining and translating in horizontal, vertical and diagonal directions. One of the important conclusions that Richard Florida grants to the flat-theory book, is that it brings emerging economies like India and China (Brazil, South Korea, Vietnam…) into the picture.

Precisely this is the point to develop: back into the picture. As recent debates on 'world history' emphasize, we have to reconsider the plots of history on a global scale, in particular by studying the relations between Asia and Europe.[26] Tracing the history of 'empire(s)' and the evolving tensions and connections between them throughout the centuries functions as an eye-opener. The history of the relation between collections, museums and other art institutions and empires is also rich and interesting, and present challenges should be considered in a long-term perspective.[27] Some of that promising work is now being conducted by scholars focussing on the fifteenth and sixteenth centuries, a framework of the new paradigm called world history. Next to the idea of contact zones between empires (defined by Mary Louise Pratt as 'social spaces where disparate cultures meet, clash, and grapple with each other, often in highly asymmetrical relations of domination and subordination'), Natalie Rothman introduced the concept of '*trans-imperial subjects*' in her study of contacts between Venice and Istanbul.[28] It is very interesting to confront this kind of research and what they are tracing with the discourses on empire in contemporary art theory; e.g. by replacing 'subjects' with 'institutions' and to see how they have functioned across all kinds of borders and thresholds. One of the zones in art history where innovative conclusions are being drawn is in the study of relations between the Ottoman Empire and empires and city-republics in Europe in that period.[29] In the historical sciences, there is a substantial evolution in the twenty-first century and what kind of global perspectives are needed: not a brief history, but moving towards an expanded world history. That can explain the depth and evolution of a spiky world with empires, states and important cities, different connections and varying bandwidths.

It may be inspiring to see how the European interlocking cultural system of the Republic of Letters was a viable way of generating knowledge and facilitating communication (also of a more erudite or vertical kind), even in very difficult and repressive circumstances. We urgently need another world art history, in analogy with the recent world history paradigm shift that puts different kinds of emphasis on, for instance, China or the Islamic world.[30] Recent discussions about developments in Asian arts in the twenty-first century come into a totally different light if they are viewed in that long-term perspective. In short, let us consider reframing in many forms. Debunk, think critically and cultivate reflexivity, over and over again in this spiky world.

26 Eric Vanhaute, Wereldgeschiedenis: Een inleiding (Ghent: Academia Press, 2012).

27 See the perspective on 'empires': Karen Barkey, Empire of Difference: The Ottomans in Comparative Perspective (Cambridge, MA: Cambridge University Press, 2008).

28 Natalie Rothman, Brokering Empire: Trans-Imperial Subjects between Venice and Istanbul (Ithaca, NY, and London: Cornell University Press, 2012).

29 See the rediscovered work by Marshall Hodgson, Rethinking World History: Essays on Europe, Islam, and World History (Cambridge, MA: Cambridge University Press, 1993); Jerry Brotton, Le bazar Renaissance: Comment l'Orient et l'islam ont inluencé l'Occident (Paris: Les Liens, 2011).

30 See André G. Frank, ReOrient: Global Economy in the Asian Age (Berkeley, CA: University of California Press, 1998).

[redacted]

Instituting Change
The Protocol as a Productive Space of Conflict

Markus Miessen

Why do we need institutions today? A question that has been asked again and again over the last 40 years, mostly with a certain degree of pessimism and frustration, from the point of view of a criticism toward the notion of limitations, editorial censorship and supposed processes of appropriation. In the context of today's cultural production, what seems urgently needed is to invert this question, while emphasizing the potentials and possible models and productive trajectories of the contemporary institution. How can the institution be understood as an enabler rather than a hindrance, an agency for critical production and discourses rather than a creature that generates stasis? A question on processes of institutionalization, its need or misuse, its potentials or backdrops, is first and foremost a question of the context in which it takes place. No one would argue that it would be most welcome if some countries in the Middle East, or in fact China, would nurture what we, in the European geography of milk and honey, would refer to as the 'civic institution'. At the same time, when we discuss the question of institutionalization, we mostly discuss models and scenarios that are of, or supersede, a certain scale, both physically and economically.

Reinstituting Hierarchies

Whether in regard to decision-making structures as well as, depending on context, understanding the formality of the institution as a structural asset rather than an element representing forms of limitation and control, the time has come to reintroduce verticality where it is needed. The (supposed) democratization of (seemingly) any process is a serious mistake. Making every process horizontal does not necessarily solve a problem. This flatness needs to be articulated by reintroducing individual specificities.

The Nightmare of Participation 2.0: An afterthought

Markus Miessen and Hannes Grassegger

From Cairo to Berlin to Occupy Wall Street. Participation is the new opium of the people. When everyone takes part in everything, everything will be fine, or so says the holy doctrine of participation. But sometimes what's better is exactly the opposite.

Everyone should be able to take part! The call to participation is the red thread of the history of political thought of our time, linking the protests on Wall Street to Cairo to the ballot boxes captured by the Pirates of Germany.

But 'participation' is a concept in need of urgent repair. Sometimes, such forms of democracy, in which everyone has a right to have a say in the matter, should be avoided at all costs. Not everyone should be invited to take part in decision-making processes. We propose that one should look at participation from the other way around: as an autocratic model.

In fact, the time has come to take a chance on more autocracy. In Germany, at least, participation is wildly romanticized. The middle seems to be lost as soon as one calls out 'join us!' on Facebook. And we're not talking about massive binge drinking. For the past decade or so, we have been experiencing an almost fundamentalist endorsement of civic participation under the mantle of 'participation'. This enthusiasm is accompanied by a grotesque harmlessness in creating the structures and basic conditions for so-called participation at both the national and local levels, for example, as with Stuttgart 21, or with newspapers such as *Freitag* (bursting with specious participatory ideas), or with the flood of participatory projects in the art world, et cetera. It's as if participation itself has taken on a value all on its own.

The disciples of this holy vision of participation are Germany's Pirate Party. For the time being they appear to have ushered in our gentle *deutscher arabischer Frühling* (German Arab Spring), as Heinrich Wefing described in one of Germany's leading newspapers, *Die Zeit*. In reality, they are radical without even knowing why. For voting they use their laptops, mostly through the voting platform Adhocracy. It offers up the possibility of voting in real time just like a representative of parliament. The Pirates stipulated 'liquid democracy' is meant to replace representative democracy (a half-democratic compromise, in the eyes of the Pirates) in favour of 'real participation' with power. All access, uncompromised, here-and-now democracy — for every question a popular vote: this is the participatory dogma of the Pirates. These 'orange activists' see participation as voting via menu, with the least possible personal effort or consequences.

A feeble push of a button, an anonymous log-in. This is Slacktivism, the vision of an all-inclusive democracy inspired by the collaborative model Web 2.0, from Facebook to Wikipedia,

[redacted]

where content is generated or edited by anyone at anytime. In theory, it sounds wonderful. In reality, it is dreadful. The Pirates have liquidized one of the foundational pillars of democracy: personal responsibility. Both on the level of the voter, who acts as an advocate for something with his real person, and on the level of the representative, who shows his face with every decision.

What the Pirates have neglected to see is that even in the Holy Grail of all Participation idolatry — Wikipedia — the participatory illusion has quietly and furtively disappeared. That is, Wikipedia has contracted a disease through the contagion of participation. Useless for scholarship due to its liquid contents, in any case, this web-encyclopedia is also becoming eventually useless to the normal user. Studies complain about the ever-more endless entries, ever-more incomprehensible terminology. The community of enthusiasts is diminishing. In fact, since 2007, the swell of Wikipedia entries has been shrinking.

The era of total participation is over. In the meanwhile, Wikipedia has been under attack by an entire arsenal of undemocratic decision-making processes for critical situations. As so-called 'administrators' have the power to completely negate editorial additions to the profiles of controversial politicians on Wikipedia — if only to prevent Edit Wars that render the site useless — content can be changed by the minute. Important 'admins' are known by name. And sometimes Jimmy Wales, the head of Wikipedia, has the last word. For example, when he deleted details from his own resume, going against the encyclopaedia's set rules. Or when media-czar John Seigenthaler used his influence to change the rules of Wikipedia, pressuring them to delete an entry about him containing defamatory content.

Participation alone doesn't work. The best proof of this are those in the realm of politics who held fast to participatory dogma and then came nowhere near close to holding power. In Egypt, the Muslim Brotherhood and the military have taken the reins; Occupy Wall Street sunk in embarrassing roundtable all-inclusive discussions held on the island of Mallorca; and while the Pirates lack concrete suggestions, they are rife with internal organizational quibbles and a continually changing leadership.

What should the participatory vision lead to? Imagine what an Edit War would mean to a participatory Pirate Utopia. An editorial war in which our constitutional laws would be changed by the minute. Or the regulations on access to weapons. It is nearly impossible to imagine how dangerous total democracy could be. It is a nightmare. In the best case, one that never comes true.

We believe that such a holy vision — the idea that radically participative open models guarantee the optimal solution for all problems — is dangerous. Participation must be viewed without romanticism. Participation is neither a quality nor a solution but rather an organizational model.

Real democracy demands much more than just voting. In parliament, ideas are created and heads are chopped off. Real participation is not innocent. In other words: participation is war. Like the political theorist Chantal Mouffe says, we should agree that we disagree. And learn to productively live and deal with this situation.

The basis for the worldwide call to participation lies in real conflicts. We demand a conflict-orientated praxis that dissents from the fashionable cyber-democratic mediation-mania and accepts the fact that sometimes one person must take responsibility for a solution. Not because we doubt democracy, but because we don't want to end up in *Harmonistan*, a pseudo-participatory superficial democracy, in which politicians shove all responsibility onto the online-voting community.

We have to turn the idea of participation on its head. Democracy is a continual process of democratization on the personal level. For this, everyone must (sometimes) grant power to an autocrat. Instead of viewing participation as an opening of the decision-making process that is dictated from above, one should see participation as an individual entrance strategy to power from down below; as a post-consensus method of getting in the door. Our join-in era of participation needs a new understanding of itself: do-it-yourself instead of picking from a menu. Even if it seems that we are standing on the other side of the door of power, uninvited: we are still a part of the party.

Architectural Space as Agent: Notes Regarding the Winter School Middle East, Kuwait

Conversation between Markus Miessen, Patricia Reed, and Kenny Cupers; introduction by Markus Miessen, founder and director of the Winter School

Initiated in January 2008 in Dubai, the Winter School Middle East was set up as a roaming, mobile institution realized in a variety of formats, including a series of workshops, seminars, mini-schools, and conferences to discuss spatial practice. In 2010, the Winter School moved to Kuwait for a longer-term involvement and local engagement regarding the establishment of a platform for critical exchange. These projects were not only tested against the criticism of the group, but also against the knowledge and expertise of local protagonists. The Winter School is now based in Kuwait, with several satellite activities taking place over the year. In 2012, the school organized a conference in Kuwait as well as being involved in the development of Kuwait's first national presentation at the Venice Architecture Biennale.

The political and cultural environment in Kuwait is very liberal: encouraging open discussion, with a tradition in platforms such as *dewaniya*, a term that stems from a very rich regional history, including the word *dewan*, which presents a typology of lounge furniture that one might sit on to hold discussions about public matters in an intimate setting.[1] It has a specific history and constituency: a spatial typology for political exchange. From the point of view of spatial practices, urbanism, and discourse, there is very little attention paid to the development and growth of a local expertise beyond a classical Western notion of urbanism, one that uses the specificities of the local context in order to generate new types of spatial practice.

The following conversation was recorded after the Winter School's 2011 workshops concluded in Kuwait.

Markus Miessen

The Winter School, which is now in its third year of programming, attempts to set up and offer a non-profit space that accommodates an opposition. An opposition not in the sense of necessarily being 'against' something, but rather a space that is based on the notion of both political, institutional, and structural autonomy, which is deliberately introduced from the outside, yet embeds itself within the actors, realities, and questions of local and regional practices. The notion of *dewaniya*, as we have discussed it during the Winter School, could be read and interpreted both as a spatial phenomenon as well as a process. The Winter School — in the way it is set up, situated, and structured — was meant to allow for a decentred perspective on politics through a *reunderstanding* of everyday communal practices. In describing the school as an autonomous space, one could arguably compare it to the *dewaniya*: a 'protected space', a congregation site and a lobbying device for political thought.

Patricia, in one of your seminars you explored the conception and understanding of what it means to set up a problematic as opposed to an understanding of the subject or object of investigation as problem. Could you please elaborate on this concept and the structure of the problematic?

Patricia Reed

Firstly, I would just like to say that I will refer to *dewaniya* without a definite article in my contributions to this multi-logue. The removal of the article treats *dewaniya* as a process rather than a thing. What became clear during our time in Kuwait was the ambiguity surrounding the defini-

1 See Abdullah Mohammad Alhajeri, 'The Development of Political Interaction in Kuwait through the "Dewaniyas" from Their Beginnings until the Year 1999', *Journal of Islamic Law and Culture* 12, no. 1 (2010), p. 24-44. Alhajeri describes the role and function of *dewaniya* today in the introduction to his study thusly: 'The dewaniya represents the first democratic institution in Kuwait in which the most important political elections have taken place free from any tribal influence. It is doubtless that the dewaniya is one of the oldest and most deeply rooted social institutions of the Gulf States, and its relationship with the political process makes it even more important. Kuwait, more than other Gulf States, has experienced various political movements that have resulted in various systems of government. Yet underlying all of these political movements has been the unofficial yet pervasive institution of the dewaniya. The political importance of the dewaniya lies in the fact that it is not solely, or even primarily, a political institution – it is equally a center of traditional culture, daily social life, and political activity. It has continued to play this multifaceted and dynamic role since the establishment of the Kuwaiti Emirate. The institution has deeply shaped Kuwaiti life and has affected the current form of the Kuwaiti Emirate. Indeed, so great has been the political influence of the dewaniya that many have called them Kuwaiti mini-parliaments.' Historically, *dewaniya* has deep roots. Alhajeri contextualizes the phenomenon as follows: 'Dewaniya in Kuwait are considered an ancient social phenomenon. They can be described as an informal political, cultural, and social outlet where common and elite people alike can meet to discuss the society's affairs. Throughout their history, the dewaniya have always been the first venue for the discussion of various issues. ... The distinguished status of the dewaniya in Arab culture goes back hundreds of years. In the past, the dewaniya took the form of what was called the "council", which was the dominant political concept of the earliest Islamic state – elders of the tribe or the clan used to meet in order to discuss the most important issues facing them and to solve any disputes that existed among clans and families. The origins of the dewaniya can, therefore, be traced to the first of these political councils.'

[redacted]

tion of *dewaniya*, so it seems only apt to respond to this question by apprehending *dewaniya* not as a static entity, but as something quite malleable, in fact. So in this sense *dewaniya* is always becoming. What I meant by introducing this more or less philosophical term of the 'problematic' was not to suggest that we identify a problem of *dewaniya* per se, but rather that we form a particular approach, or angle on the complex issues embroiled within the notion of *dewaniya* itself. The basic maxim behind this discussion of establishing our individual problematics is to say that an interesting or relevant spatial intervention is wholly dependent on setting up an equally complex and novel problematic. So, for example, when we take up this term of 'protected space', coined by Marianne Tétreault, in regards to the private/public dialectic at work within the spatial condition of *dewaniya*, we may possibly start to approach spatial problematics by further asking: *From whom is* dewaniya *protected? Who is protected through* dewaniya*? How does* dewaniya *establish boundaries of inclusion/exclusion within the* nomos *of the everyday?*

Kenny Cupers

I think these are very good questions to begin unpacking the spatial agency of the *dewaniya*. For me, the notion of the 'problematic' is less philosophical than simply analytical — i.e., it is about asking the right questions. The right questions here are the ones that open up the 'black box' of the *dewaniya*. I think our position of outsider — which, as Markus has mentioned, shapes the politics of the Winter School — is crucial in this respect. The fact that the Winter School's participants are either women or non-Kuwaiti, or both, undoubtedly shapes much of our questions — and the debates to which they have given rise. As a gathering of Kuwaiti men, the *dewaniya* is certainly a highly gendered practice. Its mechanisms of inclusion and exclusion are ambiguous, to say the least, in that the regime of hospitality in the *dewaniya* generates both an explicit openness and an implicit closure. As outsiders, our approach to the *dewaniya* is shaped to a large extent by an imaginary rather than everyday experience. This situation I think reflects the nature of the *dewaniya* as a phenomenon in Kuwaiti society at large. As Mohammed Al-Ghanim, one of the invited public speakers and an officer in the national parliament, has suggested, the *dewaniya* structures Kuwaiti society not just as a concrete social practice, but perhaps even more importantly, as an imaginary. The *dewaniya* has given rise to political contestation at key moments in Kuwaiti history and as such has entered collective memory as a place of national success — regardless of whether many of these instances constituted actual political successes or rather failures.

M.M.

Might the dewaniya *in this sense be comparable to the agora in Ancient Greek culture?*

K.C.

The agora constitutes a myth of an open public space of participatory decision-making, a myth that continues to entice the collective imagination and has led to the baptizing of 'Agoras' across Europe… in spite of the fact that historians continue to inform us of the outright exclusion of women, slaves, and non-citizens that was at its basis. The *dewaniya* seems to serve similarly as a locus of tradition in collective consciousness, yet at the same time it might be a crucial agent of Kuwaiti modernization. Some of the current uses of the *dewaniya* — a Playstation room for youth, or a space to collectively discuss weight loss goals — attest to this hypothesis. For me, the most fascinating aspect of the *dewaniya* lies in such seeming contradictions. My main question is therefore: If the *dewaniya* is a 'protected space' — a specifically designated space for politics — might it protect the political from entering the realm of the street and the spaces of everyday life? Or is it the opposite, rather: the *dewaniya* makes urban life debatable and therefore becomes the agent through which political and other tensions can be channelled into more organized, rational discussion? Certainly Jürgen Habermas would be happy with the latter possibility. But to me, the *dewaniya*'s regime of inclusion/exclusion suggests otherwise.

M.M.

In many ways, the Winter School itself acts as an uninvited outsider. Through its temporal structure and nomadic appearance, it questions both the normativity of the space of the 'school' as well as, in the case of the 2011 Winter School in Kuwait, the normativity of those communal spaces and practices defined as *dewaniya*, a historically protected space originating from tribal society in which the leader of a tribe would offer a gathering space within his private quarters. Let's talk about *dewaniya* as a means to formally register a thought in an informal setting, a means of maintaining private and public social networks. *How can one think through the written and unwritten rules as to the use and protocols of space? How does it become a site outside of itself?*

M.M.

In some of the seminars we discussed the notion of politics versus the political, both read through the goggles of Chantal Mouffe and Jacques Rancière. *Would you agree if I called* dewaniya *the Mouffian space in which one agrees to disagree, a space of potentially oppositional, non-violent encounter, a network or scaffold of sense-making, a common ground, conceptual framework, and shared space of meeting in which a political community forms?*

P.R.

I would agree. I think *dewaniya* is a potential space for debate, so very much in line (again possibly so, not always) with Mouffian agonism. Important to mention, however, is the very normative codes of conduct or common ground/ethos instantiated within *dewaniya*. For me this means *dewaniya* is still caught up within the established symbolic orders of 'the police', using the language of Rancière (and in that regard is not a political eruption).[2] Again, it depends on your understanding of 'the political' in Mouffe's language. For me, it doesn't go far enough since her toned-down antagonism as 'agonism' requires that we agree on a common grammar of disagreement, whereas for Rancière real disagreement lies in the contestation of the very grammar used, that is understood as making sense. Again, referring back to the initial dialectic of 'protected space' we deployed as a potential problematic of *dewaniya* setting up relations of inclusion/exclusion, I think Rancière's conception of politics is useful here, seeing as a moment of dissensus (a doing of politics) is always initiated by a part that has no part in the sphere of perceptibility.

Let me briefly elaborate — within a Mouffian paradigm, as I understand it, it is true that *dewaniya* can gather together a particular group of people to debate and create a presence of an oppositional position to a particular hegemonic condition. They can gather and discuss because they already have consensus on a normative grammar of presenting, contesting, and debating issues. So, in short, this potentially productive force of contestation is based on a fundamental consensus, a profound paradox. That said, we cannot have politics all the time, so *dewaniya*, as a space of consensual disagreement, can still be figured as a fruitful space for the proliferation of opinions and ideas, albeit from a part of the population fully accounted for.

M.M.

Is dewaniya *a horizontally accessible space?*

P.R.

When we use *dewaniya* as an example, it is often presented as a space open to all, yet this very notion of 'open to all' is of course determined by the normative grammar of who constitutes 'all' in the first place. We know that *dewaniya* is a particularly male-dominated institution, and, furthermore, one 'open to all' who are passport holders, and often those who are friends of friends. So challenging the very normative grammar of 'open to all' is, for me, a potential site of politics, rather than debating ideas, people, and functions within the pre-existing grammar of common sense. The larger question of politics, as such, would entail a renegotiation of the normative grammar 'open to all' in terms of who counts in making an appearance, to who and what could be understood as being a part of the order of hospitality.

K.C.

I think it is important not to impose a theory that reduces the spatial and political complexity of the *dewaniya*. I don't think it is at all possible to identify the *dewaniya* — as a space, a phenomenon, or an event — with either of the categories established by Mouffe (politics/the political) or Rancière (the police/politics). From the many invited speakers during the Winter School, we have been able to learn about an amazing diversity of potential instances in which the *dewaniya* became a political agent. I think the *dewaniya* can historically be both an institution of politics as 'business as usual' (for a privileged group of Kuwaiti men), and an agent of political contention and social change, in which women and youth can begin to play a key role. Rancière's redistribution of the sensible — the emergence of a new common sense — might already be taking place, yet whether the recent establishment of certain exclusively female *dewaniya* can be seen as such a positive change is not entirely clear. The question about social change is perhaps a question of which regimes of hospitality are imaginable in Kuwaiti society.

2 In Rancière's philosophical thought, 'the police' is a non-pejorative term referring not to the petty order of those people in uniform asserting the authority of the law, but rather the sensible modalities through which we come to apprehend identities, functions, ways of doing, ways of saying, and places, to which Rancière adopts the terms 'the distribution of the sensible' or the 'partitioning of the sensible'. Politics, on the other hand, is that which shifts the symbolic ordering of the police or the partitioning of the sensible; that is, 'It makes visible what had no business being seen, and makes heard a discourse where once there was only place for noise.' Politics is a *doing*, rather than a standalone entity, and takes place as an intervention within the aesthetical constellation of the social order; it is nothing less than the aesthetical clash with, and interruption of, the distribution of the sensible. Jacques Rancière, *Disagreement: Politics and Philosophy*, trans. Julie Rose (Minnesota, MN: University of Minnesota Press, 1998), p. 29.

[redacted]

M.M.

Patricia, in one of your talks you unpacked the notion of 'deskilling' — or what I would call 'unlearning' — as an unsettlement of normativity, an unsettling of the given coordinates and datums of convention. Could you please explain this further in the literal context of the 2011 Winter School?

P.R.

The notion of deskilling was brought up in the context of mapping the sorts of characteristics of an 'uninvited outsider' as a kind of aesthetical-political agent. In the field of visual arts, deskilling — as identified by Boris Groys in *Art Power* — was mentioned as a residue of the gesture from Marcel Duchamp with his infamous *Fountain* (1917), the purchased and signed urinal he submitted to the world as an art object, by authorizing it as art, by contextualizing it as art. So deskilling has more to do with a downplaying of a particular ability with materials and techniques, craftsmanship and virtuoso capacities, in order to be a 'professional' artist. In the specific context of the Winter School, I thought this was important to impart to students in terms of heightening the agency of non-expert abilities, that interventions and important contributions are also thinkable outside the realm of master techniques, and can also be forged through recontextualizations.

In regards to unlearning — I'm not sure if I would create a parallel between these two modes — I think unlearning is perhaps a result of deskilling (we unlearn the definition of an artist, for example, through the pervasiveness of 'deskilling' in art — so that the artist cannot be defined as a master craftsman/artisan any longer). For me, unlearning is always a kind of conceptual violence, a necessary violence and a struggle with one's own cognitive schema of the world. For Kant, the schema is the result of experience and intellect, transformed into imagination — so we can figure something without having it directly represented. I use this example quite often, but when I describe to you 'red pen' we have a common schema in mind as to 'penness' and 'redness', so we can communicate about something without having it present, simple enough. The more complicated issues arise when we start to communicate about inclusion/exclusion, the human, and even *dewaniya*! What is the schema of being human? I situate unlearning as a deforming of our schemas, what I like to call contaminating imagination.

K.C.

I would like to connect this notion of unlearning back to Markus's comment about how the Winter School's temporal structure and nomadic appearance promises to unsettle and redefine the 'school' as institution. I am wary of celebrating 'unlearning' because I think it might result from a misconception about learning. If learning is understood as the flexible adjustment to change rather than the encyclopaedic collection of data, it comes much closer to a continual becoming rather than the attainment of expertise. Similarly, I think the current infatuation with the figure of the amateur is a dubious trend. Becoming someone else (whether amateur or expert) is of more interest to me, since it denotes an active process of engagement. Unlearning then threatens to equate a purely negative or expulsive approach.

This relates back to the notion of an alternative school. The Winter School I think is unique not because of its temporal structure and nomadic appearance (study-abroad programmes of similar structure abound in US and European university institutions), but because of the more reciprocal linkages it has forged between the local and the non-local. In this sense, the Winter School works through a different regime of hospitality. And this is also where its ethics lie. Markus's notion of the 'uninvited outsider' is useful to bring up here. I agree with him that the notion of the uninvited outsider has great potential. But it also brings with it a great responsibility. The questioning of certain states of affairs, accepted knowledges, or sets of norms often happens from a realm outside of or relatively removed from this relatively coherent yet closed condition. This is, I think, the positive challenge an outside perspective can offer. That said, the outsider, in its worst incarnation, is a ruthless colonizer. Whether the outsider is a respectful instigator of debate or its opposite depends of course on the concrete ways of engagement. But it also depends on the circulation of capital — whether it be economic or cultural. And it depends on the modes of reciprocity. Patricia in her seminar mentioned the words of art critic Jan Verwoert and his suggestion that the artist's ethics lie in inhabiting the consequences of her or his making. I think this is very relevant to the Winter School. *To what extent can it live the afterlife of its own instigations?*

M.M.

Unlearning here is meant in a flexible and at the same time specific sense, moving towards the education of architects and other disciplines dealing with the conventional tools regarding the production of space — i.e., constructing buildings, infrastructure, devising master plans, thinking about and directly act-

[redacted]

ing upon the city. When we look at the way in which this/these disciplines are taught in many schools and universities, it seems to me that indeed one of the most important things to teach is how to not fall back into the default modes of practice, which is how it is being transferred in many international courses. We need experts, yes, and there are many experts already. What I am personally interested in is the person who is not so keen to be the expert, but manages to smartly manoeuvre between 'things' — not necessarily disciplines, but within the whole apparatus of a diverse set of practices, relations, and social networks in order to proactively raise questions that are usually not being raised, at least not in the environment in which they are now posed.

Concerning your point about responsibility, Kenny, yes, of course. The notion of this role, this 'uninvited outsider' of course brings with it not only a great deal of responsibility, but also consequence. If this were not the case, I would also not be interested in it. I think that any practice that denies either responsibility or consequence — or even worse, both — should not be considered critical. I agree, as I argued in my book, that one of course has to be careful as to how this role can be achieved. And it can also easily be misused. Since I am an optimist, I tend to usually think about possibilities rather than problems.

The future of the Winter School, in terms of its ongoing afterlife, mostly during the calendar year when no major workshops are taking place, is based on a relationship of trust towards those practitioners and actors in Kuwait, such as Zahra, who could potentially develop this further and elevate it to the next level. This was always the idea right from the start — that is, that it would precisely occur not just in January every year, but that it would start to build an ongoing platform for critical exchange. After the final presentation this year, local architect and educator Ali Al-Khaled told me that he could not believe that this was the first time he actually saw all these locals together in one place. This is the point: to develop a shared space for criticality in a place in which such a model does not otherwise exist.

Call me a colonizer, but I think the moment that people were realizing this, it was already Winter School 2.0 and had nothing to do with me anymore. The process had started, and this is what counts. With the little financial means we have, I hope that this also helped to have the National Council for Culture rethinking its protocols in the future. This way, we can hopefully also have an active role in the reshaping and influencing of what I would call the 'institutional everyday'. We should not forget that this is all happening in a context where a female student getting a bank account at NBK (the National Bank of Kuwait) can receive up to KWD 5,000 (approximately 13,000) when opening a bank account, which can be accessed only for plastic surgery. At the same time, there is not a single programme that the bank offers for educational loans.

The Winter School is a project of proactive instigation, a localized, self-authorized trigger of sorts. If one was to assume such a role of the 'uninvited outsider', one could describe the potentiality of such self-authorized projects as one which is based on an underlying principle of questions rather than answers, a destabilizing momentum that attempts to contaminate the imagination of others. It attempts to perform itself as an autonomous agent, enacting and producing in relation to the given context and its specific audience-producing affect. As an agent for the instigation of dissensus, the 'uninvited outsider' arguably opens up alternative avenues for the staging of new formats or frameworks of production by proactively generating and directing a set of unprovoked questions. Such practice of 'opening up' is being enabled by, as Patricia called it, the 'partial unpredictability' of a foreigner resetting the rules of engagement. *Patricia, could you please elaborate on your reading of Giorgio Agamben in the context of a playful character that allows for what you named the practice of 'inappropriating'?*

K.C.

I will insert myself as the 'uninvited outsider' here and interrupt. First of all, I think we need to question the notion of the autonomous, 'self-authorized' actor here. The success of the Winter School lies not in the way it acts autonomously, but in the way it engages contingency. I think what needs theorization here is not the actor or organizer, but the situation or the encounter that is created. How can we invite contingency and incidence instead of celebrating individual agency? That brings us back to Rancière's notion of dissensus, which I think is less about intentionality then about the afterlife of an event. *How can we make sure that what we think is 'dissensus' is not just temporary transgression — which, just like the medieval carnival or the contemporary art festival, basically threatens to reinforce rather than challenge the status quo and the reigning normativity?*

M.M.

Exactly. This is why the issue of permanence and consequence in this context is so important.

[redacted]

P.R.

I don't want to be a stickler, but I think we have to be careful when using terms like 'the foreigner' in our discussion, since they enter our imagination in a fairly specific way. I prefer the Greek term *xenos* since it has a multiplicity of meanings. It, of course, signifies a foreigner (someone from outside a given community), but also an enemy/stranger and a guest friendship. So *xenos* possesses all of these qualities simultaneously: a menacing, friendly outsider — rather than just being from the outside. In regards to playfulness, another quality we attributed to the potential agency of *xenos*, Agamben discusses this in several texts from his prolific output, but in particular he sees it as a manner of determining other uses for things that have been locked down in a reified capacity for functioning within a given symbolic order. In the discussion of play in 'In Praise of Profanation' he cites the example of the child who takes an official legal contract and transforms it into a paper airplane. So the legal contract, something most of us would regard as precious or untouchable to some degree, becomes something wholly other by transforming its symbolic functioning.

In our case of *dewaniya* I am not suggesting that we are thinking within the coordinates of 'profanation' per se, for *dewaniya* is not sacred or removed from the sphere of use. Nonetheless, if we think about play in general and as a political tactic, it is something that renders a reified use inoperative; the gesture of play is always about imagining other uses, not to mention introducing a certain lightness into the discussion of spatial politics. In play, one neglects a certain use, but a kind of neglect that opens up other possibilities of use. Play is always in a sense inappropriate — if we consider appropriateness of use to set up a relation of memesis to a given order. Henri Lefebvre describes the body in space as that which appropriates codes and materials in space to produce (and reproduce) the spatial; interfacing this description of the Lefebvrian body and his project to revolutionize the everyday with the agency of play, we could further infer that to revolutionize our experience of the everyday requires an ethos of play through inappropriating the codes and materials of the spatial. Through *inappropriation*, I think we open more possibilities of use (symbolic and actual) and thus experience, rather than a purely mimetic experience through the reproductive force of appropriation. Speaking of the body, it's time we take a break and have some lunch!

(This conversation is an abridged edit of 'Architectural Space as Agent: Notes Regarding the 2011 Winter School Middle East, Kuwait', which was first published in *Fillip* 14, Summer 2011.)

[redacted]

Institutional Mores

Alex Farquharson

I.

In this text I want to reconsider some of the practices and theories associated with 'New Institutionalism', as it came to be known a few years ago, and then loosen and broaden the terms of that debate in light of more recent experience and different potentialities. This was a debate that began to be codified around 2003, based on the practices of several art institutions at that time. By 2006, some of the critics associated with these developments felt they were in crisis and were being subjected to governmental and bureaucratic repression — funding cuts, forced merger and closure. For some, the answer was to, in a sense, de-institutionalize, to work small, with small numbers of participants, in situations that involved little money, and therefore relatively little political scrutiny; to, perhaps, follow the lead of self-organized groups, often led by artists, whose principle medium was dialogic research and experimental collective learning systems. Activist networks that shared some of the same theoretical reference points were also looked to.

Instead of this exit or exodus from the mainstream, I want to consider how these critical and experimental practices may have proliferated and multiplied amongst more mainstream institutions, and how through this expansion they have acquired different political, ethical and poetic coordinates. I have in mind institutional practices of a certain scale, that speak to publics of a certain size — *kunsthalle*-sized institutions and certain museums of contemporary art.

My initial interest in New Institutionalism stemmed from experimental exhibition-making — specifically, what happens when the kinds of curatorial innovations brought to bear on individual exhibitions are transposed to the whole institution. What are the stakes for those institutions and their publics? What does it mean for an institution to internalize and commit long-term to critical and experimental ways of working with artists, with publics and on itself? How, as a consequence, is the triangular relationship between artists, institutions and their publics reconceived, restructured and politicized in these situations, and how might that redefine the publicness of institutions of contemporary art?

I was conscious, then, as I am now, of my geocultural distance from many of these phenomena and debates. At that time there was little of this kind occurring in Britain (there is more now), and the politics of arts funding in Britain has been very different from those of the social-democratic countries of Europe where these practices and discourses have been concentrated. In Britain, the overwhelming government priority for the arts during the New Labour era had been increasing the number of visitors, or, as they prefer to call it, 'audience development' (since then, under the Conservative-Liberal Democrats, it has been cost-cutting and philanthropy). That has led to larger, more diverse publics, as a consequence of free admission, increased emphasis on marketing and outreach, and — thanks to the National Lottery — new and better buildings. There is still, no doubt, more to do here, but the presumed ties between art institutions and a solid bourgeois tradition are not as strong in Britain as they are elsewhere. While I would not want to underestimate the positive aspects of these developments, they have often led to an increase in both the marketization and the instrumentalization of art and art institutions. This pattern, of course, has been replicated across the public sector (a process Mark Fisher has called 'capitalist realism'), which even after the massive public bailout of the financial sector is required to remodel itself along corporate lines. In our own sector, directors began calling themselves 'chief executives', their institutions 'attractions', the art they presented 'product' and their publics 'customers' and 'markets'. The public sector under New Labour was a bonanza for private consultants.

I remain conscious of these circumstantial differences as I re-enter this debate, this time not in an independent capacity, but as an institutional practitioner — as the director of a medium-sized, *kunsthalle*-type institution in a medium sized, post-industrial city in the UK, which opened just four months ago in a new building: Nottingham Contemporary. When I wrote on institutions prior to this, I could do so with more detachment. Later in these reflections, I will draw on our experiences in Nottingham in the hope that they may have some general application to the situations of other more or less like-minded institutions in other regions. While our institution is unique as an assemblage, its constituent parts are variously shared with others and have some precedents.

II.

Inspired by the institutionally-reflexive practices of some artists associated with Relational Aesthetics, as well as successive waves of institutional critique, New Institutionalism developed important ways of reconceiving the socio-political function of the art institution. In general terms, this represented a move away from

[redacted]

a consumption-based model towards a more discursive one that linked institutional practice to the formation of a critical and plural public sphere. Under New Institutionalism, the cycle of exhibition programming was no longer the privileged format around which all others revolved. Instead, as Charles Esche wrote on the late Rooseum's website in 2001, the new institution aspired to be 'part community centre, part laboratory and part academy, with less need for the established showroom function'. In new institutions, closed workshops, artist-designed foyers, longitudinal research projects and performatively-installed archives have been as visible as exhibitions. Exhibition catalogues gave ground to readers and institutional journals. As in the term 'New Institutionalism' itself, the prefix 'art' was often absent, and discourses were more often drawn from political philosophy and the social sciences than art history and art theory.

The practical limitation of New Institutionalism in its more distilled forms is that it often fails to engage much more than a relatively small, invited knowledge community. New Institutionalism often conceives of the social agency of institutions in far wider terms than most conventional art institutions, and yet the actual take-up by these publics, imagined as pluralistic and agonistic (after Ernesto Laclau and Chantal Mouffe), is often small and uniform in practice. There is the sense that New Institutionalism has a model-like quality, that it is a prototype for a far larger kind of social production that may always remain deferred. In practice, new institutions often only engage relatively small constituencies, whose politics and subjectivities remain more or less aligned to those of the institutional actors. Their scale allows them to be highly focused and uncompromising.

There is value in this, I would want to maintain: their small scale and considerable autonomy enables them to work in critically and experimentally developed ways, uncompromised by the expectations of large, unknowing audiences and the scrutiny of political stakeholders. Other larger institutions, in turn, may benefit from their experimental and often far-reaching critical work. There should always be room in the infrastructure of public spaces for institutions able to work in laboratory and research-centre like conditions.

But generally speaking, what interests me more is the possibility of working on larger scales, achieving greater visibility, engaging larger and more diverse publics with varying degrees of knowledge of art and its intellectual contexts, and in having the opportunity to influence the immediate social environment in which the institution operates. With this scale comes all kinds of expectations and demands: from audiences, non-audiences, funders, tourism administrators, the local media, etc — all the various social and governmental actors that feel they have a stake in what you do as a consequence of how you are funded. What they might want from you might be quite different from your own motivations and ethics. What follows from this is a continuous process of turning necessity into desire, and this involves a continuous process of negotiation and transformation.

It also means devoting considerable energy to the more mundane areas of a larger institution's infrastructure. It means running a shop or a café well; it means efficiently communicating quite basic visitor information, as well as keeping a large building clean; it means publicizing what you do in and around your city; it means seeking sponsorship, building partnerships, responding to the reporting regimes of the political structures you are accountable to — all the everyday functions of larger scale institutions; the essential operating system on which the artistic, discursive and participatory work of the institution constantly depends.

III.

What follows is a series of attitudes and techniques that I find helpful when looking to intervene in more mainstream institutional situations and more intense political contexts. Some relate to new institutional approaches, others don't. They all relate to the situation of a medium- to large-scale art institution under some political and bureaucratic scrutiny. They are drawn from observation, relate to current experiences, and are written in the form of maxims in a rather speculative way:

Work on different scales to create spaces for participation. Build those spaces into your programme, into your building, for more developed exchange. Do what small, experimental institutions do, but in pockets or cells of the larger organization, whose other forms of mediation may be orientated towards a larger, more diffuse public. It's through these more intense encounters — varying from, say, five to fifty-five people in a room — that audiences become participants, collaborators even, in the development of what constitutes the institution. Feedback occurs, and the institution can become a mutual learning system — viewers, listeners,

[redacted]

become producers. An exhibition, an institution, may listen to its publics. The intellectual work of an exhibition need not finish when it goes live, projects can learn from themselves once public. They can acquire new, unanticipated meanings through the opening up of spaces for exchange in and around them. In keeping with Jacques Rancière's *The Emancipated Spectator*, consider the act of viewing as an active form of creative agency, the viewer authoring their own versions of what he or she finds before him; then try to find spaces within which those viewers can communicate these multiple authorships. (Michel Foucault said in an interview, 'I don't write a book so that it will be the final word; I write a book so that other books are possible, not necessarily written by me.') This process is dynamic and unpredictable, sometimes arising from unexpected subjectivites — very old, very young; people with quite different lives, but with 'equal intelligences' (as Rancière would put it). This gives rise to new perceptions, as the disciplining of thought and the hierarchizing of identities is undone.

Hospitality. Be welcoming, particularly if you want to work critically and you want what your institution produces to challenge normative wisdom, to open up new regions of thought. Try to make people feel welcome — whoever they are, whatever they are — by communicating generously. All we should look for in return for hospitality is curiosity and an open mind. Work on the assumption that everyone is invited, and what you do is for anyone at all; that art, and the thinking it gives rise to, cuts across the ways societies are segmented as markets, bracketed by class, known by power. I try to work from the assumption that the reception of art, at its best, undoes forms of identity overly determined by power, whether corporate or governmental; that it gives rise to new subjectivities and conditions of inter-subjectivity.

Generosity follows on from hospitality and the publicness of publicly-funded institutions. We are living in a new era of Enclosure: enclosures of knowledge, information, language, signs, culture, plant species, DNA and digital space. (This is a subject we recently explored through talks and performances in an eighteenth-century farm in the village of Laxton, the last surviving example of the Open Field System of farming in England.) As public institutions, we should be true to our publicness by distributing knowledge that has been publicly paid for. Like many other institutions these days, at Nottingham Contemporary we distribute the knowledge produced by and for the institution freely, whenever we can — by recording and uploading our talks, seminars and conferences along with the writing we commission. In this way, websites can function as second venues, offering access to the knowledge the institution produces beyond the constraints of geography and time. A Commons approach can also be extended to the physical spaces and resources of art institutions, putting at people's disposal the backstory, the research tools, that inform the conception of a given project. By situating all the books and journals we use in our research in 'The Study' — our resource room adjoining our exhibition spaces — we share the same space as visitors when we research; front and backstage meet and the customary divisions between the producers and publics of institutions dissolve a little.

Transdisciplinarity: art isn't just 'post-medium' anymore (as Donald Judd put it), it is 'post-discipline' (as in the writings of Dan Graham and Robert Smithson, for example). For Rancière, again the two go hand-in-hand: 'Contemporary art is, quintessentially, art defined by the erasure of medium specificity, indeed by the erasure of the visibility of art as a distinct practice.... [It is] particularly receptive to thought that shatter[s] the boundaries that separate specialists — of philosophy, art, social sciences, etc.' Art since at least the 1990s has acted as a dissolving agent on disciplinary and professional borders. Artists rarely speak from the position of specialists when they enter these other domains; their subject-position often equates more to that of the amateur, which in French means 'lover of', suggesting that that dissolving agent is indisciplined desire.

The consequences of art's post- or transdisciplinarity are far-reaching for institutions. In following the lead of artists, institutions can open up public platforms for intellectual exchange of virtually unlimited social reach. By working alongside academics and universities, art institutions can open up public spheres for intellectual energies otherwise confined to the heterotopia of campuses. By following art across the divisions of disciplines, and by doing so multiplying the number of an institution's interlocutors, debates can occur on a complex horizontal level, as opposed to a vertical pedagogic axis, with the institution above and the public below, based on relative knowledge or ignorance of a single discipline.

Yes: As an art institution, exceed what is expected of you, but do it in your own way, and according to your own values. Exceeding expectations is the most certain way of evading instru-

[redacted]

mentalization and gaining relative autonomy — you may even be turned to for solutions. The imposed goals and targets, in themselves, are often in themselves desirable anyway (such as large audience figures and socio-economic stimulus); it's what form that action then takes and what it can be made to mean that becomes critical. Try to say 'yes' to political or public expectations whenever you can, but convert these agendas to something more radical and unexpected. Achieve large new audiences, for example, through what it is that you do: the art you work with, the knowledge you produce, the debates you engender, the spaces for participation you open up, rather than through adopting the aggressive mendacities of the retail and leisure industries. In doing this, introduce different ways of thinking into the larger life of your city or local environment, to those with power and to the wider populace. Adopting the principle of the Trojan horse, smuggle something inspired into normative and predictable ways of doing things. Choose your battles carefully and sparingly. Try to harness larger energies, and convert them from conservative to progressive ones.

Popularity: Finally, don't be afraid of popularity, and don't confuse it for populism. In being critical, let us not forget pleasure.

[redacted]

Afterword
Let's Go Back to the Beginning

Bart De Baere
Ann Demeester
Nicolaus Schafhausen

This story started in Captain Cook. Captain Cook is a bar in Roosendaal, the Dutch town which until recently was the international junction for trains from Belgium and the Netherlands. It's a rather dull place where you could easily miss your connection but then might fall into an interesting conversation with someone who was in the same situation. A group of directors from contemporary art institutions in the Benelux started getting together there to discuss the state of affairs of their institutions. These meetings became known as the 'Comité van Roosendaal'. There had been a previous Comité van Roosendaal, one of two committees that organized the Brabant revolution at the end of the 18th century, which for a short time liberated the present Belgian territory from Austrian rule.

The 21st century Comité had an ambition that was more limited, yet covered a greater territory. It wanted to come up with institutional questions for contemporary art institutions in a region that doesn't officially exist. Its members were from the Benelux and North-West Germany. This zone has many, sometimes overlapping, historical regional configurations that somehow have always managed to work together as an integrated domain. Dutch architect Rem Koolhaas calls it the 'Eurocore'. It can be seen as a single megalopolis, comprising almost ten percent of Europe's population and an important part of its economy. It might also be called the 'hollowcore': the governments that administer the individual sectors of this greater urban zone define each of those sectors as if they were urban zones in their own right, neatly contained within governmental boundaries.

The Eurocore exists because of the many economic, social and cultural networks that extend from Lille to Brussels, Amsterdam and North Rhine-Westphalia. Subcultures from one side of the Eurocore know what's up on the other side. This zone was one of the key areas to shape the post-WWII international avant-garde art canon. It did so through an effective network of galleries, collectors and museums that linked up to create a lasting image.

The topic of the Roosendaal discussions was the loss of support for public institutions, and specifically contemporary art institutions. Their existence has become precarious, most clearly so in countries with a social-democratic tradition. Social democracy is falling apart, and what is left of it most often merely tolerates the state institutions that still survive. The leftovers would love to see state support reduced, at whatever cost. As a result, progressive as well as populist parties may prescribe neoliberal formulas. Western Europe is at a strange moment in its history, for it no longer has a project. It is not just politicians and fearful populations that ought to be blamed (or the 'evil powers' that disempower them, such as capitalism, globalization, etc.) but civil society also, and especially those who still have the immense luxury of being civil servants with institutions to run. They don't think. We don't think. We have become nearly as smooth operators as anyone else. We don't abstain from the 'lowest-common-denominator phenomenon' pointed out by Jimmie Durham in his astringent report for this book: 'We might complain about commercialism, yet we rent it, try to buy it.'

Although the insights gained from the discussions in Roosendaal most often led to plans that never materialized as collective efforts, several of them were adopted by individual institutions to enhance their own functioning. The committee finally hired a young aide, Nathalie Hartjes, presently coordinator of the curatorial and gallerist programmes at de Appel. She began turning the informal network of Comité van Roosendaal into an organization. The most important outcome was the 'Institutional Attitudes' conference held on 24 and 25 April 2010 in Brussels, of which this book is a further result. Isn't it strange that public institutions don't reflect upon their own significance, even though the urgency is so great?

To a certain extent the conference was a success, but to just as large an extent it was a failure that pointed up the problem it wanted to address. The last part of the conference ended in a meltdown, with the focuses that had been developed earlier devolving into in-crowd self-referentiality and even a quite spectacular moment of infighting.

Some of the insights from this conference have meanwhile been published in other settings. Irit Rogoff turned her keynote lecture 'On Being Serious in the Art World' into a separate book, published by the Swiss publishing house JRP Ringier. Zdenka Badovinac's interesting take on approaching art as part of a wider public intelligence was articulated in the 'L'Internationale' project, documented in the book *L'Internationale: Post-War Avant-Gardes Between 1957 and 1986,* by the same publisher. Several other valid texts were withheld from the present book, because after the conference we felt even more strongly than before that we did not want to continue along the lines of institutional criticism that led

[redacted]

to New Institutionalism, or base our approach on a sociological analysis of contemporary modes of economic exploitation, however important these concepts are in themselves.

Two key texts from the conference have been included as beacons in this book. One is by Marc Jacobs, who draws a parallel between the 'Republic of Letters' — with its international scholarly exchange that was constitutive for modernity — and today's network of international contemporary art institutions. The other is by Alex Farquharson, who advocates a positive take on questions and expectations addressed to institutions. Both offer a point of departure for attitudes that may differ substantially from the bulk of our present praxis.

It is a pleasure to see this book being published. We're happy we insisted on it. The questions it poses open up a broader domain than the one that the Comité van Roosendaal focussed upon; its discussion of academies, criticism and archives provides fertile ground for new insights. As Pascal Gielen points out in his linking of academies and museums in the first essay in this book: How may institutions continue an engagement with the value regimes that produced them? How can they continue to protect the 'imaginary space of the artist'? And how can they address the challenge Thijs Lijster poses in his analysis of criticism when he asks: 'If they cannot or will no longer explain what their function and importance is, why should the public bother?'

The backdrop to most of the essays is the Occupy Movement and the Italian Operaist thinkers. Their notion of 'exodus' — leaving existing structures — seems like a final deathblow to existing public institutions. Indeed, as Mark Fisher points out, at present there is a single ideology, which is adhered to by both left and right, by trade unions and the 'Big Society' alike.

Horizontality itself does not exist without aspects of verticality, as Isabell Lorey writes. This is the main axis of tension in the present book. Gerald Raunig sides with horizontality and asks how it can once again assume an emancipatory form. He wants institutions to take part in transforming the public into the common. Sonja Lavaert validates the ambiguity of social institutions when she writes that they 'navigate, to the rhythm of time, between general validity and the specificity of their origin, between equality and individual differences, between unity and the multitude of the people'. She quotes Paulo Virno (who often can be found on these pages): 'Institutions offer real protection only and exclusively if … they keep feeding on their openness to the world and the ability of negation, infinite regress and modality of possibility, and, finally, if they demonstrate at all times that they belong to the domain of that which could be something other than it is.'

Serving as a bridge from these viewpoints to the radically different stance taken by a couple of authors in this book, Chantal Mouffe bases her argument on the discursive character of the social, advocating a strategy of engagement with institutions where new modes of identification may be made available. Blake Stimson sees institutions as a check, very much in the way that the market functions as an effective check and balance for institutions. They may 'redirect the unbridled sovereignty of politicians, bankers, and ourselves' if they focus on what he calls a 'tender spot', the space that can open up between a regime of truth and truth proper, the space in which meaningfulness might still be found in any folder or object.

There seems to be a widespread aspiration to imbue institutions with new meaning. They are seen as potential locations for the perspective of a future humanity, as places that may constitute authority in a more democratic and collective fashion, and even as an instrument to reinvent the State. The political is not only happening in the sphere of politics, and — conversely - the aesthetic is not only happening in the realm of art and culture. That is the exciting undercurrent of this book.

Gerald Raunig states that in order to have a future, it is important that the art institution 'is regarded neither solely as an appendage to the State or the art market nor as a heterotopia that could function by itself as being completely other than the State and the market'. But how to go about this? Raunig gives some indications: content-wise, institutions may opt for projects which enable long-term effects and political-aesthetic experiments. As for modes of production, they may 'enable time for taking a deep breath'. And they ought to reconsider the models for audience participation and activation. There are many interesting proposals to be found in this book, yet it is not easy to carry them further into operational mode, not even if they are concrete, such as in this case or that of Farquahason. Public institutions today have to respond to three main fields of expectation that seem to be incompatible and equally demeaning.

First, there is the sphere of international developments: first and foremost, one might say, because this is the sphere in

[redacted]

which long-term developments are cooked up. In a globalized world, more qualitative knowledge and understanding is available than ever before, and aspiration urges people and institutions to search for the keenest and most recent references. What used to be an avant-garde has become a highly specialized network, like all 'state-of-the-art' developments in other fields nowadays. This may be seen as the horizon of such institutions but, on the other hand, it tends to turn them into free-floating heterotopias, weird and inaccessible Others.

Second — or first and foremost, it depends on which perspective you take — there is the sphere of the expectations of the general public, which determines what may become a blockbuster and what may serve as an attractor in a mediatized society. This is where right-wing neoliberalism and populist progressive political parties sometimes find common ground. We may very well call this, along with Jimmie Durham, the 'lowest-common-denominator phenomenon', but it is hard to argue against it in the currently prevailing system of measuring investment and output. For this is what works, doesn't it?

Last but not least, there are the unformed energies in the local art scene, which considers certain aspects of the two other spheres important and is dismissive of others. In the last decade, this sphere has tended to be a pain in the ass for institutions wanting to stay in touch with recent developments. It would be a defective analysis to envisage this as yet another result of the horizontalization of society, with mediocre, underdeveloped artistic positions now claiming equality. People who take mediocre, old-fashioned artistic positions have always bluntly felt that all this modernism was utterly worthless. What has really changed over the past two decades is the enlightened positions of people around institutions. Artists and other actors in civil society who used to be the hardcore defenders of these places have become globalized themselves. They now exist within their own networks of expertise; the institution around the corner simply offers them less immediate rewards and they validate it anyhow on their own highest international levels, not as a matter of principle.

If institutions wish to take up the aspirations raised by various authors in this book in response to 'institutional attitudes', the initial theme of the conference and book title, they will have to reconfigure the relation between these three spheres and place equal value on all of them. Each of the three is important. The sphere of international developments indeed is the one that ultimately determines the future; this is where public institutions can be strategically successful or defective. The sphere of popular expectations would seem to be the one for tactical moves but actually is where institutions negotiate with society as a whole. They should not necessarily be submissive to it; they can be aware of the fact that they also unavoidably change popular expectations by their actions and that they can be proactive by setting new agendas. Finally, the local sphere is complementary to the other two; it offers a litmus test for institutional significance. It may be the most important of the three, if one can be called most important. A horizon is not so much determined by what is visible at the edge of visibility, but first and foremost by the location from which one looks and how this is cultivated or not. The alternative to the old hierarchical institutions, which pretended to be self-sufficient in their encyclopaedia-like structuring of phenomena, lies precisely in this sense of locatedness that is part of the notion of a horizon. Horizontality then becomes a concrete and very factual challenge: How to enhance local validation in such a way that the edges of the world become visible. To start with, the local is the horizontal. It is the ground on which one stands, the humus, one might also say, in a slightly more organic metaphoric register. Verticality only makes sense if it is rooted in the local.

At the end of this trajectory from Captain Cook to the last pages of this book, the questions that have been posed still remain unresolved; the problematics surrounding institutions have not become possibilities. It is possible, however, to feel a bit more sure about the idea that institutions are basically able to give their presence a twist. Perhaps they cannot become institutions of a common — grass roots movements seem to have a monopoly on that radicalism for the time being — but they may surely aim to become institutions *for* the common.

[redacted]

Arts in **Society Series**

Arts in Society Series

Institutional Attitudes: Instituting Art in a Flat World is the twelfth publication in a series of books that map the interaction between changes in society (social, economical, political, technological and ecological transformations) and artistic practices. Inspired by critical theory, the research group Arts *in* Society studies the possibilities of a (re) positioning of the arts in society. The series is open for publishing proposals in the form of essays, theoretical explanations, practically orientated research in the arts, and research studies.

Earlier publications in this series:

— Gielen, P., Corsten, M.-J., Niesten, Ch. and Fens, H. (eds., 2013), *Autonomie als waarde: Dilemma's in kunst en onderwijs.* Amsterdam: Valiz.
— Gielen, P. and De Bruyne P. (eds., 2012, 2013 — 2nd ed.), *Teaching Art in the Neoliberal Realm: Realism versus Cynicism.* Amsterdam: Valiz.
— De Bruyne, P. and Gielen, P. (eds., 2011, 2013 — 2nd ed.), *Community Art: The Politics of Trespassing.* Amsterdam: Valiz.
— Gielen, P. (2010), *Hasselt: Op weg naar een artistieke biotoop?* Hasselt: Ballien & Maris.
— Gielen, P. (2009, 2011 — 2nd ed.), *The Murmuring of the Artistic Multitude: Global Art, Memory and Post-Fordism.* Amsterdam: Valiz.
— Gielen, P. and De Bruyne, P. (eds., 2009), *Being an Artist in Post-Fordist Times.* Rotterdam: NAi Publishers.
— Gielen, P. and Jorinde, S. (eds., 2009), *The Art Biennial as a Global Phenomenon: Strategies in Neo-Political Times.* Rotterdam and Amsterdam: NAi Publishers and SKOR.
— De Bruyne, P. (2009), *Een stoet van kleur en klanken: De muziek van Luc Mishalle & Co.* Gent: Academia Press.
— Gielen, P. (2008), *Het gemurmel van de artistieke menigte: Over kunst en postfordisme.* Tilburg: Fontys.
— Gielen, P. (2007), *De Kunstinstitutie: De identiteit en maatschappelijke positie van de artistieke instellingen van de Vlaamse Gemeenschap.* Antwerpen: OIV.
— Gielen, P. (2003, 2005, 2008 and 2011 — 4th ed.), *Kunst in Netwerken: Artistieke selecties in de hedendaagse dans en de beeldende kunst.* Leuven: LannooCampus.

[redacted]

Contributors

Kenny Cupers (b. 1977) is an architectural and urban historian and Assistant Professor at the School of Architecture of the University of Illinois at Urbana-Champaign.

Bart De Baere is director of the MuHKA, the Antwerp contemporary art museum. He is active as a curator and as a writer, has been chair of both the Council for Museums and the Cultural Council of Flanders, was a member of the International Advisory Council for the Soros Center for Contemporary Art network and consultant for the city of Johannesburg to establish its biennial. He is a cofounder of the Kunsthalle Wiels in Brussels.

Ann Demeester (b. 1975) has been the director of de Appel arts centre in Amsterdam since 2006. From 2003 to 2006 she was the director of W139 art space in Amsterdam. Together with The Fair Gallery she initiated the Gallerist Programme in October 2012 and has co-presented the Dutch television programme '4Art' since 2009.

Jimmie Durham (b. 1940) is a sculptor, poet and writer who currently lives in Europe. His sculptural work has been shown in numerous international exhibitions such as the Whitney Biennial of New York (1993, 2003), the Venice Biennial (1999, 2001, 2003, 2005), Documenta in Kassel (1992, 2012), Museum Ludwig in Cologne, ICA in London, Palais des Beaux-Arts in Brussels and Madre Museum in Naples. In 2012, a retrospective of his oeuvre with the title *A Matter of Life and Death and Singing* was shown at MuHKA, Antwerp.

Alex Farquharson (b. 1969) is Director of Nottingham Contemporary, UK, which opened in 2009. Recent exhibitions he has co-curated there include *Kafou: Haiti, Art and Vodou* (2012), *Jean Genet Acts 1 and 2* (2011), *Uneven Geographies* (2010), and *Star City: The Future Under Communism* (2010). He is also curating *Aquatopia: the Imaginary of the Deep* at Nottingham Contemporary and Tate St Ives. He has written on art and curating in various art magazines and journals, including *Frieze*, *Artforum*, *Manifesta Journal* and *Art Monthly* and has written essays for publications on John McCracken, Thomas Demand, Isa Genzken, Richard Wright, Sean Landers and Klaus Weber, amongst others.

Mark Fisher (b. 1968) is the author of *Capitalist Realism* (ZerO Books, 2009) and the forthcoming *Ghosts of My Life: Writings on Depression, Hauntology and Lost Futures* (Zer0 Books, 2013). His writing appears in many publications, including *The Guardian*, *Sight&Sound*, *The Wire* and *Frieze*. He teaches at Goldsmiths, University of London and the University of East London.

Pascal Gielen (b. 1970) is director of the research centre Arts in Society at Groningen University, where he is Associate Professor of Sociology of Art. Gielen leads also the research group and book series 'Arts in Society' (Fontys School of Fine and Performing Arts, Tilburg). His research focuses on contemporary art, cultural heritage and cultural politics. With Paul De Bruyne, Gielen has co-edited *Being an Artist in Post-Fordist Times* (2009, NAi Publishers), *Community Art. The Politics of Trespassing* (2011, Valiz) and *Teaching Art in the Neoliberal Realm: Realism versus Cynicism* (2012, Valiz). Gielen's English-language monographs are *The Murmuring of the Artistic Multitude: Global Art, Memory and Post-Fordism* (2009, Valiz) and *Creativity and Other Fundamentalisms* (2013, Mondriaan).

Marc Jacobs (b. 1963) is director of FARO, Flemish Interface for Cultural Heritage (www.faronet.be) and professor at the Free University of Brussels VUB, Department of Arts Sciences and Archaeology (www.vub.ac.be).

Sonja Lavaert (b. 1958) is a philosopher and Italianist, lecturer at the Department of Applied Linguistics of the Erasmus College at the Free University of Brussels VUB. She has written about Machiavelli, Spinoza, contemporary radical philosophy, Italian studies, and art. In 2011, she published *Het perspectief van de multitude: Agamben, Machiavelli, Negri, Spinoza, Virno* (Vubpress, 2011). Her current research focuses on the genealogy of political and ethical concepts in the area of philosophy, literature and translation, between the present, the late 17th century and the early Renaissance. Contact sonja.lavaert@vub.ac.be

Thijs Lijster (b. 1981) studied philosophy at the University of Groningen and the New School for Social Research in New York. In 2012, he received his PhD in philosophy (*cum laude*) at the University of Groningen, for a dissertation about Walter Benjamin's and Theodor W. Adorno's concepts of art criticism. Currently he is a researcher and coordinator of the research centre Arts in Society at the same university. He has published in *Algemeen Nederlands tijdschrift*

[redacted]

voor wijsbegeerte, *Krisis: Journal for Contemporary Philosophy* and *Esthetica: Tijdschrift voor filosofie en kunst*. He also regularly publishes in Dutch newspapers and magazines. In 2009, he received the ABG/VN Essay prize and in 2010 the Dutch/Flemish Prize for Young Art Criticism.

Isabell Lorey (b. 1964) Dr. phil. habil., political scientist, teaches political theory, social sciences, cultural and gender studies as a visiting professor at several universities. Find more here: www.eipcp.net/bio/lorey

Markus Miessen (b. 1978) is an architect and writer. The initiator of the Participation Quadrilogy, his work revolves around the question of critical spatial practice, institution building, and spatial politics. In various collaborations, Miessen has published, amongst other titles: *Actors, Agents and Attendants* (Sternberg Press/SKOR, 2011), *Waking Up From the Nightmare of Participation* (Expodium, 2011), *The Nightmare of Participation* (Sternberg Press, 2010), *Institution Building* (Sternberg Press, 2009), *East Coast Europe* (Sternberg Press, 2008), *The Violence of Participation* (Sternberg Press, 2007), *With/Without: Spatial Products, Practices, and Politics in the Middle East* (Bidoun, 2007), *Did Someone Say Participate? An Atlas of Spatial Practice* (MIT Press, 2006), and *Spaces of Uncertainty* (Müller & Busmann, 2002). His work has been published and exhibited internationally, including at the Lyon, Venice, Performa, Manifesta, Gwangju, and Shenzhen biennials. Architectural projects include LU Arts Centre (UK), Gwangju Biennial Hub (Korea), Performa Hubs 09/11 (US), the reappropriation of a former post-office for Manifesta 8 (Spain), a new interior for Witte de With (NL), and the largest project to date: a masterplan and *Kunsthalle* building for a former NATO nuclear-warhead bunker facility in Germany.

Chantal Mouffe (b. 1943) is Professor of Political Theory and Director of the Centre for the Study of Democracy at the University of Westminster in London. She is the co-author with Ernesto Laclau of *Hegemony and Socialist Strategy: Towards a Radical Democratic Politics* (Verso, 1985) and the author of *The Return of the Political* (Verso, 1993) *The Democratic Paradox* (Verso, 2000) and *On the Political* (Routledge, 2005).

Gerald Raunig is philosopher at the Zürcher Hochschule der Künste and at the eipcp (European Institute for Progressive Cultural

Policies). His books have been translated into English, Serbian, Spanish, Slovenian, Russian and Italian. Books available in English: *Art and Revolution: Transversal Activism in the Long Twentieth Century* (Semiotext(e)/MIT Press, 2007), *Art and Contemporary Critical Practice: Reinventing Institutional Critique* (ed., with Gene Ray, MayFly Books, 2009), *A Thousand Machines* (Semiotext(e)/MIT Press, 2010), *Critique of Creativity* (ed., with Gene Ray and Ulf Wuggenig, MayFly Books, 2011), *Factories of Knowledge, Industries of Creativity* (Semiotext(e)/MIT Press, 2013).

Patricia Reed (b. 1977) is a Canadian artist and writer based in Berlin.

Nicolaus Schafhausen (b. 1965) is director of Kunsthalle Wien since October 2012. From 2006 until 2011 he served as the director of the Witte de With Center for Contemporary Art in Rotterdam. Among other projects, Schafhausen was the curator of the German Pavilion for the 52nd in 2007 and the 53rd in 2009 Venice Biennial and the Media City Seoul Festival in 2010. Schafhausen is Visiting Lecturer at HISK, Ghent and Strategic director of Fogo Island Arts."

Blake Stimson teaches contemporary art, the history of photography, and critical theory at the University of Illinois, Chicago. He is the author of *The Pivot of the World: Photography and Its Nation* and, forthcoming from Reaktion Books, *Citizen Warhol*. He has also edited a number of volumes including, with Gregory Sholette, *Collectivism After Modernism: The Art of Social Imagination After 1945*, and, with Alexander Alberro, *Institutional Critique: An Anthology of Artists' Writings*.

Index of Names, Institutes, Organizations and Movements

[redacted]

[redacted]

Colophon

Institutional Attitudes: Instituting Art in a Flat World
Editor Pascal Gielen
Antennae Series n°8 by Valiz, Amsterdam
Part of the Fontys-series 'Arts *in* Society'

Contributors Kenny Cupers, Bart De Baere, Ann Demeester, Jimmie Durham, Alex Farquharson, Mark Fisher, Pascal Gielen, Marc Jacobs, Sonja Lavaert, Thijs Lijster, Isabell Lorey, Markus Miessen, Chantal Mouffe, Gerald Raunig, Patricia Reed, Nicolaus Schafhausen, Blake Stimson
Translation Jane Bemont (Dutch-English), Aileen Derieg (text Isabell Lorey), April Lamm (text Markus Miessen & Hannes Grassegger)
Copy editing Jane Bemont, Els Brinkman
Design Metahaven
Paper inside Munken Print White 100gr, 1.5 hv satinated mc 115gr
Paper cover Bioset 240 gr
Printing and binding Ten Brink/Euradius, Meppel
Published by Valiz, Amsterdam, 2013

This publication was made possible through the generous support of
de Appel arts centre, Amsterdam
BAM, Flemish institute for visual, audiovisual and media art, Gent
European Cultural Foundation, Amsterdam
Fontys School of Fine and Performing Arts, Tilburg
MuHKA, Museum van Hedendaagse Kunst Antwerpen
University of Groningen
Witte de With, Center for Contemporary Art, Rotterdam

Colophon

Distribution:
USA: D.A.P., www.artbook.com
GB/IE: Art Data, www.artdata.co.uk
NL/BE/LU: Coen Sligting, www.coensligtingbookimport.nl
Europe/Asia: Idea Books, www.ideabooks.nl

ISBN 978-90-78088-68-4
NUR 658, 657
Printed and bound in the Netherlands, 2013
www.valiz.nl

[redacted]

Antennae Series:

The Fall of the Studio: Artists at Work
edited by Wouter Davidts & Kim Paice
Amsterdam: Valiz, 2009 (2nd ed.: 2010),
ISBN 978-90-78088-29-5

Take Place: Photography and Place from Multiple Perspectives
edited by Helen Westgeest
Amsterdam: Valiz, 2009, ISBN 978-90-78088-35-6

The Murmuring of the Artistic Multitude: Global Art, Memory and Post-Fordism
Pascal Gielen (author)
Arts *in* Society
Amsterdam: Valiz, 2009 (2nd ed.: 2011), ISBN 978-90-78088-34-9

Locating the Producers: Durational Approaches to Public Art
edited by Paul O'Neill & Claire Doherty
Amsterdam: Valiz, 2011, ISBN 978-90-78088-51-6

Community Art: The Politics of Trespassing
edited by Paul De Bruyne, Pascal Gielen
Arts *in* Society
Amsterdam: Valiz, 2011 (2nd ed.: 2013), ISBN 978-90-78088-50-9

See it Again, Say it Again: The Artist as Researcher
edited by Janneke Wesseling
Amsterdam: Valiz, 2011, ISBN 978-90-78088-49-3

Teaching Art in the Neoliberal Realm: Realism versus Cynicism
edited by Pascal Gielen, Paul De Bruyne
Arts *in* Society
Amsterdam: Valiz, 2012 (2nd ed.: 2013), ISBN 978-90-78088-57-8